Studies in Major Literary Authors

Edited by
William E. Cain
Professor of English
Wellesley College

A Routledge Series

STUDIES IN MAJOR LITERARY AUTHORS
WILLIAM E. CAIN, *General Editor*

EDITH WHARTON'S "EVOLUTIONARY CONCEPTION"
Darwinian Allegory in Her Major Novels
Paul J. Ohler

THE END OF LEARNING
Milton and Education
Thomas Festa

READING AND MAPPING HARDY'S ROADS
Scott Rode

CREATING YOKNAPATAWPHA
Readers and Writers in Faulkner's Fiction
Owen Robinson

NO PLACE FOR HOME
Spatial Constraint and Character Flight in the Novels of Cormac McCarthy
Jay Ellis

THE MACHINE THAT SINGS
Modernism, Hart Crane, and the Culture of the Body
Gordon A. Tapper

INFLUENTIAL GHOSTS
A Study of Auden's Sources
Rachel Wetzsteon

D.H. LAWRENCE'S BORDER CROSSING
Colonialism in His Travel Writings and "Leadership" Novels
Eunyoung Oh

DOROTHY WORDSWORTH'S ECOLOGY
Kenneth R. Cervelli

SPORTS, NARRATIVE, AND NATION IN THE FICTION OF F. SCOTT FITZGERALD
Jarom Lyle McDonald

SHELLEY'S INTELLECTUAL SYSTEM AND ITS EPICUREAN BACKGROUND
Michael A. Vicario

MODERNIST AESTHETICS AND CONSUMER CULTURE IN THE WRITINGS OF OSCAR WILDE
Paul L. Fortunato

MILTON'S UNCERTAIN EDEN
Understanding Place in Paradise Lost
Andrew Mattison

HENRY MILLER AND RELIGION
Thomas Nesbit

THE MAGIC LANTERN
Representation of the Double in Dickens
Maria Cristina Paganoni

THE ENVIRONMENTAL UNCONSCIOUS IN THE FICTION OF DON DELILLO
Elise A. Martucci

JAMES MERRILL
Knowing Innocence
Reena Sastri

YEATS AND THEOSOPHY
Ken Monteith

PYNCHON AND THE POLITICAL
Samuel Thomas

PAUL AUSTER'S POSTMODERNITY
Brendan Martin

EDITING EMILY DICKINSON
The Production of an Author
Lena Christensen

EDITING EMILY DICKINSON
The Production of an Author

Lena Christensen

NEW YORK AND LONDON

First published 2008
by Routledge

711 Third Avenue, New York, NY 10017

Simultaneously published in the UK
by Routledge
2 Park Square, Milton Park, Abingdon, Oxon OX14 4RN

Routledge is an imprint of the Taylor & Francis Group, an informa business

© 2008 Taylor & Francis

Poems are reprinted by permission of the publishers and the Trustees of Amherst College from THE POEMS OF EMILY DICKINSON: VARIORUM EDITION, Ralph W. Franklin, ed., Cambridge, Mass.: The Belknap Press of Harvard University Press, Copyright © 1998 by the President and Fellows of Harvard College, Copyright ©1951, 1955, 1979, 1983 by the President and Fellows of Harvard College.

Letters are reproduced by publishers and the Trustees of Amherst College from THE LETTERS OF EMILY DICKINSON: VARIORUM EDITION, Thomas H. Johnson, ed., Cambridge, Mass.: The Belknap Press of Harvard University Press, Copyright © 1958, 1986 by the President and Fellows of Harvard College.

Typeset in Adobe Garamond by IBT Global

All rights reserved. No part of this book may be reprinted or reproduced or utilised in any form or by any electronic, mechanical, or other means, now known or hereafter invented, including photocopying and recording, or in any information storage or retrieval system, without permission in writing from the publishers.

Trademark Notice: Product or corporate names may be trademarks or registered trademarks, and are used only for identification and explanation without intent to infringe.

Library of Congress Cataloging-in-Publication Data
Holm Christensen, Lena
  Editing Emily Dickinson : the production of an author / by Lena Christensen.
    p. cm. — (Studies in major literary authors)
  Includes bibliographical references and index.
  ISBN 0-415-95586-6 (acid-free paper)
   1. Dickinson, Emily, 1830–1886—Criticism, Textual. 2. Dickinson, Emily, 1830–1886—Technique. 3. Dickinson, Emily, 1830–1886—Manuscripts. 4. Manuscripts, American—Editing. I. Title.
  PS1541.Z5H57 2007
   811'.4--dc22   2007022103

ISBN13: 978-0-415-95586-7 (hbk)
ISBN13: 978-0-203-93191-2 (ebk)
ISBN13: 978-0-415-54122-0 (pbk)

Contents

Acknowledgments · vii

Introduction · 1

Chapter One
Authoring Emily Dickinson · 33

Chapter Two
Material Dickinson: The Function of the Manuscript
in Dickinson Studies · 67

Chapter Three
Digital Dickinson: From Editions to Archives · 115

Conclusion · 157

Notes · 163

Bibliography · 181

Index · 189

Acknowledgments

This book started out as a doctoral project. In 2005 I defended my thesis at Lund University, Sweden. The following pages are the result of that event. I would like to thank a number of people that have been engaged in my work along the way. Lars-Håkan Svensson served as my supervisor and deserves many thanks for patiently reading and commenting on drafts of all kinds for a long period of time. Thank you to Domhnall Mitchell for serving as external examiner at my public defense. A number of people at the Department of English at Lund University have shown me how important a sense of community is when embarking on research—a trip that can oftentimes seem a lonely one. To have been a part of this group is a privilege. Thank you, then, *Valvet* people and friends. Since finishing my thesis, I have had the opportunity to teach in both Canada and Sweden. I would like to thank my students at Dawson College in Montréal and at Växjö University for inspiring me with their curiosity and interest in literary studies but also challenging me with their critique of the discipline. This book took shape on both sides of the Atlantic. I have been supported in so many ways by family and friends in both Canada and Sweden. My parents have been there from the beginning supporting me in every possible way. Jonathan and Liv have offered their unconditional love throughout. This book is for them.

Introduction

> I wonder what made Emily Dickinson as she was
>
> Amy Lowell, "Emily Dickinson"

On April 16, 1862, Thomas Higginson received a letter from a then unknown poet. The letter lacked a signature. But the sender

> had written her name on a card, and put it under the shelter of a smaller envelope inclosed in the larger; and even this name was written—as if the shy writer wished to recede as far as possible from view—in pencil, not in ink. The name was Emily Dickinson. ("Emily Dickinson's Letters" 444)

Far from being a sign of shyness, Emily Dickinson's decision to leave her autograph on a separate note may be interpreted as a professional strategy, eerily pointing to the practice of her relatives and editors to, as Martha Nell Smith notes, tear her signature away from letters after her death, thus giving away autographs of the author (*Rowing* 148). Dickinson created an interpretive framework by thus supplying her name—indicating that she knew that she was a writer of importance and more boldly, that she wanted to be recognized as such. A person's name is not a simple affair, as J. Hillis Miller reminds us in "The Critic as Host." Weaving the notion of the name into a discussion of (inter)textual instability Miller asks, "Who, however, is 'Shelley'? To what does this word refer if any work signed with this name has no identifiable borders, and no interior walls either? It has no edges because it has been invaded from all sides as well as from within by other 'names,' other powers of writing" (243). In this study I want to consider in more detail how it is that a name, an author's name, may in this way be understood as an effect or production of various discourses. The name Emily Dickinson does not so much refer to the biographical person as to what (many things) has come to fill a certain author-function. To a greater extent than many other canonical writers, 'Emily Dickinson' is certainly an (inter)text that has been invaded in a similar fashion on all sides by "other 'names,' other powers of writing." The name 'Emily Dickinson' is a text and, more so, this text is set in continual re-reading and hence re-writing, by every reader. Susan Howe has perhaps most explicitly theorized this problematic status of the proper name in the very title of her book on Dickinson, *MY Emily Dickinson*. Howe's self-conscious appropriation of an author's name acknowledges—in fact, announces—that such re-readings, as subjective versions, are all we can ever aspire to: there can be no definitive Emily Dickinson. Nevertheless, Howe's title also makes clear that there is a possessive need, a desire, to appropriate, to make sense: and hence we produce 'our' specific 'Shelleys,' 'our' specific 'Dickinsons.' This study engages such critical productions of 'Emily Dickinson' in the twentieth century. More precisely, it examines what I take to be particularly anxious stages of producing the Dickinson text for publication and critical periods in which the production of 'Emily Dickinson' because of these editorial queries has been seen as particularly problematic. That is, this study analyzes specific periods of Dickinson studies for which the status of the texts of Dickinson, and the editorial questions related to the editing of those texts as works, have been articulated as problematic. There are so many versions of 'Emily Dickinson' available that the critic who wants to 'figure her out' finds herself wandering through a maze of different and differing voices. Fully aware of this situation, this study does not attempt to figure Dickinson out. Rather, 'Emily Dickinson' is treated as an intertextual constellation of editorial and critical narratives. This is not to deny that there are historical facts but each critic must choose to interpret those 'facts' according to their own desires, aims, and theses. As poststructuralist critiques of essentialism suggest, a life story can never be more than another construction, another critical imagination. 'Emily Dickinson,' then, is understood here as a weave of editorial and critical narratives. But then, again, if that point is settled, it is, indeed, such critical imaginations that must be the 'stuff' that makes the kind of criticism literary scholars pursue meaningful in the first place. This is true for both literary criticism and textual criticism. Hence authors are given a certain stability, a certain biographical groundedness; hence texts are established as works if ever so tentatively. Needless to say, we must continue to tell stories of authors and texts, because such stories are what keep them alive, keep them within our archives of the past that also shape our future. So in different ways we continue to write about Emily Dickinson as the person who lived in Amherst and we continue to read her letters and poems as artistic textual productions. But we need also to consider how Emily Dickinson and her work are produced through our readings of her through the archive of editorial representations and critical interpretations of her.

Such a consideration would include both the historical situation in which Emily Dickinson lived and wrote and the various ways in which her work has been disseminated. This means that we must study not only the historical situation that produced Emily Dickinson but also the various editions and interpretations that shape her into 'Emily Dickinson(s).' That is to say that a historicizing reading of the transmission of Dickinson offers clues to how the author has come to serve particular functions. This strategy emphasizes the belatedness of any portrait of the artist. The production of Emily Dickinson into 'Emily Dickinson(s)' could have been studied by recourse to the critical heritage that is constituted by biographical studies, contemporary reviews, the editions of her work (from the earliest to the latest), anthologies that include her work, and criticism. Because this study is itself conditioned by a specific period of Dickinson criticism that has brought to the fore the significance of how a text is edited into a 'work,' this study, however, focuses on how twentieth-century editing, and recently, electronic archiving, of Emily Dickinson's work and the specific critical debates and considerations (about Emily Dickinson and the ontological status of her texts) that have emerged through these editions and archives constitute a specific kind of 'authoring'(through editing and archiving) of 'Emily Dickinson.'

Indicative of the poet's ubiquitous presence in the academic marketplace—indicative of her canonical status that is—is the enormous amount of critical engagement with Emily Dickinson. Numerous attitudes and approaches compete in the construction of the figure of the author and her work. This introduction does not provide a diachronically comprehensive bibliography of such research: its purpose is not to relate such a comprehensive 'critical biography' but to consider how particular discourses related to editorial practices, in the verb-sense of the word, *author* Emily Dickinson. This selectivity does not mean that my study of the production of Emily Dickinson in the twentieth century assumes that there is only 'one' (that is, scholarly) Dickinson. But it necessarily implies a choice: this choice has been, as related above, to read Emily Dickinson through editorial process as I see such editorial processes to be crucial, indeed key, elements in the authoring of Emily Dickinson. Thus embedded in my study is the argument that in order to read an author we must consider how editions and critical debates about editing constitute the poet. Thus this study, in its exploration of various but specific Dickinsons produces its own *version* of Emily Dickinson, a Dickinson who is the product of my readings of what I see as particularly anxious stages of Dickinson editing-criticism, of which the present time is one. This Dickinson is precisely versioned rather than in any sense monolithic. I use the term version here in analogy with the term's usage in textual criticism. George Bornstein writes "the literary work might be said to exist not in any one version, but in all the versions put together" (6). Thus Emily Dickinson can be understood as a continual negotiation of competing figures of the author.

All readings of Emily Dickinson's work are of edited texts. All editions are interpretations. These seemingly innocuous facts have become increasingly problematized in the late twentieth century in Dickinson editing and criticism. As the temporary stability offered by Johnson's *Variorum* editions of Dickinson's poems and letters was queried, these questions became foundational questions for Dickinson studies. This study builds on and develops the critical inquiry of these questions. I seize upon the critical interest, since the publication in 1981 of *The Manuscript Books of Emily Dickinson*, in editorial questions for the study of Emily Dickinson. 'Who' is Emily Dickinson? 'What' is a poem of Emily Dickinson? Emily Dickinson is a set of *figures* made out of 'our' imaginations about the biographical person who lived in Amherst, Massachusetts, USA, between the years 1830 and 1886. Her 'poems' are the result of editorial and critical negotiations of 'our' notions of the female author, the poetic text, and the manuscripts of Emily Dickinson. The author and her text are not separable. As the 'work' is edited, made into a specific shape, so the 'author' is edited, shaped into a particular figure. This is, then, a study of the author 'Emily Dickinson' as a continual production, an 'edited' figure of the author, a figure who is intricately bound up in the editions of her work and the readings which are contingent on those editions. This study understands the task of 'editing' as a kind of 'criticism.' Similarly, the 'biographies' and 'literary criticism' based in all these editorial projects can, in an extended meaning of the word 'editing,' be seen as contributions toward a wider 'editing' of the received 'texts' of 'Emily Dickinson:' 'texts' implying both the editions and the criticism of the poet, all of which produce or authorize Emily Dickinson.

This study, then, explores how 'Emily Dickinson' is constructed in twentieth-century editorial and critical debates. The general aim is to explore the following question: how has 'Emily Dickinson' been constructed through the major editorial projects 'about' this writer in the twentieth century?[1] And, as a consequence of these editorial projects, how has the critical construct 'Emily Dickinson' emerged? These questions were born out of the particular scene of reading Emily Dickinson in the 1990s, which emphasized the problems in editing Emily Dickinson's work for the printed page and which in its subsequent insistence on the reading of Dickinson in the 'original' handwritten text has proposed to 'unedit' the printed editions through which the poet has been disseminated.[2]

The study asks these questions by considering three critical practices or processes: 'authoring,' 'editing,' and 'archiving.' The result of this is in itself a construct, a specific figure—'Emily Dickinson'—as I understand this figure in the early twenty-first century. The particular figure that emerges in this study is not monolithic but versioned, as I do not offer my Dickinson as a particular or unique author whose poetics I have refined through my critical evaluation; instead, this figure is not mine but conventional because socialized. With a reading of the author as versioned I allude to the term as used by Donald Reiman in his privileging of a text's versions instead of a theoretical ideal work; with a reading of the figure as not mine I mean to emphasize radically the way in which an author is always the production of numerous voices. This introduction first presents an outline of the theoretical framework and methodological strategies of my study, which includes a consideration of the main concepts employed. A brief consideration of editions of Emily Dickinson's poems and the critical responses to those editions leads on to a presentation of 'Emily Dickinson' as she has been constructed in critical debates. This is in itself an 'inventory' of the material examined in this study. I thus construct the field of Emily Dickinson studies, consider previous research pertinent to this study and situate my work in the context of metacritical studies of Emily Dickinson. The introduction concludes with an outline of the study as a whole.

AUTHORING UN/EDITING ARCHIVING

The production of the author that concerns me in this study is manifold: it is really a matter of productions. In this section I consider some important concepts or terms that structure the present study's consideration of how Emily Dickinson and her work are disciplined into specific editorial and critical (academic) grids. The concepts of the 'author,' 'editing,' 'archiving,' but also the concept of text, that finally contains them all, in themselves have extensive critical histories: my scope does not allow for an elaboration of these histories: instead my discussions of these concepts are intended to pragmatically organize this particular study. This study traces the authoring of Emily Dickinson from the Book to the Electronic Archive through an analytical grid that is constituted by recourse to the theorization of 'unediting the Renaissance' and the methods of French archival-oriented genetic criticism. With such a combination of critical resources the study contributes to a widening of Dickinson studies, by fruitfully situating 'Emily Dickinson' (and the editorial and critical production of her) in the context of other periods, genres, and critical approaches.

Authoring

Timothy Morris suggests that before New Criticism, the typical "unit for study" in literary criticism was not so much the work as the author, around whom literary texts were studied as part of that author's life achievement (2). The task of the critic was to unify all texts of an author into such a coherent oeuvre. Dickinson was first seriously studied around the same time as New Criticism had begun to replace the 'author' as the unit for study with 'the work.' Study of literature in the academic classroom thus shifted from a focus on literary history structured on the idea of the centrality of major authors to a focus on the similarly select and canonical literary work, as what Lawrence Buell calls the "supposedly autonomous artifact as the privileged object of study" (5). But of course the author remained a potent figure even in such text-oriented practice as New Criticism, as will be explored at more length in Chapter One. Literary criticism in the wake of New Historicism, Cultural Materialism and other critical practices that emphasize the social and cultural aspects of literary production has reinserted the 'author' into critical practice.

This study is conspicuously author-centered: it reads and analyzes the editorial-critical production, or 'authoring,' of 'Emily Dickinson' in the twentieth century. But it approaches such a formation of an 'author' from a metacritical perspective that aims to query that very formation. This 'production' of 'Emily Dickinson' is clearly multiple: there are many figures of Dickinson in the critical marketplace. Typical of Dickinson criticism is, however, the notion of this author as having a 'clear referent,' as a locus from which we may derive the meaning of 'her work:' that is, specific studies may produce specific interpretations of Emily Dickinson's work but they all lead back to this referent, this 'author.' In this sense Dickinson studies is based in essentially unquestioned notions of 'originality,' 'intention,' and 'radicality.' Emily Dickinson as author exists within a powerful context of 'canonicity' that seems impossible to challenge. We will see that even though there may be as many 'Emily Dickinson' figures as there are readers, critical study is, as it seems, bound to produce this figure as a great, major author. The purpose of this study is not to question 'Emily Dickinson's' position as author, but rather to engage the ways in which she has been authored, been canonized.[3]

One risk with an author-oriented study like this one clearly is that 'Emily Dickinson' comes to serve as a stable figure pointing to the biographical person

Introduction 7

in precisely the idealist fashion that it seeks to query. The point, however, of this study is that 'Emily Dickinson' is a socially constructed and constituted figure; moreover this figure depends for its constitution on critical investments. I engage two levels of producing this figure: while 'editing' is the central trope through which I read Dickinson, such editorial discourses are reproduced in 'criticism' as well (it may appear here that I somehow 'forget' the self-fashioning of the author in her own writings: such textual self-fashioning of 'Emily Dickinson' is, however, the object of another study). Editorial discourses that emerge in all these three domains of critical practice will be the subject of this study.

In the analysis of 'authorship' as conducted by theorists like Michel Foucault and Raymond Williams, the term becomes a tool with which to analyze the externalization of a writer's position in a marketplace in which 'authors' have certain functions. In this sense the term 'author,' is clearly connected with terms that reflect power positions, 'authority' and 'authorization.' Both the 'author' and the 'work' are, of course, as for example the debate between Michel Foucault and Roland Barthes in the 1970s reveals, socio-cultural constructs that carry significant, powerful connotations. Hence, the 'author' becomes a Foucauldian 'function.' From a specifically Marxist perspective (that is important to a study of *material* culture), this 'author function' has served, in modern western culture, according to Raymond Williams, as a vehicle for bourgeois thought (193). In this tradition, the concept is connected to that of the individual subject: it has come to represent precisely the key markers of such presumed individuality, originality and uniqueness. But as Williams argues, subjectivity and individuality are constructs of this bourgeois ideology and what is under the bourgeois rubric described as 'individuality' is in fact socially and historically produced. Williams proposes an analysis of authorship that grants a certain space for the 'individual' within a model of the 'trans-individual' in which "the emergence of an individual project, and the real history of other contemporary projects and of the developing forms and structures, are continuously and substantially interactive" (196). Such a model refuses both the reduction of the 'author,' according to the traditional Marxist model, to a "representative" of a particular class or to the equally idealistic 'bourgeois' construct of the unique and significant individual as the result of an individual emulation of a background of "shared facts, ideas and influences" (196).

In this sense, the author is what a writer becomes through processes such as publication and criticism. As the name Emily Dickinson has come to serve such a function by being attached to specific edited texts—versions of her writings—both those writings and 'Emily Dickinson' have been legitimized into specific forms, forms that I here explore as the production of 'Emily Dickinson. Michel Foucault's construction of the notion of the 'author-function' is to the point here. His essay "What is an Author?" is a standard starting-point for discussions of authorship. In this essay he establishes the notion of the 'author-function'—a means by which to classify texts, to reign texts in according to certain discursive norms regarding authority.

As a response to Roland Barthes' polemical "Death of the Author," Foucault's essay is an attempt to produce a constructive account of 'authorship' without taking recourse to that idealistic biographical subject that was Barthes' target, thus retaining the figure of the author within the analysis of literary texts. By constructing this level of analysis Foucault can move away from the notion of the biographical subject (who is clearly empirically verifiable in several ways) to a wider definition and means of analyzing the authoring of (for example) literary works. In Foucault's analysis, the literary text emerged as an 'individual' project that was dependent on an 'author-function' in the eighteenth century. As the name of an author thus is offered a sense of individuality and of a unique imprint, the idea of being an author of a literary work moves towards the 'public' of a commercial publication and legalistic system of controlling the text. This, as Roger Chartier notes, reflects a general shift from the anonymous gentleman writer of early modern aristocratic circles, that could no longer be sustained, to a commercial and public means of authoring texts and writers. The important point is, for the discussion of authorship, that the author becomes the result of operations that refer the unity, coherence, and historical belonging of a literary work back to such a subject (Chartier 41).[4] As Kevin Pask points out, drawing on Foucault's considerations, this process of becoming an author through publication came, in the early modern period to be "constituted by the juridical dynamic of censorship and, from the eighteenth century onward, copyright law" (3). While such analysis of the 'author' as a construct dependent on various legal power relations in its wide discursive sense requires a structural analysis of an entire period, the scope of this study is limited to specific editions of Dickinson's work and specific editorially-inflected critical discussions of that work. Although it is inspired by and draws on wider-scale studies of the production of authorship this study is thus limited to discuss such disciplinary contests within the confines of the editorial and critical construction, in effect 'authorization' (or 'canonization') of 'Emily Dickinson.'

Un/Editing

"This book is an event of large importance:" the hyperbolic tone of Mark Van Doren's "Foreword" to *Bolts of Melody: New Poems of Emily Dickinson* is indicative of the investments made in the editing of Emily Dickinson and symbolic of editorial projects generally. Editorial projects, after all, strive to offer readers better access to an author's work. Van Doren continues

> The task of editing her, as scholars at least are sure to know, is both a tease and a torment. The materials, the manuscripts, are either chaotic or elusive; sometimes they require so many decisions by the editor as to constitute him, provided his choices are wise, a poet himself. (v)

In his formulation of the editor as 'poet,' Van Doren implicitly reveals that editing is both interpretation and collaboration: the editor is indeed a 'co-author' of the social text that is the historical dissemination of an author. I wish here to situate my own study and the field of Dickinson studies in the context of a changing textual criticism, a changing editorial practice characterized by a turn from the ideology of 'ideal' works to a theorization of 'social' texts, in which the serious interest in Emily Dickinson's manuscripts must be understood. David Greetham outlines the decisive shift in textual criticism that took place in the 1980s. The tradition of 'eclectic,' 'intentionalist,' 'Platonist,' or 'Modernist' editions of the modern textual criticism tradition has increasingly become critiqued for being founded on an idealist theory of the text 'that never was.' In short, the text produced in this theoretical tradition encouraged the (ideal) reader to accept a Romantic notion of the ideal artifact, 'created' rather than 'produced' by the author, an author isolated from the corruption of social and cultural pressures (*Theories* 370).

Greetham constructs the modern textual critical tradition as a scheme where the concrete manifestation of the text, along with the concrete, material work of editors, scribes and publishers, is simply an evanescent, because material, representation of the thought emanating from the sole intention of the author (370). Rather than making the ideal text, thought, or intention the basis for critical inquiry, Jerome McGann and other critics of modern textual criticism have made the text's "negotiations with its own history" the basis of textual operations. Intention, in this contemporary scheme, becomes, in Foucauldian vocabulary, a "function," an historically conditioned effect of critical reading (Greetham, *Theories* 370). Because it was supported by an ideology of essentialism and idealism, eclecticism could produce 'definitive editions' of works "that would never have to be edited again." The eclectic ideology thus posits itself outside of history's contingencies. In the eclectic edition, the notes recording variance and textual 'corruption' are relegated to the back of the book, constructing a closed clear text that, to Greetham, "smack[s] of old-fashioned privilege and authority" (374). Modern textual criticism posited that an 'ideal' text corresponding to the author's 'final intentions' could be established by an editor. Contemporary editorial theory refutes that premise as an idealist ideology.

As part of his project to socialize the study of literary texts, Jerome McGann famously distinguishes between a literary work's 'linguistic' and 'bibliographic' codes: these terms allow us to deal analytically with how a literary work's meaning is shaped historically and materially (*The Textual Condition* 9, 13, 62–65). McGann theorizes a social approach to texts and to editing where texts are seen as evolving social constructs. As such, a text cannot be seen as a silent repository for hidden meanings 'already there:' "In this world, time, space, and physicality are not the emblems of a fall from grace, but the bounding conditions which turn gracefulness abounding" (9). McGann argues against linguistic prejudice among most literary critics, a prejudice which yields only linguistic meaning and which ignores a text's other codes, codes that McGann calls 'bibliographic.' This concept resembles Gérard Genette's idea of 'paratextual' features but extends it, as the latter only includes linguistic material (including headings, copyright information, and bibliographic information although he certainly opens up for wider implications) while McGann's notion includes the material shape of the book/text itself, as well.

In *Paratexts* Genette defines the literary work as essentially a linguistic text but also speaks of "a certain number of verbal or other productions" that "adorn" that linguistic text; he writes of the concept of paratexts that it designates that which makes a text present in the world, that is, it shapes a text into a material object among other objects (1). The material pages, spine and covers of a book; ink marks, lineation, paper type, spine and cover design; and how the linguistic signs are shaped and placed on the page along with other visual features of a textual object—all need to be taken into consideration for a full understanding of a work. While a work's 'linguistic' codes have typically been the stuff that critics analyze—interpret—its bibliographic codes have often been either disregarded completely or dealt with by historians of the book for the purposes not of engaging with the meaning of the work but in more general genealogies of book publishing. The notions of bibliographic codes and paratextual features, extending as they do the study of literary texts to the socio-material forms that texts 'are,' guide the following chapters' historicizing analyses of editions of Emily Dickinson's texts.

Archiving

The concept of the archive has been put to various and variant uses in critical discourses in the social and human sciences. Michael Sheringham suggests that there is a "fascination with archives in contemporary western culture" generally (48).[5] In textual criticism, the notion of the 'archive' has increasingly come to serve an important function in the development of new forms of publishing literary texts electronically: indeed, it is possible to see a tendency of a move from editing towards archiving. As will be discussed at more length in Chapter Three the 'archive' traces an etymological link between 'house' as in the Greek 'magisterial residence' and "government." Archives are created by governments, municipalities, universities, libraries, and churches—for the sake of recording common and individual histories. As such archives must be understood as 'public.' But access to Emily Dickinson's manuscripts, as administrated and archived by Harvard University's Houghton Library, is of course limited. Designated editors and the rare researcher are the only ones to view such 'viewed by-experts-only objects'—other readers make do with facsimile versions of the originals. There is of course a common-sense reason for such restriction: the papers are fragile and need to be protected from too much handling. This lack of presence of these documents in the public domain is a driving logic for the production of such a website as *Dickinson Electronic Archives*. Put simply, such an archive is hypothesized as a tool to democratize access to rare documents. Hence Martha Nell Smith writes that the digital environment makes "BE-O objects" or "viewed by-experts-only objects" available for general readers. Hence only specialists may view for example Emily Dickinson's manuscripts (837).

Yet we need to think more about the possible democratic effect of web-based archiving. An archive is an argument and a definition of what a poet's work and life is. The etymology of the archive cautions us to not theorize the archive in utopian terms and encourages us instead to interrogate the practice of archiving—in the context of literary studies, we need to ask what role the archive has in the continual production of the text as 'work' and the writer as 'author.' We need to remember that all space is public and that, in fact, the 'access denied' label of the 'original' documents produces a privileging of that document as rare.

Text

Clearly the author, the edition and the archive would be of no interest unless there were materials to authorize, edit and archive in the first place. Such materials, in the context of literary study, are usually texts. The above-discussed categories need to be considered in the context of the notion of 'text.' For the purposes of this study, we need to consider two traditions of thinking about this notion as the history of textual criticism and literary criticism reveal two different ways of approaching it. But, because this study engages what can be called electronic text, we must also consider how such 'text' might 'differ' from these two traditions.

The notion of the 'text' is of course not neutral. In the context of textual criticism, the idea of the 'work' traditionally implied abstract category—the ideal version of the material text/s that makes up the work (Johan Svedjedal, "A Note on the Concept of 'Hypertext'" 1). Peter Shillingsburg represents a traditional textual critical understanding of text and work when he writes that 'text' is "the actual order of words and punctuation as contained in any one physical form, such as manuscript, proof, or book" (46). The text is the result of an author's attempt to store "in tangible form the version the author currently intends" (46). But, he continues, "a text (the order of the words) has no substantial or material existence, since it is not restricted by time and space [. . .] the same text can exist simultaneously in more than one form. The text is contained and stabilized by the physical form but is not the physical form itself. A manuscript can include one or more texts: that represented by the original reading including those portions now cancelled and that represented by the final revision or that represented by intermediate readings" (46). This is precisely where the critique of modern textual criticism steps in to argue that, indeed, not only does 'the physical form' 'contain' and 'stabilize' the text but the physical form *is* the text and as such *matters*.

Hence traditional textual criticism came under attack in the 1970s and 1980s by textual critics engaging a social theory of text, privileging the material instantiations, or 'texts' of the 'work.' Instead the notion of the literary 'work' is radically inverted from the New Bibliography's idealist conception of the 'ideal' text somehow existing outside the material instantiations of 'documents' to being embraced, as exactly that physical or material composite of the historical transmission of that work, in different 'texts' (Leah Marcus, *Unediting the Renaissance* 29–30). Its richness stems from its historical condition and not from its 'creator.' Such historical conditions were, in the modern textual tradition, 'cleared' away as the noise of corruption. Contemporary editorial theorists engage in such 'corruption' precisely to understand how the meaning of a work of art is historically conditioned, how its meaning is part of a larger cultural context rather than derived from some intentional source. The work of art is therefore not a stable concept and the particular text not a receptacle of an original 'truth' ready to be excavated by the conjecturing editor. Each material text, in handwritten and print instantiations of a work, contributes to the full story of that work. This means that we 'unedit' both the notion that there is a 'final authorial intention' to guide the production of an ideally 'best' text, and that we 'unedit' the resistance to bibliographic codes that has shaped editing and criticism: the text is material, physical.⁶ But the concept of 'work' has been otherwise formulated and theorized in literary theory and criticism. Rather than ideal abstract, for Roland Barthes 'work' is the concrete category, the books we find in bookstores and that we hold in our hands, while 'text' is the abstract 'writerly' construction that the 'reader' (as in 'reader-writer') produces from the experience of the work ("From Work to Text" 156–157: Barthes calls the 'text' a "methodological field" whereas the 'work' is something we can find in a library). We notice an idealist tendency in both ways of thinking about the work/text construct. In textual criticism the 'work' is that ideal form of the text, that representing, perhaps, the author's final intentions, somehow imaginatively deduced by the editor. In Barthes' theory, on the other hand, the 'text' takes on similar ideal forms, signifying a utopian writerly production.

For the purposes of this study, it will be important to remember the idealisms at stake in both these models of text and work, and consider the potential in rethinking text through electronic text, which, Katherine Hayles writes, offers a vantage point from which to rethink 'text' as it has been formulated in both these traditions. For example, she suggests that "our assumptions about text are shot through with assumptions specific to print" (264). As such, 'text' has not been problematized as materially variant and versioned, and hence processual and consequently the object from which literary criticism has theorized intertextuality and readers' productions of variant meanings has remained solid, printed in 'final' form. Hence both textual criticism and literary criticism have conceived of 'text' and 'work' as fixed (and ideal) objects rather than material processes: electronic text, on the other hand, needs to be understood precisely as processual. In fact, the encoding of text in the electronic medium makes explicit the concreteness, materiality, of that text, as "an ordered hierarchy of content objects" (269).

I would like to consider, finally, a critical approach to 'text' that has theorized the text as materially versioned and variant: French *critique génétique*. Even though seldom referred to explicitly by Dickinson scholars, it is clear that genetic criticism has important significance for the study of Emily Dickinson's texts in manuscript. Its formulation of the notion of the 'avant-texte' destabilizes the notion of the 'work' (Deppman et al. 10). Its insistence on the process of writing as an object of study, its ambition to map the process, or to be more precise, the birth, of the literary work in fact serves as a heuristic for an engagement with text as process in general and with the study of Emily Dickinson's manuscripts and editions of her work in particular. For the purposes of this metacritical study, which stipulates manuscript criticism as a particular way of figuring Emily Dickinson, in Chapters Two and Three I consider genetic criticism as an important critical intertext to the manuscript criticism of Dickinson's work. Genetic criticism, in its quest for the traces of the process of writing rather than the finished work, in important ways points to a study of the materials of 'text, problematizes both the idea of the 'finished work' but also, perhaps inadvertently, by drawing attention to such ephemeral notions as the 'birth' of the literary work, suggests both difficulties with manuscript study and the potentials of such an approach to the literary text. Text needs to be understood materially and non-ideally, in the way Hayles figures it: "There are only physical objects such as books and computers, foci of attention, and codes that entrain attention and organize material operations" (270).

PRODUCING AN AUTHOR

This study is intended as a contribution to the ongoing study of the historicity of Emily Dickinson and her work as produced textual objects as to the metacritical concerns of how 'Emily Dickinson' and her 'work' are produced. This metacritical approach seems especially pertinent at the present time. At certain times, a scholarly field experiences shifts in direction that demand metacritical inquiry. As Cristanne Miller points out, in the 1990s 'Emily Dickinson' became the site for such argument and debate ("Whose Dickinson?" 230). Miller writes "Textual editors and scholars debate questions as basic as what constitutes a Dickinson poem, how many poems she wrote, whether her handscripted manuscript booklets constitute publication and determine the order in which poems should now be printed, and how the poems are most accurately transcribed in print" (230). As Miller points out "Because this debate has to do with basic assumptions about how Dickinson conceived her poetry and what constitutes a poem, no discussion of her work is untouched by them" (230). I take such a critical self-consciousness to be a serious call for meta-critical engagement.

We can employ the notion of 'unediting' as a heuristic to investigate the recent shift in critical direction in Dickinson studies. Such a perspective, as outlined by Leah Marcus, necessitates a historicizing and materialist critical practice. In this study 'unediting' serves as a lens through which to consider the formation of specific editorial projects regarding the texts of Emily Dickinson: Thomas Johnson's 1955 Variorum, R. W. Franklin's 1981 facsimile edition, Franklin's 1998 Variorum, and the ongoing *Dickinson Electronic Archives,* edited by Martha Nell Smith, Ellen Louise Hart, Marta Werner, and Lara Vetter. As Marcus notes, the critical task consists of being continually aware of "the subtle, pervasive rhetorical power exerted by the editions we use" in the study of literary texts (3).

Introduction

In order to consider such "rhetorical power" we need to employ a methodology that is historicizing and materialist. For editions are historically and materially specific. But as Paul Hamilton writes, the historicist project entails not only a concern "to situate any statement—philosophical, historical, aesthetic or whatever—in its historical context" but also a critical "[doubling] back on itself to explore the extent to which any historical enterprise inevitably reflects the interests and bias of the period in which it was written" (3). Emphasizing the importance of a consideration of the historical specifics of any edition, Marcus writes

> No single version of a literary work, whether Renaissance or modern, can offer us the fond dream of unmediated access to an author or to his or her era; the more aware we are of the processes of mediation to which a given edition has been subject, the less likely we are to be caught up in a constricting hermeneutic knot by which the shaping hand of the editor is mistaken for the intent of the author, or for some lost, 'perfect' version of the author's creation. (*Unediting* 3)

Thus bringing up the question of the conflation of edited text and author's intention, Marcus points to a problem with 'unediting:' how to formulate the return to the 'original' historically specific text without committing precisely that "fond dream of unmediated access" to that 'lost' period, that 'lost' intention. It is crucial to emphasize the mediation of any reading of any text, whether it is the manuscript in the author's script, a first edition, or a paperback edition of the work.

If 'unediting' is a tool which serves the present day, then, it is worth keeping in mind, as Marcus writes, that "We might well find ourselves repeating the past—assembling new standard editions if only to have a stable reference point for future departures from them" (4). It is thus imperative to continually evaluate editorial projects, not simply those that seem safely lodged in the 'past' but also those that produce 'Emily Dickinson' at the moment. This study engages in such an analysis of current editorial projects, considering the point that the 'unediting' project might very well be the new 'editing' of the specific text, cementing the text again, according to specific assumptions and norms.

Guiding me through the writing of this study is a belief that it is important to move away from a heroic narrative of Emily Dickinson's life and the connected assumption of a heroic rescue of her texts. My purpose has been to see and explore those kinds of appropriating narratives as producing a composite "Dickinson Text." One risk involved with this metacritical approach is to fall prey to an illusory objectification of 'Dickinson studies' as if this study could somehow step outside of such a discourse when in fact it participates in it. A further risk is that the particular editorial and critical discourses that I have selected here for discussion and analysis are defined too narrowly or widely, as if they could, in fact, be defined. The selection has been made with the objective to engage what I perceive to be dominant discourses about 'Emily Dickinson.' By such 'dominant' discourses is understood the major editorial ventures (that are clearly by the publishing industry and critics taken as 'major') and critical tendencies (that can be gleaned not only from what kinds of monographs are published but also from what kinds of topics are discussed in current 'textbooks' about the poet) with regard to this enigmatic figure 'Emily Dickinson.'

Part of a research project that is concerned with a specific author, it could be argued, should be to offer new insights into her biography or a new model for interpreting her work but the purpose here is rather to *undo* such statements that produce a contained coherent picture of the artist or the poem, if ever so desirable (for our own purposes, for our own goals of closure). Indeed, it is the refusal to explain, fix or otherwise catch the Dickinson text that is, in a sense, the 'meaning' of this study. It is hoped that the study will be received as precisely a critique of the way in which authorship is produced, the way in which the academic institution canonizes its authors. In this way this study participates in the general project of 'unediting' Emily Dickinson, in the employment of that term to mean an insistence on challenging the received editorial constructs of a particular set of texts and a particular author. I think about what appears from this method of reading the author as a kind of editorial or textual biography that seeks to elaborate how the author is produced through the editorial ventures that present her work to an audience.

EDITING DICKINSON

We must state from the beginning that Emily Dickinson was a known poet in her lifetime and that in specific ways she 'edited' her work for 'publication' in ways perhaps deviant from the print norm but nevertheless in ways public. The lore surrounding Emily Dickinson may covet the idea of the reclusive poet wrapping up her work in a chest of drawers in her bedroom but in fact Emily Dickinson's work was not radically discovered in that mythical moment when Lavinia, her sister, opened the chest of drawers and found the poet's manuscript books and other writings. Emily Dickinson had sent her poems to family and friends, in an epistolary kind of publication: the poet's scene of writing was very much a scene of publication.[7] She had many correspondents, and the writing of letters entailed the writing and rewriting of poems, for letters came with poems (letters are poems, poems are letters: the 'letter-poem' is a genre assigned to Dickinson). Among her friends she counted editors of influential newspapers and the popular writer Helen Hunt Jackson. Samuel Bowles, the editor of the *Springfield Daily Republican* was a close friend of the Dickinsons. Dickinson's correspondence with Thomas W. Higginson might have for a long time been stressed as the most significant one by critics but, as Martha Nell Smith has made clear, the recipient of the most extensive number of poems is Susan Dickinson, married to Emily Dickinson's brother, Austin. Anna Mary Wells wrote, in a 1929 survey of early Dickinson criticism, that the poet's "sister Lavinia and sister-in-law Susan treasured every scrap [of Dickinson's hand] they could find, as did most of the friends to whom she sent verses in letters" and suggests that "the family of Emily Dickinson seem to have joined with her friends in urging her to publish her poems" (247).

But Emily Dickinson did not print-publish her work and hence the chest of drawers now on display in the Houghton Library at Harvard University symbolically offers the clichéd notion of the poet writing for secrecy in her Amherst bedroom. Pulling its drawers out at the time of the writer's death in 1886, the story goes, Lavinia found the large trove of poems that had been stored there (Johnson, *Poems* xxxix). The magnitude of this production, once hidden from the world (in the sense of a general public), has slowly been unraveled during subsequent decades of publication and critical attention. The chest of drawers is now, of course, emptied of its contents, and remains only a token symbol of this writer's practices. But as it carries with it notions of privacy and isolation, it is a misleading symbol if we wish to consider Emily Dickinson' life and work as in some sense public in her own lifetime.

The history of the dispersal and re-collection of the poet's work needs here to be recounted briefly. The manuscripts are preserved in different libraries far flung from that 'original' scene of storage. The manuscripts in the possession of the last of the Dickinson line are archived in the Houghton Library at Harvard University. The manuscripts in the possession of the last of the Todd line are archived at Amherst College Library.

This division reflects the 'war of the houses' that erupted in full force and seemingly became cemented in the subsequent history of Dickinson, when Lavinia decided to have her sister's work published and turned first to Susan Dickinson and then to Mabel Loomis Todd, the mistress of Dickinson's brother Austin Dickinson. This war of sorts between families has been narrated at length in various introductions to the editorial and critical history of Emily Dickinson's work.[8] For the purposes of this study, it is important to note that this 'war' has infiltrated not only the relations between the various members of the rivaling families, and hence the various editorial projects embarked upon by them; as a consequence critical voices too have wavered. On the one hand, in the vein of Richard Sewall's biographical account in *Emily Dickinson,* some critics have seen Mabel Loomis Todd and her daughter Millicent Todd Bingham as the heroic rescuers of Dickinson's work, thereby quite explicitly disregarding the work of Susan Dickinson (and her daughter) in the same direction. On the other hand, other critics have condemned Mabel Loomis Todd for being the adulterous intruder into the Dickinson compound of the Homestead and the Evergreens, and have chosen to privilege Susan Dickinson's role in the poet's life. The roles these women played in the editorial and critical dissemination of Dickinson's work have challenged critics to refuse an objective role (not practically achievable anyway), clearly indicating their subjective preferences. In particular, critics seem to have had to choose for or against Susan Dickinson in this narrative. Some have seen her as Dickinson's friend-turned-sour, whereas contemporary critics, most strongly Martha Nell Smith, have 'recovered' Susan Dickinson to her rightful role as friend, potential lover and recipient of more letters from Dickinson than any other single correspondent. The story of the making public-through-print of Emily Dickinson's work, then, is intimately connected to the family dynamics of the Dickinsons and to the divergent critical interpretations of those dynamics: furthermore, these dynamics and interpretations still shape Dickinson editing and study.

From the very beginning, in this family 'war' we can see the interconnectedness, not only between 'text' and 'life,' but between the interpretive tasks of 'editing' and 'criticism' in the construction of 'Emily Dickinson.' All editions of Emily Dickinson's work, even Johnson's presumably more 'neutral' and 'scholarly' edition of 1955 are inflected with the family politics stemming from the triangular affairs between the Homestead (where Emily Dickinson lived with her father, mother and sister Lavinia Dickinson), the Evergreens (where Austin and Susan lived), and the Todd house.

The early editing that started out as collaboration between Thomas Higginson and Mabel Loomis Todd was shaped by a severe distrust in the market potential of Dickinson's work. Higginson dubbed the "sudden" success of the first edition of her work as the "curious" effect of a publication venture that had launched quietly and "without any expectation of a wide audience" ("Letters" 444). The volume, as Higginson mentions in an article in *The Atlantic Monthly,* sold in six consecutive editions within six months

Introduction 19

of the first publication. Higginson calls this a "suddenness of success almost without a parallel in American literature" ("Letters" 444).

Thomas Higginson described Emily Dickinson as a woman who had "no reference, in all the rest, to anything but her own thought and a few friends" ("Letters" 444). Considering the fact that Higginson had corresponded with Emily Dickinson for a number of decades, this is a remarkable comment but clearly made with a certain end in mind: the article in which Higginson thus describes Dickinson was meant as a promotion of the forthcoming edition of the poet's *Letters* and, indeed, the market value of that edition was calculated on the presumed 'privacy' and 'reclusiveness' of the poet and the presumed 'revelations' that her letters would have for a world feeding of the idea of the lonely and misunderstood spinster of Amherst.

This idea of Emily Dickinson as isolated recluse was aggravated by the infamous 'war between the houses,' which resulted in a large number of Dickinson's poems being stacked away for several decades in the very private belongings of Austin's mistress, Mabel Loomis Todd. A large number of Dickinson's poems, that is, were not made public even after her death. The problems that haunted the Dickinson family were hence intricately woven into the fabric of the Dickinson text.

The early twentieth century editorial dissemination of 'Emily Dickinson' was a confusing replay of that infamous "war between the houses" that in Richard Sewall's version involves "all three of the younger Dickinsons, plus two outsiders, Susan Gilbert Dickinson and (beginning in 1882) Mabel Loomis Todd" (*Emily Dickinson* 161). Through various editorial projects Martha Dickinson Bianchi and Millicent Todd Bingham attempted to furnish the legacy not only of Emily Dickinson but also of their respective mothers. Because this process of establishing Emily Dickinson's poems and letters in the literary marketplace was not simply conditioned by a desire to see those writings in print but also structured by family affairs, it was characterized by a blurring of text and life: of, on the one hand 'further' and 'new' poems and, on the other, 'revelations' and 'ancestors' brocades.'

Dickinson's niece Martha Dickinson Bianchi put out an impressive set of editions. In 1914, *The Single Hound: Poems of a Lifetime* was published. In 1924, *The Life and Letters of Emily Dickinson* as well as *The Complete Poems of Emily Dickinson* appeared. But, already in 1929, *Further Poems of Emily Dickinson*, with the telling subtitle *Withheld from Publication by her Sister Lavinia*, co-edited with Alfred Leete Hampson, was added to that supposed 'completeness.' In 1930, one hundred years after the poet's birth, Dickinson Bianchi and Leete Hampson published *The Poems of Emily Dickinson: Centenary Edition*. *Emily Dickinson Face to Face: Unpublished Letters with Notes and Reminiscences by Her Niece,* by Martha Dickinson Bianchi, appeared in 1932. In 1935, another round of poems appeared in *Unpublished Poems of Emily Dickinson* and, finally, in 1937, *Poems by Emily Dickinson* was published. From the other 'house' emerged Mabel Loomis Todd's edition of *Letters of Emily Dickinson: New and Enlarged Edition* in 1931. *Bolts of Melody: New Poems of Emily Dickinson,* edited by Mabel Loomis Todd and Millicent Todd Bingham, appeared in 1945, after the death of Martha Dickinson Bianchi. This edition could have had the subtitle 'Withheld from publication by Mabel Loomis Todd' but of course did not: the edition is another instance of the personal politics of the Dickinson wars, for this edition contained a number of poems that Millicent had 'discovered' in the camphor-wood chest in which her mother had stored, locked up, a significant number of Dickinson documents in the wake of the lawsuit with Lavinia over a strip of land in 1898. Finally Todd Bingham published *Ancestors' Brocades: the Literary Debut of Emily Dickinson* in 1945 and *Emily Dickinson: A Revelation* in 1954.

This confusing array of editorial ventures impacted on the reception of the poet, to the extent that the canonization of the poet, her inclusion, that is, in American literary history, was to some extent hindered by the critical suspicion regarding the textual accuracy of the editions. To make the point somewhat extreme: instead of criticism, there were reviews of new editions; and, moreover, instead of textual uncertainty, there was 'biography,' as if the textual uncertainty would be mended by biographical certainties.[9] It is here, in the interstices between an uncertain text and an (un)certain biography, that the figure of Emily Dickinson has developed into an enigma that feeds an industry of scholarly engagement: it is this interconnectedness between editing, criticism, and the figuring of an author that is the subject of this study.

In spite of the confusing textual situation, there was, of course, criticism in the sense of serious studies of Emily Dickinson's art. Many of these considerations came from poets whom we associate with Modernism: Amy Lowell, Marianne Moore, Hart Crane, and William Carlos Williams. The 'southern' critics that we associate with New Criticism also paid significant attention to Emily Dickinson.[10]

In 1955 Thomas Johnson published *The Poems of Emily Dickinson.* This edition, a three-volume variorum, was seen as that final scholarly answer to the previous textual disarray. But the war between the houses insidiously shaped Johnson's work as he was only offered photostat access to the manuscripts in the possession of Mabel Loomis Todd's line. In recent years critics like Martha Nell Smith and Ellen Louise Hart have seized on the inaccuracies that such photostats yield in terms of the material status of a document, such as whether it is written in pen or pencil ("Gifts and Ghosts" 27). R. W.

Franklin's 1967 "reconsideration" of Johnson's editing was instigated by Millicent Loomis Todd's offering him access to her mother's editorial project: we can see how his work, then, is shaped by certain 'family' investments as well. Martha Nell Smith's work, too, is intricately bound up in 'family matters,' or the 'Dickinson wars' both in her general argument that Susan Dickinson must be considered central to Dickinson's poetic project and in her reconsiderations of Martha Dickinson Bianchi's editing.

We must consider how that more particular 'war' between the families implicated in the triangular relations in Amherst circa 1898 is still raging, very much 'alive,' in spite of the literal death of all of its original participants. In a very literal sense, these family wars came full circle, in 1998, with the very personal politics invested in and investing the editing of *Open me Carefully: Emily Dickinson's Intimate Letters to Susan Huntington Dickinson.*

This edition's very interpretive force challenges the 'neutrality' conferred by the other 1998 publication: R. W. Franklin's revisioning of *The Poems of Emily Dickinson.* Yet again a three-volume variorum edition emerged from Harvard University Press, with the message that Emily Dickinson's poetry is possible to bind into the luxuries of silver and pale blue.[11]

The ongoing project of archiving Emily Dickinson's work electronically is governed by an explicit interpretive drive that is also explicitly located in the original family dynamics of the Homestead and the Evergreens: *The Dickinson Electronic Archives* is not meant as a storage space for the work of Emily Dickinson but of several Dickinson figures, most prominently Susan Dickinson and her son Ned's writings.[12] Such a production of the archive is based in a consideration of authorship as collaborative rather than strictly 'individual,' in the idealist sense that has produced our literary histories of individual talents: it nevertheless succumbs to the privileging of a particular Dickinson narrative.

In this description of the editorial history of Dickinson we have seen how 'Emily Dickinson' is a textual production of editorial investments in her texts as 'poems' and of 'Emily Dickinson' as 'poet.' 'Emily Dickinson' is furthermore the continual production of critical readings based on these editorial investments. I now move on to a brief consideration of this critical figuring of Emily Dickinson through anthologizing, biographical and critical work about her.

AUTHORING DICKINSON: BIOGRAPHY

In this section I consider previous Dickinson research that problematizes the stability of the Dickinson text. The web of editions and criticism that produces an author can be thought of as classificatory: as a canonical author Emily Dickinson has indeed been neatly organized into entries in an encyclopedia. Emily Dickinson is hence reproduced not only in editions but also in titles like *An Emily Dickinson Encyclopedia, The Emily Dickinson Handbook, A Historical Guide to Emily Dickinson* and *The Cambridge Companion to Emily Dickinson*. I interpret these kinds of anthologies of critical perspectives on Dickinson as a specific form of 'editing' the poet: like the major editorial projects, these kinds of books reinforce the poet's canonicity, and in specific ways they not simply establish the 'foundations' for Dickinson studies but, I argue, limit it too. Encyclopedias are selective. This means that I agree with Jane Donahue Eberwein, who reassuringly writes about *An Emily Dickinson Encyclopedia*, "this encyclopedia remains only a starting point for research" (xii). But such a cheerful proposition needs to be qualified and queried, for that starting point is in itself already a production of Dickinson and indeed suggests that 'Emily Dickinson' takes shapes, as a figure, through such projects: and the particular shape she takes is the canonical. Tellingly shared by these encyclopedic projects is the insistence on 'Emily Dickinson' as a separate, singular, unique author: as a proper and disciplined object of study.

In spite of this seeming coherence of the object of study 'Emily Dickinson,' Karl Keller writes about Emily Dickinson that to "a great extent she is unknowable. Those students of hers who have not learnt this have been, with few exceptions, fooled by their certainties." He describes biography as a "hall of tortures" (1–2). Vivian Pollak writes of an "omitted center" in Dickinson's poetry and life, a center constituted by one or several traumatic narratives that "[press] against language" and that need to be recovered. She produces an image of the author as 'isolated' but hypothesizes that the effect of this social isolation is non-recoverable, the question to what the effects on the poet's poetics this isolation may have had, "unanswerable" (6). Keller is right that we cannot ever 'know' Emily Dickinson, in the sense of a biographical revelation. We cannot know that particular Emily Dickinson who "writing for honor and herself, not for fame and publication, and not for the academic or editorial or even general community—did not know (however much she may have hoped) that she would one day become 'Emily Dickinson'" (Judith Farr, *The Passion of Emily Dickinson* 246). But we can interpret the textualized history that is 'Emily Dickinson.'

We can say that Emily Dickinson was her own 'un-biographer' even it that first letter to Higginson where she intriguingly disconnected her artistic work from her personal name. From the very beginnings of her public life, she defied the conventions of modern authorship, refusing to take an active position in the field of literary production. Clearly, Dickinson did offer her work to the select world of her correspondents. The idea of Dickinson as enigmatic spinster is as Shawn Alfrey points out, a result precisely of her first editor Thomas Higginson who produced this notion of the poet as isolated from the world by precisely beginning the first published volume of her work with a poem that speaks about letters as a kind of biography (9). Emily Dickinson's poems, while typically considered lyrical, cannot be read literally biographically. The only 'access' we may get to 'Emily Dickinson' is precisely textual, contextual but nevertheless textual, 'located' in the ever-increasing production of the figure of Emily Dickinson. Sewall describes Dickinson's life as a "mystery" that, one assumes, is about to be solved (4). Genetic critics play on this notion of a mystery in their tracing of an intention in the documents that precede a published work. But there is no ur-text to which to turn. Katherine Sutherland writes, in a discussion of the similarities in method between biographer and textual critic that their work is "ultimately self-defeating since its outcome can only be another text and another site of authority and disorder" (*Jane Austen* 103). Is it possible to envision biography and textual criticism without authority, without disorder? Or is perhaps the positivist desire for a progression towards what Sutherland describes as "better text/life" so much part of the task of the very formulation of the professional scholar that it is impossible to break?

Raymond Williams offers the example of the conventional biography to elucidate his theorization of the "dynamic senses of social formation, of individual development, and of cultural creation, which have to be seen as in radical relationship without any categorical or procedural assumption of priorities" (197). Reading a biography of an individual, we get the impression of this figure's centrality, around which other characters figure in more or less marginal positions. When, then, we pick up a biography of one of those other, marginal, figures, we realize the relativity of the biographical project: we see that "key events appear and disappear; the decisive relationships shift" (196–97). Of course, we can compare different biographies about the same person in a similar way: although biographies of the same person, different biographies of Emily Dickinson ask different questions, shift focus, privilege one event over another.[13]

MANUSCRIPT DICKINSON

From the time of the publication of Johnson's Variorum edition in 1955 to the time of the publication of *The Manuscript Books of Emily Dickinson* in 1981, the Dickinson text had been considered reproduced in correct and reliable form by the critical community.[14] But the 'revelations' of *The Manuscript*

Books of Emily Dickinson in 1981 of the poet's handwritten pages led to a multiple-dimensioned fascination with Dickinson's handwritten manuscripts. As a consequence, editorial concerns regarding the translation of such handwritten pages into typographic form were moved to the center of Dickinson studies. Before considering the 'manuscript criticism' that was born out of this edition, I wish first to consider the more general effects this publication has had on Dickinson studies.

As any reader of Johnson's and Franklin's respective three-volume editions of Dickinson's work knows, Emily Dickinson not only produced versions of poems but furthermore experimented with variant word readings. Like so many other writers, Emily Dickinson produced numerous versions of 'the same' text.[15] Such variant texts have traditionally constituted an editorial problem: which version, that is, is to be chosen for representation in the edition? Of course, in both Johnson and Franklin's variorum editions (1955 and 1998 respectively) every variant is accounted for, but in the commentary and footnote apparatus, thereby organizing the text in a very particular, scholarly way. The goal has normally been to establish one text as the 'work.' The history of editing Dickinson's work has been shaped by such desires to fix texts into solid works. As outlined above, such a desire for the 'fixity' of the 'work' has been increasingly challenged.

In a study that situates Dickinson in the critical context of deconstruction, Sharon Cameron suggests that Emily Dickinson "chose not to choose" among her versions. In one of the most important and influential early readings of Dickinson's fascicles, *Choosing Not Choosing*, Cameron argues that Dickinson's fascicle poetry challenges the theoretical understanding of the lyric poem as 'closed' or 'limited.' Dickinson's fascicles, in spite of their appearance (as formal 'booklets'), in fact problematize the very notion of poetic or textual 'identity' (4). What constitutes a poem? Where is the boundary of a poem? How can a poem with variants both internal and external be limited, shaped and explained? That is, how can a poem such as a fascicle poem be 'controlled' (that is, made sense of, grasped) by a reader or editor?

Dickinson's fascicles, with their status wavering between the form of the book and the loose leaf, challenge the traditional idea of the lyric as spatially limited, organically self-contained. Cameron departs from the supposition of "boundedness" that comes with identifying lyrics as such individual productions, and that also comes with supposing relations between individual poems in a 'sequence' in order "to consider poems as not discrete but also as not related is to complicate the negotiations between interior and exterior" (5). The poems, Cameron argues, with their variants and versions, must be read as a (meta) consideration of what the identity of a text may be—that is, of how we make sense of a literary work that refuses to mold itself according the model of the organic whole, tightly wrought urn: "[t]he question raised is if this word—or this second poem—conventionally understood to be outside the poem is rather integral to the poem, how is the poem delimited? What is the poem?" (6) Cameron's questions have been pursued by manuscript critics and have even been revamped into questions of what Emily Dickinson wrote. For example, moving away from the 'book' as the necessary form of publication, Martha Nell Smith has proposed that Dickinson's specific correspondences be seen as metaphorical books, as epistolary publications.[16]

Hence the questions asked by Cameron regarding the fascicles today extend to the entire Dickinson corpus, and Martha Nell Smith's questions, echoing Cameron's, still provoke and lurk in each critic's dealings with this writer's work: "What counts as a Dickinson poem? What counts as Dickinson's 'work'?" ("Corporealizations" 216) The Dickinson corpus—writings that conventionally have been categorized according to strict genre conventions—poetry and letters—has been opened up to an extent that leaves little stability. Each reader-critic must become an editor of these texts.[17] This is then the context for manuscript criticism, with its particular focus on handwriting and the manuscript page, to which I now turn.

In the wake of *The Manuscript Books of Emily Dickinson,* David Porter noted a "new viewpoint" in Dickinson studies that "involves a fresh look at the poet's worksheets, including the scraps of paper on which she sometimes wrote" (2). Further, and importantly, "[t]o examine the scraps that fall out of the acid-free envelopes now protecting them from disintegration-corners of wrapping paper, slit-open envelopes, a cooking-chocolate wrapper is to realize that printed versions of the poems necessarily recreate the figure of the artist" (2). Thus, in the 1980s, what Domhnall Mitchell calls the 'manuscript school' brought about what I consider to be a paradigmatic change in Dickinson studies ("'A Foreign Country'" 176). To this effect, poet-critic Susan Howe states that "[i]n the long run, the best way to read Dickinson is to read the facsimiles, because her calligraphy influences her meaning" (*The Birth-mark:* 153).[18]

In the Dickinson studies marketplace circulate a number of strong and related discourses connected to this argument. While arguing the privilege of the material "artifact" over the immaterial "work;" and substituting collaborative ventures for authoritative editions (Smith, "Corporealizations" 215–216), the liberation of Dickinson from the high culture editions sealed with the Harvard University Press insignia is promised (Werner, *Open Folios* 12–13), as is the encounter with a flesh-and-blood Dickinsonian text (Smith,

"Corporealizations" 195, 203). What these discourses have in common is a suspicion of pinning down 'meaning'—of the kind of organic, closed, meaning of a poem as codified by New Criticism and New Bibliography. Instead of limiting Dickinson's texts by enclosing them in a book, these discourses elaborate a poetics of writing and a poetics of reading. Central to these is the idea of open-endedness, of a dwelling in possibility-of-sorts. These critical discourses trace the texts' meanings through explorations of the poetics of Dickinson and the poetics of the reader: *The Dickinson Electronic Archives* is a putting-into-practice of these theories of the Dickinson text.[19]

I wish here to make a contribution to central metacritical arguments in what I see as a context of metacritical debates in Emily Dickinson studies. In "The Emily Dickinson Wars" Betsy Erkkila sets out to sketch an answer regarding the question of what are "the precise kinds of cultural, political, and ideological work that the figure of Emily Dickinson and her writings have been called upon to do" (12). This study engages that question by considering how the Dickinson text has been valorized in different periods. The twentieth-century history of editing and of critically reading Dickinson is explored with the aim to discern what kinds of meanings the editorial 'figures' (forms) of Emily Dickinson's texts have been imbued with. Discussing what she sees a serious suppression of the "facts" of Dickinson's relationship with Susan Dickinson, Martha Nell Smith reminds us that such "facts" need not simply to be articulated but engaged with in order to matter ("Susan and Emily" 53–54). Similarly, while editing may earlier have been theorized as objective by neutrally presenting information about a text, contemporary textual criticism emphasizes how editions are indeed productions of a specific kind of knowledge, they are never simply informational, non-interpretive. It is the uses to which editorial projects (and critical projects concerned with editorial questions) have figured and put to use 'Emily Dickinson' that I explore.

As the 1998 Franklin edition would seem to implicitly suggest, not everyone is content with the construction of a 'scriptural' Dickinson. From various theoretical positions, critics have produced critiques of manuscript criticism. Shawn Alfrey considers the putting into play an ideology of the sublime and notes the danger of turning Dickinson and her manuscripts into icons similar in function to a saint (10). Similarly, Robert McClure Smith assesses critically such manuscript critics as "engage in a flight from history and sexuality (and, more *strikingly,* from the history of sexuality) in order to fetishize fascicle manuscripts, to pursue somatic contact with documents the poet fingered, to pilgrimage to Harvard and Amherst to touch the relics, to ponder lost and irrecoverable intentions in new hypertextual scriptures ("seductions" 10)." He suggests, "it may be a more than opportune moment to ask pointedly what makes of this particular poet, at this particular critical juncture, a consummate saint or martyr?" ("Dickinson and the Masochistic Aesthetic"15). From a historicizing perspective, that insists on 'materiality' in more senses than that particular kind of the pure manuscript body, Domhnall Mitchell notes too that manuscript criticism pursues an ahistoricist formalism in its approach to Dickinson's autograph poems ("Grammar" 479–480, 508; *Monarch* 260). Similarly, Shira Wolosky articulates a concern that Dickinson may not only be liberated from editorial convention and cultural stereotypes but also from history: "Having been so long locked in her room, Dickinson now seems in danger of being locked in her drawer" (92).

These critics voice important questions with regard to manuscript criticism: I interpret the sheer amount of critical responses to this particularly potent merger of textual criticism, biography and literary criticism as indicative precisely of its potency and force. Nevertheless, if the surfaces of the Dickinson manuscripts were somewhat novel in the 1980s and 1990s, at the beginning of the twenty-first century manuscript criticism itself demands to be historicized. It thus seems pertinent to contextualize further the question of the significance of Dickinson's handwriting and other manuscript features. Other critics have contributed towards such a contextualization and written about the risks of manuscript criticism. Heinz Ickstadt describes how critics like Susan Howe and Jerome McGann insert Dickinson into a genealogy of visual Modernist writing, pointing to McGann's allusion to Charles Olson's concept of 'composition by field' (65).[20] His summary of these manuscript critics suggests that one of the risks of such manuscript study is a paradoxical departure from matter altogether. For by privileging matter, critics run the risk of essentializing it, attributing to it a foundational meaning. Marta Werner, Ickstadt argues, explores the manuscript's surfaces to reach a kind of spiritual reading of "marks and signs" (65). In Chapter Two, I will analyze further this problematic connection, made by Werner, between material page and some kind of 'spiritual' beyond.

Melanie Hubbard's article "As there are Apartments: Emily Dickinson's Manuscripts and Critical Desire at the Scene of Reading" begins with an ironic description of such manuscript oriented criticism: in a critical environment where only the handwritten manuscript suffices, is the editorial task not redundant? In fact, is not "only a pilgrimage to the archives" the only meaningful way of encountering Dickinson's hand/writing? In order to move away from such appropriations of manuscripts as somehow signifying the dead author's mind or hand, Hubbard stresses the reader's construction of meaning in such documents: we will not, of course, find Dickinson in her signature or in shopping lists (53). That ultimate desire to somehow 'find' Emily Dickinson, that ultimate figure of the author, yields a paradoxical constraint to manuscript criticism's avowed privileging of multiple and versioned texts. Ickstadt suggests they have "converted the uncertainty surrounding Dickinson's texts [. . .] into a radical assertion of their subversive richness, their infinite textual and textural suggestiveness" (56). That is to say that the dogmatic rhetoric of their arguments clashes with the very multiplicity they propose.[21] Ickstadt concludes by zooming in on manuscript criticism as a "zero point in Dickinson scholarship," which with its offering of "ultimate uncertainty, the doubt in the very possibility of an authentic text" "makes us inevitably aware that to confront Dickinson's mysteries is to confront our own individual, professional or cultural preconceptions and constructions" (56). It is from this position, where the metacritical mode turns self-conscious, that I consider the strongest metacritical engagement in Dickinson studies today. As outlined above, several critics before me have adopted a metacritical analytical perspective to elucidate the ways in which 'Emily Dickinson' has been figured a central author through editions and criticism. I contribute to such metacritical investigation by considering the continual instability of the 'object' of study. I will argue that each edition of Emily Dickinson's work is bound to be unedited, is bound to be cancelled by a subsequent edition: there is no Dickinson text to which we can 'return' as 'proper' or 'best.'

The aim of this study is to show how each editorial project and subsequent critical body of work shape the Dickinson text and, as a consequence, the figure of Dickinson, in important ways. In the following chapters it is my aim to explore how editorial-critical voices that propose 'radical' change are quickly neutralized into the latest figure of Dickinson, thereby succumbing to the conservatism of the editorial and critical task, which is essentially a task of canonizing an author or a critical model. This study hence engages the body of editorial productions that constitute the 'scholarly' representation of 'Emily Dickinson' in the twentieth century. In order to do so, editions and important critical debates are analyzed through a historicizing and materialist methodology. By 'historicizing' I mean an approach that understands 'history' as an ever-evolving construct of critical imaginations, rather than a progressive linear development that, from a 'later' vantage point, criticism may 'reveal.' Instead, the current notions of what the past represents shape any kind of 'historical' narrative. By 'materialist' I mean specifically a critical approach that takes into consideration the *matter* of text, that is, textual materiality in the senses of paper, pen and ink, but also, extending the usage of the term, the conditions through which such texts emerge. These are not simple terms but for the purposes of this study these provisory definitions will be applied. This study then challenges the idealizing momentum that drives all Dickinson editing, even in the digital versions of the early twenty-first century. Such a challenge is important because such idealization of the author and her texts (texts that almost become materializations of her, the poet, or her mind) creates a critical environment in which the author's insertion into canons of 'good' literature is simply assumed, rather than demanded.

This study consists of three chapters. The order of the chapters is chronological in the sense that they deal chronologically with the editing and reception of 'Emily Dickinson.' It is also chronological in the sense that the move from 'authoring' (as in establishing the author) to 'un/editing' to 'archiving' the poet represents, schematically, a chronology of the general goals of editorial-critical practices in the twentieth century. Of course, all these notions are continual practices, so that the 'authoring' of the author of course is a practice of all criticism of Dickinson, so that the 'unediting' of her texts can in one sense be understood as the rationale of any editorial project (in the sense of 'making better' the previous editions), and so that 'archiving' Dickinson is a continual practice of preserving the poet's work for posterity. But the various practices have been valorized as 'central' in the chronology that the chapters suggest.

The first chapter presents the early twentieth-century critical formulations of Emily Dickinson. This early twentieth-century reception was conditioned by a number of different and differing editorial projects. Much critical attention has been given the unselfconscious heterosexism in the figuring of this early twentieth-century Dickinson. Several critics have also offered analyses of this period as conditioned by both nostalgic readings of the poet as a representative of a lost (and better) historical New England and by a conflation of the author and her texts as 'one.' I build on these critics' work in my presentation of how Emily Dickinson was made a major American poet in these decades leading up to the publication, in 1955, of Thomas H. Johnson's three-volume edition of the poet's work, the edition that definitely established Dickinson as 'major author.' In the wake of the publication of a number of conflicting editions critical attention to Emily Dickinson's poetry reignited in the 1930s.

Parallel with this renewed interest in the author was a sense of discomfort with the edited forms through which the poet's work was encountered, a desire to establish an 'accurate' printed edition of Emily Dickinson's work. This desire was answered by the appearance in 1955 of Thomas Johnson's variorum edition. But even though this edition served, in effect, as the scholarly edition of Emily Dickinson's poetry until very recently, dissatisfaction with its editorial theory and method was articulated already in the first reviews. In the period 1924 through 1967, which this chapter is concerned with, we sense then a certain anxiety regarding the possibility of editing Emily Dickinson's work satisfactorily. Hence even in the period when Emily Dickinson criticism turned professional and when her work was established as central to the study of American literature the stability of her texts was never ascertained. In this chapter I read the early twentieth-century reception of Dickinson as a specific period of critical anxiety regarding the Dickinson text, an anxiety about the unstable text that led the New Critics to strongly 'define' the author (rather than the text, as they purported to do) and that finally led to the temporary scholarly 'sealing' of those restless texts into Johnson's variorum edition (an edition which itself was quickly queried and problematized). This sets the stage for the study's analysis of various periods of critical-editorial anxieties regarding the question, "what is a Dickinson text?," so common in contemporary critical investigations of 'Emily Dickinson.' The notoriously problematic history of editions of the poet's work based in the 'war of the houses,' is, I argue, reflected in the definition-urgency among New Critics regarding the 'author' associated with these unstable texts.

The second chapter seizes on the tropes of 'the editor' and 'editing' and the theorization of the 'unediting' of texts and periods in order to elucidate the late twentieth-century field of Dickinson studies. The chapter argues that the questioning of the edited Dickinson page that developed as a result of *The Manuscript Books of Emily Dickinson* in the late twentieth century has important implications for anyone picking up a book or visiting a web site where Emily Dickinson's work is published because it seriously undermines the traditional notion that Emily Dickinson's work can be read in print. The chapter proposes that while the 'novelty' of the Dickinson manuscript's visual shapes is transformed into one among several ways of approaching Dickinson, manuscript criticism's arguments have had a paradigmatic impact on Dickinson's recent reception. Consequently, the effects of manuscript criticism need to be contextualized as an important model of theorizing Dickinson's texts. In this second chapter I hence approach Dickinson's manuscripts and manuscript criticism through a review of the late twentieth-century editing of Dickinson.

Literary texts are transmitted to readers through various media. Increasingly, the material forms of such media have been explored as constitutive of the meaning of the work.

Little metacritical analysis has considered the recent digital/electronic editorial ventures to construct an 'archived' Emily Dickinson. But there is an urgent need for critics to engage these developments. The third chapter of this book is a study of such a method of 'archiving' rather than 'editing' a poet. I ask what this means for our understanding of 'an author' and a 'text.' This chapter explores the idea of archiving a poet and a text in the context of current trends in hypertext and digital media. It considers the difference between 'archiving' and 'editing.' On the Internet, literary culture is increasingly 'preserved' in virtual 'archives' of text.

The chapter begins with a consideration of the notion of the (electronic) 'archive' as a liberating answer to the 'limitedness' of print editing. A discussion of the textual criticism that informs current reading and criticism of Dickinson in a fruitful cross-fertilization between disciplines provides an analysis of the electronic editing and criticism of Emily Dickinson's texts that manuscript criticism has spawned. Contemporary 'readers' of Emily Dickinson's work are very likely to encounter her by logging on to a computer connected to the Internet: the future reception of her work is hence conditioned by the ever-growing sophistication of the capacity of digital media to represent non-digital cultural objects.

This study engages with the Dickinson text chronologically, from the early twentieth- century to the early twenty-first century editing and reception of this poet. This, however, is not meant to indicate a simple narrative of diachronic 'progression' from an earlier ideology of the 'final' work towards a current postmodern ideal of the fragmentary text as reflected in the critical desire to explore versions and variants. Dickinson studies in many ways in fact upholds the figure of Dickinson as unique and ultimately different, as well as the notion of her work as a material objectivity that can simply be reached for in the quest towards a final realization of the import of this poet and her writings. In the conclusion some reflections are provided on how editing and criticism shape the object of study—how the principles of academic canonization change while the aim seems always, regardless of critical persuasion, to be an even-better reader-editor of this Dickinson text, to be an even-better propagator of the Dickinson text. This study contributes to the critical discussion about such critical practices, rather than seeking to argue some kind of 'development' in the field of Dickinson studies as it has taken shape in the past one hundred years. The Dickinson text cannot be understood as a linear development of 'better' editions; it must be understood as an evolving and growing body of edited texts (both literally and metaphorically edited) that compete in the academic marketplace that is 'Dickinson studies.' In the following I consider the emergence of Emily Dickinson as canonical author in American literary history. By examining a number of discussions regarding the 'correct' way of editing Dickinson's manuscripts I argue that the negotiations over the correct means of editing her work can be seen as an editing of her biography, of 'Emily Dickinson' as a literary construct. In the recent past, editing has been reformulated as a historicizing practice through which readers receive not objective works but indeed socially and historically conditioned texts. This study ties in with this trend.

Chapter One
Authoring Emily Dickinson

> We must never forget this paradox: what was written before and had, at first, no after, we meet only after , and this tempts us to supply a before in the sense of a priority, cause or origin
>
> (Jean Bellemin-Noël)

> Once literary criticism is viewed as a form of 're-production,' literary debates must shift from positions of 'intrinsic' meaning to considerations of their own modes of working
>
> (Moyra Haslett)

"The basic need is to determine the Dickinson canon," wrote Thomas Johnson in 1950, five years before he was to publish the first variorum edition of Emily Dickinson's poems in three Harvard University Press volumes ("Prisms of a Poet" 263). This "need" to determine and settle Emily Dickinson's work has been and continues to be a fundamental problem in Dickinson studies, even as such determination is recast as liberation of texts from the idea of the final 'work.' We can thus understand editing as a *topos* or critical place among others that most Dickinson critics at some point pay a visit to. In the early twentieth century this critical place was informed by a desire to establish and settle Emily Dickinson as an author in American literature. A number of conflicting editions were published, continually revising the canon of poems of Emily Dickinson, offering ever 'new,' 'further,' and 'unpublished' poems. Implicitly revealing the contingency of any editorial project these editions in their confusing disarray triggered the articulation of a need to edit definitively Dickinson's work. In this chapter I explore the editorial-critical debates of the early part of the twentieth century that resulted in Johnson's 1955 volumes, thus contextualizing Johnson's variorum edition in its critical discursive field, while also linking it to current trends in Dickinson studies.

Because this edition did in so many respects establish Dickinson's texts as canonical to study the period leading up to it means to delineate how such an official canonization of the poet came about in terms of both an internal canon of Dickinson's work (her poems) and external canon of her work's place in the wider academic construct of an 'American literary history.'

In the first section of the chapter I turn to what must be characterized as the renewed interest in Emily Dickinson in the 1920s and 1930s, as key New Critics engaged with Dickinson's work. I furthermore consider the relationship of modernist writers to Dickinson that is interesting from today's critical engagements with Emily Dickinson as an avant-garde artist. Several critics, in particular Christopher Benfey, Timothy Morris, Martha Nell Smith and Betsy Erkkila, have offered meta-critical considerations of the period's production of the figure of Emily Dickinson, in particular highlighting the sexism that informs this figure. However, rather than seeing intellectual history as a linear progression (or as defined by clear paradigm shifts) I wish to accentuate similarities or continuities in critical thinking and writing between this period and today.

In the final part of the first section I test these various meta-critical notions that center on concepts like the canon and American literary history. In the second section I first consider the status of Emily Dickinson's manuscripts in the early twentieth century before I turn to the 1955 publication of *The Poems of Emily Dickinson Including Variant Readings Critically Compared with all Known Manuscripts* to elucidate Johnson's influential construction of the artist and of her work. While other editions are now superseding this edition, it is still central to readings of Dickinson's work as much of the key Dickinson criticism of the late twentieth century must be understood as conditioned by a decisive critique of this work. Rather than continuing such a critique of Johnson's edition my aim is to historicize its argument and to situate it as a defining and important answer to a scene of anxieties regarding the Dickinson text. However, while this edition has served as the standard edition of the poet's work until 1998, it almost immediately raised serious questions from reviewers and critics, regarding its editorial practice and the material results of that practice. Hence we can see that the reception of Dickinson has always been heavily conditioned by editorial problems, considerations, and debates.

NEW CRITICISM'S EMILY DICKINSON

To study the New Critical reception of Emily Dickinson is not a new undertaking by any means: it is, of course a historical period in Dickinson studies, through and from which later criticism has had to move. Hence, according to Roland Hagenbüchle New Criticism's engagement with Dickinson signifies the first serious critical analysis of her work (358–59); Robert McClure Smith writes that New Criticism "established the formal evaluative criteria that would assure Dickinson's later canonization as a key figure in American Romanticism" ("New Critical" 206); Betsy Erkkila describes Dickinson as a major figure in New Criticism's methodology of close reading that would ultimately develop into a strict delineation of "the individual poem as self-enclosed aesthetic object" ("Emily Dickinson Wars" 16); and Marjorie Perloff notes how Dickinson's work was included in *Understanding Poetry,* the New Critical pedagogical toolbox that would promote close reading as method in the undergraduate classroom for most of the twentieth century (n.pag.). This means that to engage with New Criticism is to engage with a critical period of Dickinson reception that consolidated her work as serious and worthy of inclusion in an academic canon of American literature. Thus, in his 1968 survey of Dickinson scholarship and commentary, Klaus Lubbers describes the period beginning in 1930, roughly equivalent to the earliest New Critical engagement with Dickinson, as a "period of consolidation and steadily increasing scholarly concern with Emily Dickinson" (198). But the establishing of Emily Dickinson as a key writer for New Critical methods was not a simple affair by any means. Feminist criticism, in particular, has challenged the unselfconsciously heterosexist vocabulary employed by these male New Critics in their production of Emily Dickinson and her work. Such criticism also reveals how difficult it was for critics to move beyond the biographical bias that New Criticism in theory rejected as part of an old fashioned study of literature as literary history in a limited sense of the life of authors. Put simply, gender—a social category—governs New Critical analyzes of Dickinson to the point that we can say that New Criticism canonized Emily Dickinson in spite of her gender.[1]

The life of the woman writer creeps into the narratives of these critics. One of the first critiques of such patriarchal descriptions of the poet was offered by Adrienne Rich in her important essay "Vesuvius at home: The Power of Emily Dickinson," where she cites John Crowe Ransom's verdict of the poet as "a little house-keeping person" who "while she had a proper notion of the final destiny of her poem [. . .] was not one of those poets who had advanced to that later stage of operations where manuscripts are prepared for the printer, and the poet's diction has to make concessions to the publisher's stylebook" (quoted in Rich 182). In this pungent quotation Rich captures Ransom's utter discomfort with both the female and the domestic or private aspects of Dickinson's life and with her work. Ransom's verdict of course comes across as both a diminutive portrayal of 'Emily Dickinson' and, significantly for this study's consideration of specifically editorial concerns as a disciplining of poetic language's bibliographic codes, as connecting 'real' poetry (or, at the very least the 'advanced' poet) with typography, and, in particular, with the typography of that 'publisher's stylebook.' Since Rich's essay was published in 1976, feminist criticism has thoroughly *revisioned* the figure of Emily Dickinson.

Does the New Critical period, then, have anything to offer the present? As the very ground on which New Criticism 'canonized' Emily Dickinson has since been radically questioned as partial, sexist and otherwise untheorized, the New Critical version of Emily Dickinson has come to serve two roles in recent criticism: it functions as both the first 'positive' criticism of her work from an organized and increasingly academic point of view that led to a further solidification of her presence in critical study and the negative ground from which recent critics can make their cases in antagonism, polemic and opposition. While praising and establishing Emily Dickinson, critics like Allen Tate and Richard Blackmur also produced her as the token female, as the anomalous 'poetess' who was only awkwardly fitted into the narrative of literary history. This begs the question of whether New Critical narratives may serve as anything else but a useful 'negative' background, a part of literary history from which to depart without much ado. Or can we rather see literary history, here represented by the history of reception of one author, as a continuous presence? Is criticism a linear progression of ever more informed narratives or can we see it as an on-going debate? I will here trace some connections between New Criticism and the present. In their attempts to 'locate' Emily Dickinson, critics in the early twentieth century dealt in a symbolic geography, variously inflected as 'Europe' and 'America,' the rural and the urban, the genteel and the capitalist, the conservative and the modern, and the traditional and the experimental, and of the old and the new. These binaries have continued to shape the study of Emily Dickinson until the present time. Amy Lowell's uprooting of the poet from her rural Amherst in order to posit her as an Imagist on the experimental vanguard is reflected in contemporary criticism that figures Dickinson as a protomodernist experimenter with form.[2] Similarly Tate's nostalgic reading of the poet as essentially and importantly part of that rural Amherst for his reading of the poet as a conservative cultivator of lost values can be understood as a (however problematic) precursor of contemporary criticism that attempts to figure the poet in her time.

Timothy Morris argues by employing the metaphor of a symbolic mapping of the body (of the poet, of the text) that critics associated with the New Criticism made use of and employed 'Emily Dickinson' as the final virginal site in American literary history (*Becoming Canonical* 73). But it is not only Emily Dickinson who has been mapped: her work, too, is continually mapped as a territory. Morris' analysis of the New Critical love affair with Dickinson as basically an enactment of the critical desire for the "ultimate virginal" site of interpretation, points, in poignant ways, to Martha Nell Smith's exploration of the 'New World' that she sees in the (we could say 'Virginal') material body of the manuscript page Exploiting the poet's own employments of "geographical and cartographical metaphors of exploration," Smith develops her critique of 'Old World' means of editing and reading the poet (*Rowing* 51). Employing the symbolism of such metaphors in the particular context of an American imagination, Smith develops her thesis that Dickinson's manuscripts offer a new kind of poetics, visual, antibookish, and reader-oriented.[3] Metaphorically, such a poetics offers a "New World" of poetic form. Rather than offering the reader an 'Old World' poetics of finished and organic poems (such as her print editors have offered the reader), Smith suggests that, if "we are prepared to step out of the critical circumference" of such Old World editing and criticism, we will discover "new, Edenic modes of appreciation and interpretation of the holographs" (*Rowing* 51). Smith's positing of a binary opposition between print and handwriting according to such a symbolic geography inevitably reminds us of the continual struggle to fit Emily Dickinson's work into a narrative of 'old' and 'new.' Smith's formulation of the critical task as specifically pursuing 'new ways' of reading, according to a "New World" of form, pays allegiance to Lowell's modernist reading of Emily Dickinson as part of the "vanguard" of the new: it implicitly challenges Tate's reading of the poet as part of a 'tradition' of the genteel as opposed to the modern and experimental.

If we consider the editions of Emily Dickinson's work that appeared after the slump in editorial concern with the poet in the first one and a half decades of the twentieth century, we see that these tensions between 'old' and 'new' are effected by (however implicit) editorial choices. Anna Mary Wells writes about how the radical absence of Emily Dickinson in American literature in the first fifteen years of the twentieth century triggered a feeling of 'discovery' and generational shift from Victorian to Modern among those readers who encountered Dickinson in the 1920s. Wells writes in 1929 that "it was the 15 years of obscurity between 1900 and 1915 that led to the popular misconception that no one before our own generation had appreciated Emily Dickinson" (258). But in 1914 *The Single Hound: Poems of a Lifetime* was published, an edition of Dickinson's work that, as Linda Leavell points out, numbered poems instead of entitling them and did not interfere with punctuation, rhyme and meter as had Higginson and Todd (3). The visual impression of the poems of *The Single Hound,* the edition that would 'revive' interest in Emily Dickinson, is as Leavell writes "strikingly modern" to the reader (3). Amy Lowell considers this editorial shift from "an editorial eye to conciliating criticism" in her praise of *The Single Hound* as representing Emily Dickinson's 'genius' better than the three previous volumes of her work (345). Lowell's consideration of Dickinson champions the older poet for her 'Imagistic' form. But her appraisal of Dickinson is not without implicit criticisms: Dickinson achieved her modern style without "knowing that a battle was on and that she had been selected for a place in the vanguard" (339). Hence Dickinson's modern poetic persona somehow creeps into her texts "in spite of [herself]" (348). In her analysis, Lowell brands Dickinson a fighting revolutionary of Imagism but also declares that Dickinson "was of too unanalytical a nature" to have discovered theoretically the difference between conventional verse based on units of accents and modern verse based on a unit of time: again, Dickinson's modern traits were not consciously practiced poetic art but serendipitous events (348). Nevertheless, Lowell's essay speaks mostly praise, and it contributes to a historicizing narrative of modernism itself as she writes that what Dickinson "did seemed insignificant and individual, but thirty years after her death the flag under which she fought had become a great banner, the symbol of a militant revolt" (339). Lowell's essay is a precursor to recent reconsiderations of Emily Dickinson in the context of modernism, studies that expand the notion of modernism by tracing its historical links to poets past. But Lowell's New Critical contemporaries preferred to read Emily Dickinson in her past as essentially disconnected from the modern vantage point of their own position. From an antagonistic position Blackmur, in his rigorously negative estimate of Dickinson, echoes Lowell's concern with the poet's 'unanalytical' personality when he laments that, "she never undertook the great profession of controlling the means of objective expression" (223). Rather than seeing the poet's lifetime as that "perfect literary scene," as Tate was to formulate it in his praise of the poet, Blackmur criticizes not only the poet but "the habit of her society as she knew it" through which she could never have learned that "that poetry is a rational and objective art and most so when the theme is self-expression" (223).

Tate's estimate of the poet is based in a nostalgic reading of a mythical lost New England that brought solace against modern life. In Dickinson's work Tate saw a potential to articulate such a past as a remedy to the present; and the present concern, implicit in the essay, is the development of an American literature, not provincial but on a par with the literature of the 'old' world. For Tate this does not mean that literature of the 'new' world (or any poetry) could be 'revolutionary' (as Lowell would have it) but rather that it would surface as the equal of an inherited tradition (of the old world). Hence he constructs the notion of 'the perfect literary situation' and claims Dickinson and John Donne to have been two poets to have occupied and exploited such a situation (164). Dickinson, the American author, is on a par with Donne, the poet of tradition. For Tate, Dickinson's poem "Because I could not stop for death–" becomes a central argument for Dickinson's part in a tradition; an American inflection of such a tradition. In this respect Tate's analysis of "Because I could not stop for death–" is paradigmatic. I consider here this poem and the early twentieth century's reception of it at length, as an example of the politics of both editing and criticism.

Tate's 1932 essay "New England Culture and Emily Dickinson" served to inaugurate New Critical attention to the poet. Tate has been variously been granted a major role in the reception and production of Emily Dickinson. Christopher Benfey calls the essay a "real trumpet blast" through which Dickinson's texts were included into the map or canon of American literature (35). But the essay was contested by Yvor Winters who argued that Tate's reading of Dickinson's work as great was "fraudulent" and "unconvincing" and generally "unsound" (192–93).

Tate's essay employs the symbolic geography of the 'old' and 'new' world in at least two senses. His aim was two-fold: to situate Dickinson as a specifically American author in opposition to the 'old world' literary history and to situate her as the upholder of a tradition, a rural and historical America that was disappearing in the midst of modernity. I wish here to explore these tensions through Tate's treatment of "Because I could not stop for death–." The poem emerges through Tate's essay as both a supreme Dickinson poem and a poem of powerful cultural nostalgia, serving well Tate's desire for a national literary-cultural history. Indeed, this poem builds on what was already in Emily Dickinson's lifetime starting to fade into a cliché: the genteel woman, the genteel driver, and the carriage, as stock figures, hark back to an era of nostalgic middle-class gentility. For Tate this was part of the poet's genius, her negotiation in the midst of the decline of her very culture, of that culture.

But the question, from the current scene of reading this poem, with all its editorial versions laid bare, is how to relate to Tate's reading of the poem, in which not only the added title but also a removed stanza from our perspective play serious bibliographic and linguistic havoc with Emily Dickinson's manuscript page and the potential cultural critique conveyed by the poem. First of all we need to acknowledge that our possible readings are always contingent on the textual and theoretical tools available. This articulates a problem of critical blindness and proposes the question of to what extent a reader can 'trust' an edition. Clearly, the temporal agreement on what a 'Dickinson poem' is is relative and so readers must at some level accept the current version as trustworthy. At the present time, the agreement on how to read Dickinson's texts suggests that no holographic version of a poem can be said to be final. They all inform our interpretation. Therefore editions which privilege one version over another offer only a certain sense of blindness. Yet reading cannot always be based in suspicion that the text one reads is not in some sense 'correct.' To historicize readings of textual versions that have been revealed as in some sense editorially corrupt should mean to consider the conventions of a period—they help us to better understand the critical heritage of a field. Here is the poem that Tate read (lines that have been changed, that is, censored, are italicized):

The Chariot

Because I could not stop for death,
He kindly stopped for me;
The carriage held but just ourselves
And immortality.

We slowly drove, he knew no haste
And I had put away
My labor and my leisure too,
For his civility.
We passed the school where children played
Their lessons scarcely done;
We passed the fields of gazing grain,
We passed the setting sun.

We paused before a house that seemed
A swelling of the ground;
The roof was scarcely visible,
The cornice but a mound.

Since then 'tis centuries; but each
Feels shorter than the day
I first surmised the horses' heads
Were toward eternity.

Authoring Emily Dickinson

In Tate's reading of this poem editing and criticism of 'Emily Dickinson' meet and reveal the politics of any edition, the politics of any critical reading, but in particular the politics of reading a poem of Emily Dickinson in the pre-Johnson period. For the poem that Tate read was based on the 'censored' version of 1890, with the pivotal fourth stanza cut out, a title added and four lines altered. But on top of this 1890 edition, the New Critic reader could use Martha Dickinson Bianchi's edition of the poem from 1924 (again, changes are italicized):

> Because I could not stop for Death
> He kindly stopped for me;
> The carriage held but just ourselves
> And Immortality.
>
> We slowly drove, he knew no haste
> And I had put away
> My labor and my leisure too,
> For his civility.
>
> *We passed the school where Children played*
> *At wrestling in a ring;*
> We passed the fields of gazing grain,
> We passed the setting sun.
>
> We paused before a house that seemed
> A swelling of the ground;
> The roof was scarcely visible,
> *The cornice but a mound.*
>
> *Since then 'tis Centuries; but each*
> Feels shorter than the day
> I first surmised the horses' heads
> Were toward eternity.

The critical genealogy of this poem, then, becomes a clear and important marker of how different readings of the different pages of 'the same' poem have led to very different results. Tate's reading of the poem as essentially conservative was conditioned by the absence of a stanza 'crucial' for the poem's potential critique of that conservative culture. Here it is reproduced as Franklin edits it in *Poems of Emily Dickinson* (lineation is according to Franklin's annotation rather than the bibliographic presentation):

>Or rather—He passed Us–
>The Dews drew quivering and Chill–
>For only Gossamer, my Gown–
>My Tippet—only Tulle–

Let us then return to the poem and Tate's analysis. The scene is seemingly straightforward. The speaker is being taken out for a drive in a carriage. The added title in the first edition of the poem describes this carriage: it is a 'chariot.' "The Chariot" proved an infectious title: Thomas Johnson, who 'critically' removed the added title in his 'scholarly edition' of the poet's work nevertheless chose to read the poem in the light of that title: in the 'pleasure carriage' sense of 'chariot.' His biographical reading hypothesizes the driver as one of those Amherst gentlemen who might, at one point or another have "acted as the poet's squire" (222). Similarly, in Tate's reading, the word's connotations of a pleasure drive lead into a scene of genteel love as a metaphor for death. In the Romantic tradition, Tate points out, the ideas of death and love are often conflated, and this trope is used in the poem to provide the hopeful assertion that there is no reason to fear the potential terror of death; and, after all, the speaker is carried forth on her pleasure drive by the reigns of a lover. The speaker, that is, is taken good care of by the figure of death as personified by the driver. The scene is one of polite gentility, effacing the potentially fearful emotional state of dying: as Tate puts it, "the terror of death" is "objectified" in the image of the squire driver.

To Tate the poem refuses the potentially "ludicrous" or "incredible" in such an old-fashioned genteel scene (161). But Cristanne Miller reads the first stanzas of the poem through the fourth stanza (which Tate did not have access to) and finds it ironic: "The poem becomes a satiric portrait of Victorian gentility and repression" in which death-as-gentleman-lover is revealed as a fraudulent marauder who will not release his brides to any "promised wedding ceremony and new family fold" ("Because" 14). If Tate thought the poem held together the metaphorical merger of love and death (in the Romantic trope and in its Victorian religious strain), Miller finds the fourth stanza's physical "chill" a reminder that such fusion of 'love' and 'death' is, in fact, for the speaker, a fragile cultural construct. The stanza, Miller argues, turns an otherwise genteel scene into a gothic questioning of the "clarity and comfort promised in Victorian accounts of Christian death or marriage with God" ("Because" 14). Interpreting the poem in this Christian context, Miller argues that the "chill" of the fourth stanza "undercuts the apparent calm certainties" of the previous stanzas:

> Or rather—He passed Us–
> The Dews drew quivering and Chill–
> For only Gossamer, my Gown–
> My Tippet—only Tulle–

In the fourth stanza of "Because I could not stop for Death" the speaker realizes a predicament: the air is growing chill as her clothing consists, inappropriately for the ride in the 'chariot,' of sheer "gossamer" and "tulle." Gossamer and tulle, Miller reminds us, symbolizes both marriage and funeral, adding to the poem's metaphoric conflation of death and marriage (with God). But the fabric imagery in conjunction with the figures in the poem suggests more than such marriage and/or death rhetoric. In an analysis of Emily Dickinson's employment of textile imagery, Peter Stoneley interprets the poem "I pay in—Satin Cash–(Fr 402)." Stoneley argues that the poem stages an anxiety regarding women's place in the marketplace, by suggesting that "satin as a luxurious fabric" is "too good for everyday use" (585). Implying the "exclusion or unsuitability of feminine values in the marketplace," because excluding women from the 'everyday' involvement in that marketplace, the poet's speaker, with her "satin," is left outside of the circulation of goods, a circulation dependent on 'real' cash rather than on the feminine dainties of 'satin.' The middle-class woman without cash is left behind, trapped in the house of her father or husband with a chimera of power shimmering in that satin. Just like poems like "I pay in—Satin Cash–" and "What Soft-Cherubic Creatures–" that Stoneley enlists for his argument, "Because I could not stop for death" is part of such a self-conscious critique of the paradoxes of the situation of the genteel woman. Cutting short the stanza with those telling garments, Mabel Loomis Todd and Thomas Higginson cut short, too, the potential social critique of the poem.

In the light of Stoneley's analysis, the "gossamer" and "tulle" become not so much part of a gothic narrative and sarcastic critique of Victorian sugary Christianity as part of a wider complex of images in Dickinson's poetry that conjure up a problematic relationship to the marketplace in a general sense of modern society, a society in which the narrative of "Because I could not stop for death" was a fading cliché. Miller's interpretation of the poem's "sarcastic" attitude towards genteel culture in this light becomes problematic. It is not so much sarcastic as self-consciously anxious. Stoneley's analysis of textile imagery from a cultural-materialist perspective ironically fuses both Tate's early conservative analysis of the poem and recent feminist reconsiderations of the poem. Tate is correct in his reading of 'nostalgia' into the poem. But Tate read a different poem than we do today. We must allow for the 'blindness' of Tate's reading and use his reading not as an example of a necessarily naïve reader in contrast to later feminist engagements with (another) poem with the same first line. This does not make Tate's nostalgia less sentimental. But the tulle and gossamer of the censored stanza, as impractical garments for a carriage ride, contributes to a richer sense of the speaker's problematic relationship to modernity. Just as the carriage ride itself is implicitly old-fashioned and a cliché, so the garments of such softness and sheerness must be understood as impractical and unsuitable for that "modern professionalized woman" that was to compete with the gentlewoman of past days: signaling, in turn, the unsuitability of that gentlewoman's very material foundations. It is in this way that Dickinson, as Vivian Pollak argues, "emerges as the spokeswoman for a whole generation of nineteenth century women" (quoted in Stoneley 578): through an anxious staging of an old-fashioned yet familiar and romanticized spectacle. This anxiety is not so much shaped by what Tate interprets as a simple nostalgic glancing backwards but by a realization of the ideological predicament facing the middle-class woman in the (domestic, sexual and capitalist) marketplace.

The New Critical readers of this poem did not have the luxury of seeing this stanza. What is surprising is that the editors of *Understanding Poetry*, in the third printing of the textbook of 1960 still relied on the 1890 version, in spite of the publication of Johnson's edition in 1955. Symbolically, such a continual erasure of the 'gossamer' and 'tulle' in influential publications suggests an erasure of the anxieties of Dickinson's text. It is here that the editing and 'criticism' of 'Emily Dickinson meet and reveal the politics of any edition, the politics of any critical reading. For, the poem that Tate read was, of course, based on the 'censored' version of 1890, with the pivotal fourth stanza cut out. Jerome McGann urges the literary critic to engage with the materiality of text, with the matter of text, with the bibliographic codes of the literary work. For even linguistically identical versions of a text differ and affect readers differently:

> [. . .] consider a poem like Emily Dickinson's "Because I could not stop for Death," which has an identical verbal text in Johnson's critical edition,

in *The Norton Anthology of Modern Poetry*, and in Franklin's recent *The Manuscript Books of Emily Dickinson*. These three apparently 'identical' texts are in fact very different, for they exist in bibliographical environments (as it were) that enforce very different reading experiences. The analysis of these environments will only yield to an applied textual criticism. ("The Monks and the Giants" 195)

If the bibliographic codes that embed 'the same' linguistic text in a socio-material 'context' contribute to the text's meaning, then even further "different reading experiences" are produced by such editorial decisions as the deletion of stanza four of Emily Dickinson's "Because I could not stop for death–." This blatant censuring of a poem reveals the precariousness of assuming textual stability in any 'literary work' and the ideological underpinnings of any formulation of the edited text as 'authorial' or 'ideal' or 'critical.' But rather than simply critiquing the censored edition or the critical responses based on that text we can understand them as part of the literary text's critical history, part of its 'composite' meaning—as part of how Dickinson's texts have been understood. To this effect Gary Waller writes

> [. . .] the significance of any text is not inherent only in its original production: it is generated by criticism, by use in educational institutions, by appropriation into courses and literary histories and by being made to serve different ideological and political purposes. (267)

But not only is the text reproduced in criticism and literary history—those institutions depend on the work of editing. What meaning do editions and readings of those editions take on when an edition is reevaluated? While later readers may see the blindness of earlier readers, this also inspires a self-conscious reading of current texts. By the sheer accumulation of textual matter in the archive of an author, they contribute to the canonization of an author (an author with whom so much editorial effort is invested is typically considered to be of significance). We can interpret these critical engagements with the text as part of the making of an author. Genette's concept of the paratextual explicitly includes in the subcategory 'epitext' interviews, reviews, and other considerations/extensions of the work outside the physical limits of the 'peritext' (the actual book) and allows for an understanding of the critical readings of the peritextual object as part of the coding of the work. Critical readings and college anthologies contribute to the poem's material history and become part of what may be called an archive of the poem. And thus the Tate-ian reading of "Because I could not stop for death—" becomes part of the poem, part of its wider bibliographic and paratextual meanings. It has from the strict critical vantage point changed the course of criticism. One way to make use of Tate's reading is to read it in the light of such an archive. We can read Tate's reading—as we can any other interpretation—as part of the wider archive of Dickinson studies; part of what has produced Dickinson as an author. Positioned with later readings of 'the same' but 'not the same' poem, Tate's reading both reveals the instability of any text and urges each critical reader to carefully engage with a text's material history, a history that is part editorial and part critical.

NEW CRITICISM, MODERNISM AND THE PRESENT MOMENT

It is typically understood that Emily Dickinson did not have a direct impact on modernist writers, the generation of poets contemporary with New Criticism's reception of the poet. Morris thus writes that "the canonical American authors of the early twentieth century—Eliot, Stevens, Pound, and, except for a few stray comments, Frost—were silent about Dickinson" (*Becoming Canonical* 76). Benfey similarly focuses on the "negligible presence" Dickinson seems to have had for the Imagists (34). As Jay Ladin points out, this might be partly explained by the fact that the more experimental aspects of Dickinson's work were largely censored from view until the mid-twentieth century ("Soldering the Abyss" 8–9). Benfey proposes that "perhaps" "a sense that Dickinson's life—or at least what little was known of it—" did not depart enough from the Victorian conventions of her time and place for modernists to feel quite at ease with her person and her work (34). Indeed, in Amy Lowell's essay on Dickinson, such a tension between the modern and the old may be traced, but this binary is, as we have seen, perhaps the strongest in Tate's positive analysis of the poet. Another reason for this modernist blindness is the blatantly sexist ideology that infects William Carlos Williams' notorious comment in *In the American Grain* that Emily Dickinson was the closest American literature had been to a female poet: "starving of passion in her Father's garden, is the nearest we have ever been—starving. Never a Woman: never a Poet. That's an axiom. Never a poet saw sun here" (quoted in Benfey 34). Yet while Lowell wrote an important essay about Emily Dickinson and this essay calls for a revision of the canon of received Dickinson criticism: Lowell's presence in the critical canon is not obvious. Benfey's essay is a case in point of the muting of the gender of the voice. While quoting both from Williams' sexist commentary and from Hart Crane's poetic engagement with Dickinson, Benfey does not cite Lowell and indeed when describing Lowell appropriates Williams' image of the starving poet when he writes "'Starving of passion in her father's garden' is a pretty good description of what we know of Amy Lowell's life—until her imposing father's death and his generous bequest made it possible to move in with her female lover and become the poet she had always wished to become" (35). By reducing the modernist writer who did engage with Dickinson's work to a woman "starving of passion," Benfey curiously maintains that master narrative that holds Dickinson in her house. Lowell was a 'minor' figure in modernism but she did read Dickinson as a major precursor according to the protocols of Imagism. By choosing to dwell on two male artists, Williams and Crane, Benfey inadvertently replays Lowell as both 'minor' author and 'minor' critical voice—thus perpetuating the critical blindness that he sets out to critique.

While the key modernist writers may not have engaged with Emily Dickinson, New Critical readings of Emily Dickinson maintain a hold on criticism even in the late twentieth century. The figure of the author as received through the work of critics like Tate and Blackmur has since been challenged for its patriarchal structure, but nevertheless this critical period still serves as sparring partner to contemporary criticism. This may be explained variously. One reason for the seminal role of Tate's essay is its insistence on Dickinson as a uniquely American author. In this way the essay points towards later readings of Emily Dickinson in an American tradition by, for example Susan Howe, who similarly situates Dickinson in a mythical America. Benfey historicizes the essay in Tate's own historical situation of a Southerner who offered a pastoral critique of the Industrialism that had overtaken both rural New England and the South (36–39). As such the essay, as discussed above, is a nostalgic consideration of an author, in 'her' time and place.

But more than offering the point of departure for any reading of the poet as paradigmatically American, the essay remains a generic template for any 'positive' estimate of the poet in the battlefield of Dickinson studies, in which what Morris calls a "poetics of presence" is played out as critics strive to establish their version of Emily Dickinson according to specific (and changing) values of "originality, organicism, and monologism" (2).[4] These notions point towards a formulation of the author as the authentic origin of her thought, of her art, rather than as the mediated production of, for example, editorial and critical engagement.

Morris suggests that in a model based on a poetics of presence, the author "becomes the guarantee for the worth of studying the text and for the values that are supposedly conveyed in it" (2). Paradoxically the values through which New Criticism endorsed Dickinson still challenge the critical environment. This is not only because these values were conservative and essentially heterosexist and therefore may strike contemporary readers as directly affronting but, importantly, because the very critical template through which such values were promoted is a direct analogue to any later project that aims to establish the poet according to a particular positive model, that is, according to a 'poetics of presence.' The logic that drives a criticism of 'presence' situates the 'author' as the locus of 'authenticity' and 'originality' and we can say that such a criticism becomes 'monologic' because it insists so strongly on its own 'positive' understanding of the author and her work. Similarly producing a meta-reading of the production of Emily Dickinson as the "guarantee" that validates the work by her "genius," Betsy Erkkila has challenged criticism that enlists the poet for various purposes ("Emily Dickinson Wars" 13–14). In the early twentieth century, such a model of reading is found in Tate, whose criticism while putting the poet on a genius pedestal necessarily ignores the 'actual' and 'biographical' as the gossip that was below serious criticism. Hence we see that Tate's thesis of Dickinson as custodian of an old and inevitably nostalgic and mythic past uproots the poet from her actual situation, a situation that was too biographically graphic (because the poet was a woman) to quite fit the model of the genius author.

Of particular interest for this study, the poetics of presence and the idea of the poet as 'genius' seem to produce a critical desire for an 'authentic' text equaled with the author's voice or authority. Thus we can explain Blackmur's anxiety regarding the textual state of Dickinson's work: with such a disarray of editions, how could the reader be certain what was the poet's authentic voice and what not? Indeed for Blackmur the disarray of her texts proved his rigorously negative estimate of Dickinson, seized on the poet's privateness and on her eccentric "relation to the business of poetry" (223). Coming sharply down not only on Dickinson's "personal education" but also on "the habit of her society as she knew it," he fiercely contends that she could have no idea "that poetry is a rational and objective art and most so when the theme is self-expression," and concludes that a great flaw in Dickinson is that "she never undertook the great profession of controlling the means of objective expression" (223).

As the example of "Because I could not stop for death–" reveals the question of how to editorially deal with Dickinson's manuscripts was a vexed one in the years preceding Johnson's edition, and indeed never was settled even then. The critical attention currently given to Dickinson's manuscripts, her particular use of manuscript page, pen, pencil and her non print-publication, were debated in the early twentieth century too, as critics conducted meta-editorial analyses, refusing to see the thus-far printed editions as anything near a reliable source for the interpretation of Dickinson's art. The question of how to 'define' a 'Dickinson poem' has, however, always been important to the critical community, and the early twentieth century is no exception to this. Blackmur hypothesized in 1937 that

> Perhaps it is not plain, but it is plausible, to imagine that a full and open view of the manuscripts would show the poet far less fragmentary and repetitious than the published work makes her seem. Most poets have a desk full of beginnings, a barrel of fragments and anything up to an attic full of notes. The manner of notation, if it were known, might make a beginning at the establishment of a canon. With the obvious fragments cut out, or put in an appendix, a clean, self-characterizing, responsive, and responding body of poetry, with limits and a fate and a quaking sensibility, might then be made to show itself. (200)

Beginnings, fragments and notes: these are in an ideology of finality the things that may be safely "cut out" or allocated to "an appendix" in order to establish a solid Emily Dickinson text, delineating an oeuvre worthy of the name. Blackmur asserts that, without the help of comparative scholarship, "it is impossible to determine whether a poem is a finished poem, an early version of a poem, a note for a poem, a part of a poem, or a prose fragment" (201). The tensions between these various categories of text documents served as a problem to overcome in order to evaluate Emily Dickinson's *oeuvre*. Blackmur's preference for the finished poem, for the closure that only a perfected composition (whatever that may be) yields, turns him into an editor-reader from which position he goes on to suggest changes in Dickinson's poems, poems that to him often presents misplaced stanzas and otherwise non-finished aspects (215).

In "The Private Poet: Emily Dickinson," F. O. Matthiessen, reviewing *Bolts of Melody* and *Ancestors' Brocades,* expands on a critique of the history of editing Dickinson's poetry. He writes, "Hitherto it has been generally assumed that the Higginson-Todd editions gave their poems as Emily Dickinson wrote them, but it now appears that the case was more complicated" (226). In 1945, it was clear that these late-nineteenth century editors did not want to give the audience a poet too far removed from the conventions that their ears and eyes were accustomed to. Issues of editorial propriety had been central in Dickinson studies ever since those first editions were published. The problematic status of Dickinson's work in edited form forced critics to engage with questions that led them beyond the norm of the 'final' poem, however reluctant they were to accept 'unfinished' poems as potentially challenging the very idea of 'finality.' Hence Matthiessen's estimate of Emily Dickinson's poetic practices is in a way very similar to contemporary criticism, although in one respect diametrically opposed. He took great interest in the fact that a 'single' Dickinson poem, such as 'A sparrow took a slice of twig,' presents "at least a dozen choices for its final line" (231). In Matthiessen's ideology of the finished poem, of the closure achieved in such finality, such poems such as 'A sparrow' cannot be considered as 'finished.' Dickinson was a private poet, and such poems belonged to her eyes only. It is thus impossible to tell "what she finally intended or whether she had made up her mind" (231).

In a similar fashion as manuscript critics today take great interest in Dickinson's poetic practices, Matthiessen argues that such 'unfinished' work must be printed 'as is' and that such printing in fact is important because

> a leading value of such fragments is to give us an insight into the poet's process of creation, and that our sense of her verbal resources is heightened by watching her alternate from 'the blissful oriole' to the 'reeling oriole,' and remain undecided as to whether to call him also 'confiding prodigal' or 'minute Domingo.' (231)

Matthiessen demandes that "creative editing" be abandoned in relation to such variant poems as "He preached upon 'breadth' till it argued him narrow" where in the final line Dickinson "thought of calling this individual, with varying shades of irony 'so religious (enabled, accomplished, discerning, accoutred, established, conclusive) a man!'" (231). Thus "If we are to enter into the full nature of what it meant to be a poet in her circumstances, we must print each manuscript *in toto* as the special case it is" (231). Here we can see a nascent exploration of Emily Dickinson's versions and variants, providing an important historical precedent for contemporary manuscript criticism.

Similarly engaging the question of lineation, Gay Wilson Allen writes in 1935 that "there are many people that believe that Emily Dickinson's irregular line divisions were intentional and that they are more expressive than a regular arrangement could be" (178). Allen reflects on such interpretations of her manuscripts and comes to the conclusion that the poet was not original or experimental in her lineation, but rather that line breaks are erratic results of the "shape and size of the scrap of paper" (177). Still, in spite of his own more conservative interpretation of Dickinson's meter and consequent execution of lineation, Allen provides important historicizing information when he writes that the "free versifiers" had seized on Dickinson's line divisions "as a valuable precedent for them. And Mr. Aiken's characterization of her thought as 'hard, bright, and clear' is the central ideal of the 'Imagists'"(186). In the 1930s, in the wake of the growth of imagist and 'free verse' experiments, Dickinson's poetry did not look so strange anymore, at least from the perspective of such imagist and free verse practitioners. From the vantage point of 1944, Alfred Leete Hampson could similarly draw connections between Dickinson and modernism, writing that "as long ago as 1860 Emily was outdating the imagists and writing free verse of her own invention" (xi).

JOHNSON'S DICKINSON: THE SCHOLARLY EDITION

David Porter, in a recent assessment of Emily Dickinson, writes that she is "the foremost woman poet in the American canon" ("Searching for Dickinson's Themes" 183). I move on, here, to consider how such a conception of Emily Dickinson came about and to trace more precisely how such a canonical status was structured in the mid-twentieth century according to a New Critical paradigm leading up to the publication of Johnson's monumental *Poems of Emily Dickinson* in 1955. I wish to situate the current 'unediting' of Emily Dickinson's texts in the period which solidly edited her, both literally and metaphorically, into Porter's "foremost woman poet." Johnson's editorial projects in the mid-twentieth century can, in hindsight, be understood as a singularly successful attempt to fix the Dickinson text. Perched mid-century between the conflicting editions resulting from the 'war of the houses' and late twentieth-century reformulations of the editorial task from bottom-up, Johnson's *Variorum* edition can be seen as both a serious editorial project that would spawn the rapid "critical revolution" of Klaus Lubbers' title but that would also, by the close of the century, be seen as a dead end of sorts, a final fixing of Emily Dickinson that cemented the poet and her work according to a theory of editing and the literary work that serves as an obstacle to readers' appreciation of the poet's poetic processes. In spite of this seeming dead end, I wish to stress the continuities between Johnson's edition and later editors of Emily Dickinson's work. For, to stress the historical connections between this edition and the editions of the early twenty-first century is to reveal a continual editorial obsession with 'getting it right,' with embracing and rejoicing in the editorial task of 'unediting' the poet's work in ever better ways. Editing is the coveted place to return to in order to gain insight into Emily Dickinson.

Studying Thomas Johnson's reasoning in the introductory sections to *The Poems of Emily Dickinson* yields a trove of metacritical queries regarding the critical task of editing a literary text. This edition has been questioned: but its arguments have not so much been historicized as appropriated as the convenient antagonist to later 'uneditors' of Dickinson's work.

Like his New Critic precursors, Johnson produces his authoritative and objective critical voice seemingly unselfconsciously. Central to the narrative of Emily Dickinson's poetic career is her various relationships to a number of men, or so it would seem if we turn to most twentieth century narratives about the poet, including that paradigmatic event of 1955, the publication of Thomas Johnson's *The Poems of Emily Dickinson Including Variant Readings Critically Compared with all Known Manuscripts*. I turn here to the introductory sections of this edition, sections that create the framework for interpreting the poems. From the very start, Emily Dickinson, the apparent center of the edition, is de-centered in order to provide commentary on various male figures. Primary in this narrative is Thomas Higginson to whom Emily Dickinson sent a letter inquiring about her work. In this narrative, Higginson is the busy man-of-letters to whom a shy writer of poetry addressed herself: she "dared" bring herself to his attention. She felt "emboldened" (xvii). And, in spite of his own busy life, Higginson immediately answered her letter. Thus we get the picture of a woman just brave enough to send the busy man-of-letters her poems—and of a man not too busy to condescend to this inquiry. And so the beginning of a life-long correspondence serves a seminal event in the construction of Dickinson as the quivering woman asking for advice. We must briefly consider Higginson's contribution to the construction of Emily Dickinson. As the author of the essay "Letter to a Young Contributor" that made Emily Dickinson write for an opinion as to whether her verse "breathed" or not, Higginson as the poet's long time 'mentor' and correspondent, is central. In an essay promoting the publication of the second series of *The Poems of Emily Dickinson* in 1891, Higginson advertised the construction of Emily Dickinson's life as that of an "utterly reclusive character" and without any "reference" to "anything but her own thoughts and a few friends" ("Emily Dickinson's Letters" 444). In this essay, Higginson produces that discourse of paternalistic protection that later critics would continue. It was hence "with much reluctance" that he had selected a number of the poet's letters that bring readers "intimately the peculiar quality and aroma of her nature." In describing his meeting with this reclusive woman, he "could only sit still and watch, as one does in the woods; I must name my bird without a gun as recommended by Emerson" (444, 453). Higginson's characterization of the poet fits into the general nineteenth-century construction of women's poetry as emotive, natural and unpremeditated, as an "unconscious wellspring of emotion" (Elizabeth Petrino 28). Such 'naturalness' was associated with smooth, regular rhyme and rhythm, with a strict adherence to form. Importantly, Elizabeth Petrino points out that a recurring trope in nineteenth-century (male) criticism of women's poetry is the analogy between text and body. Hence, in a review of Helen Hunt Jackson's *Verses* one reviewer conflates poetic text with female body in the complaint that the effect of her poetry is a feeling "clothed in a somewhat enigmatic form" and that, attempting to interpret this form, "one finds it almost laborious to unclothe it and discover it" (anonymous reviewer in *The Nation*, quoted in Petrino 28). Higginson's description of the poet's 'nature' points to future considerations of this poet's emotive life, radically domestic, natural and pure rather than public and professional. Higginson's essay functions as a kind of go-between: through Higginson, Dickinson's letters come to life, and the reader of the essay is invited to partake in the most 'intimate' of the poet's expressions. Another man, that is, becomes, or makes himself, a key to the revelations of this poet, this text. Hence a foundation was laid for that definition of Emily Dickinson's poetic success as dependent on the presence of particular men in her life, as if her poems, in fact, were the creation of a number of men acquainted with her. Furthermore, the foundation for conflating text/body or work/poet was solidified. We need here, in the consideration of the authoring of the poet, or the mediation of the artist, to consider again that essay that spurred Emily Dickinson to send Higginson a letter. Here, the figure of the editor as that crucial go-between is established in almost uncanny terms:

> Do not despise any honest propriation, however small, in dealing with your editor. Look to the physical aspect of your manuscript, and prepare your page so neatly that it shall allure instead of repelling. Use good pens, black ink, nice white paper, and plenty of it. Do not emulate "paper-sparing Pope," whose chaotic manuscript of the "Illiad," written chiefly on the backs of old letters, still remains in the British Museum. If your document be slovenly, the presumption is that its literary execution is the same, Pope to the contrary notwithstanding. An editor's eye becomes carnal, and is easily attracted by a comely outside. ("Letter to a Young Contributor" 402)

Here Petrino's reminder of the symbolic means of reading the text as physical body is to the point. Importantly Higginson theorizes the 'editor' as precisely a judge of 'pure' texts: away go the untidy orthography and the scraps of paper that a frugal writer might need to resort to. Furthermore, of course, we note the irony in Higginson's advice regarding the matter of writing polished fair copies. As we know, Dickinson's editors have attempted in various ways, with their "carnal eye" to clear away the 'mess' of deviant orthography, calligraphy, and, more recently, as I will consider at length in the following chapters, to employ that "carnal eye" for the opposite reason, to valorize, rather than critique, such deviance. Higginson thus recognizes that the body of the text matters and emphasizing the disciplinary role of the editor he assigns for the editor, a pivotal role in defining what is 'legible' according to the norms of aesthetic conventions, and hence the body of the text matters.

Returning to Thomas Johnson's narrative, we see that it builds on an established tradition, then, of reading Dickinson's work through her life. Dickinson is represented as a completely emotive character, who responds to male instruction and help, who would not be able to 'control' her emotions without such support (*Poems* xxiii). Building on George Whicher's biography, Johnson launches the law student Benjamin Newton, who worked in Emily Dickinson's father's office, and the Reverend Charles Wadsworth as her "Muses" (*Poems* xxi). Newton "awakened" her as "when she was about twenty years old her latent talents were invigorated by a gentle, grave young man who taught her how to observe the world" (*Poems* xxi). After Newton's death her poetic energy left her, and she had to wait "the coming of another" (*Poems* xxi). In Johnson's simple narrative of cause and effect, the poet, then, simply fell in love with Wadsworth (*Poems* xxi). She 'adored' him: he was the object of her "adoration" (*Poems* xxiii). It was "terrifying" when he moved to California—what would she do without his strength as support? (*Poems* xxiii) Around the time Wadsworth left for California (1861) Dickinson began dressing in white, a very convenient coincidence for this particular narrative that clearly serves to juxtapose speculations regarding the poet's attachments to various men with the creativity of her poetic writing.

Typical Dickinson lore has it that the poet experienced her 'flood years' from 1861 through 1865. Johnson writes, "her creative energies were at flood, and she was being overwhelmed by forces which she could not control" (*Poems* xviii). In these years, the editor speculates, Dickinson must almost have been "frightened" by her own production, her "creative drive," just as she was terrified, scared, by being alone on the east side of the American continent, with Wadsworth on the west coast (*Poems* xviii). In 1863–65 she achieved "intensity, passionate and often despairing" (*Poems* xix). She wrote poetry with "daemonic energy" around the time she wrote Higginson (*Poems* xxiii). Thus Johnson perpetuates the ideology of the intuitive, innocent, emotional character that Matthiessen, for example, described similarly in 1945 ("A Private Poet" 230).

Johnson's picture of the poet concludes that she grew more and more reclusive, that this was a conscious choice, based on the realization that nobody else could chart her life. But in the context of 'print' such a choice was based, according to Johnson, on incapacity to psychologically deal with print publication (note that Johnson uses the term 'print' and not 'publish,' exactly in the same way as manuscript critics prefer to set the terms for Dickinson's refusal to print/publish) (xxix).

The Need of a Variorum Edition

For years, then, it had been clear to many that an edition of Dickinson's work that was based on the entire corpus was necessary. As mentioned above, five years before he published the three-volume edition of Emily Dickinson's poems, Johnson wrote, "The basic need is to determine the Dickinson canon" ("Prisms of a Poet" 263). The confusing abundance of different and differing (and also competing) editions of the poet's work on the market in the late 1940s meant that "At the moment there is no certainty that her poems as they now exist in print represent what she intended to write" ("Prisms of a Poet" 263). Thus, Johnson's ambition was to finally establish Dickinson as a major poet in American literary history by thoroughly establishing the study object 'Emily Dickinson's poems.' This canonical edition of Dickinson's poems, produced under the label of Harvard University Press, came out in 1955. Produced under the auspices of the New Critical conceit of organic and closed form, the edition set the course for the critical industry that learned to refer to Dickinson's writings as short, even taut, poems. The ambition of the "variorum" edition of *The Poems of Emily Dickinson: Including Variant Readings Critically Compared with all Known Manuscripts* was thus to represent Dickinson's entire production, as well as is possible, in print. All known variants of poems are shown, with word variants marked. The edition clearly marks which version, in the case of existing versions, is deemed, by the editor, to be the 'best' in terms of authorial intention. Johnson's intention with his three-volume edition was, as is the case with so much editorial intention, to offer readers a more "accurate" version of Dickinson than had previously been presented (lxi). As an editor, Johnson was determined to present Emily Dickinson to the world the way he imagined that she herself would have liked to present 'her texts' to the world, had she ever had the opportunity. This desire to reveal a purer Dickinson text is in fact a feature that marks *all* editions of Dickinson's work; they differ in their rationales for such presentations (consider the recent editions of Dickinson's work by Martha Nell Smith, Ellen Louise Hart and Marta Werner: perhaps there can be no other reason or rationale for producing an 'edition'?). His specific desire was to compensate for the failings of earlier editors, in particular Thomas Higginson and Mabel Loomis Todd, whose efforts to "give the poetry of Emily Dickinson the sort of finish which the sensibilities of the time were thought to demand" to Johnson seemed "misguided" (xlliii). Their editorial practices were constrained by the aesthetic conventions of the late nineteenth century, and the resulting poems were altered to fit such standards (xliii). Conversely, the ideal Johnsonian Dickinson text was in accordance with his New Bibliographic/New Critical theoretical perspective, supposedly uncorrupted by such historically contaminated prejudices.

Writing at the end of the twentieth century, Peter Shillingsburg inscribes that the "word definitive should be banished from editorial discussion" (*Scholarly Editing* 90). He argues this point in the light of the paradigmatic shift in editorial theory and practice that took place in the 1980s, a shift that moved editorial preference from the definitive work to the work conceived of in its variant and versioned state. That is to say that editions can only ever, even in the particular editor's particular formulation of the 'ideal' text, be 'tentative' (*Scholarly Editing* 91). In the 1960s, however, the idea of such a definitive goal in editing prevailed.

Introducing Johnson as an important critic of Dickinson, Caesar R. Blake and Carlton F. Wells thus describe him as having "established definitively the texts of the whole Dickinson canon of poetry" (*The Recognition of Emily Dickinson* 260). Indeed, when it came out, Johnson's edition was welcomed by some as a 'definitive' edition of Dickinson's work. Perry Miller, who had been collaborating with Johnson in other editing projects, and Charles Anderson, in separate reviews of Johnson's *Poems,* call the edition 'definitive' ("An Interpretive Biography"101–103, "The Poems of Emily Dickinson" 390). Anderson continued to praise the edition for setting a standard in American literary editing: American writers had not, until then, received the kind of definitive editorial projects needed to make their status permanent (386).

Exploring Johnson's Dickinson: Order in the Workshop

The material that Johnson did have access to he chose to categorize according to its apparent state of finality and with regard to a chronology accomplished by the study of the poet's handwriting. He built this structure on an examination of handwriting and stationery and by interpreting manuscript variants as rough draft through semifinal draft to fair copy, constructing thus both a chronological and a hierarchical order of Dickinson's production. In Johnson's narrative, Emily Dickinson produced 'rough drafts,' 'semi-final drafts' and 'fair copies' in her poetry workshop. Around two hundred poems (out of the 1,775) "survive in worksheet draft only" (xxxiii). Such rough drafts are written in pencil on a range of different kinds of surfaces: flaps or backs of envelopes, discarded letters, wrapping-paper, edges of newspapers. Such drafts allow the critic a wealth of information about the poet's creative processes: they give the critic the sense of "[watching] the creative spirit in action" (xxxiii). The working papers of a writer are the material a genetic critic would use to study the genesis of a work. Such a 'genetic' study of a writer's habits would not privilege the 'final product;' it would, in fact, not be very interested in such finality at all: it is the process, the genesis of a work of art, that guides such criticism (albeit, necessarily implicitly dependent on a concept of 'finality' in its insistence on the 'birth' of the 'work of art,' something that the process *leads to*). It is important to emphasize that all editing 'creates' poems, represents and ultimately interprets particular texts for a chosen audience. Of course there cannot be an 'objective' text, and Johnson was as much in need of an editorial structure as Higginson and Todd, even if he believed that his was less subjective.

Johnson writes that relatively few poems show Dickinson's creative method. But "even so [. . .] they are an impressive body of documents in the manifold history of artistic generation" (xxxiv). To Johnson, though, there is a difference between studying such a process of creation and the final product that is 'the poem.' As an editor, he saw it as his task to produce that final, complete, fixed poem. He was firmly convinced of the notion of 'finality' and 'final intentions,' and it is these notions that guided his interpretation of the manuscripts as 'final' or not (xxxv). The important thing to keep in mind today is that editors like Johnson certainly registered the same workshop processes, registered the details of paper and pencil. The difference is the critical use, based in the interpretation of such materialities.

The period after Johnson's edition was concerned with establishing the Dickinson internal canon. An apparently important task in 1950s Dickinson criticism was to establish a seeming order in the writer's work. Hence, one of Charles Anderson's demands was that a "winnowing process" of selecting the poet's good poems from the mediocre majority of her poems should begin ("The Poems" 389). Similarly, John Crowe Ransom writes, "Shall we say that the poems which are destined to become a common public property might be in the proportion of one out of seventeen of the 1,775? They will hardly be more. But it will take time to tell" (288).

Johnson himself cleared much of Dickinson's irregularity by shaping lineation according to his standards. Johnson interpreted Dickinson as a writer of lyric poetry based in metrical conventions. He standardized her lineation typographically, accordingly. In particular, Johnson fixed on the quatrain of which Emily Dickinson "has achieved fulfillment" with a sureness of no one else (xxxvi). The crux was that the editor himself constructed this quatrain out of Dickinson's manuscripts; the quatrain was a poetic form he expected to see and consequently saw. These poems were not, of course, the manuscript poems that Dickinson left behind. Nevertheless, in his scheme of following an assumed 'authorial intention' that he, himself, conjectured to be accurate, Johnson consequently numbered the poems, 1 through 1,775, and a new kind of order was imposed on the manuscripts.

Popularizing and Fixing the Dickinson Text: The Reader's Edition

In the wake of the 1955 publication of his variorum edition, Johnson brought out a 'reader's volume' of all 1,775 poems. The sense one gets from reading the one-volume reader's edition that Johnson published in 1960, entitled *Complete Poems of Emily Dickinson,* is one of finality. But rather than establishing Dickinson's final intentions, this is an edition steeped in Johnson's editorial policies. This *Complete Poems of Emily Dickinson* presents one version of each poem, imposed more heavily editorially on the manuscripts, perhaps most obviously with regard to those poems that Johnson categorizes as 'semi-final' and 'rough drafts.'

In the reader's edition, word variation was edited out in poems deemed 'semi-final,' thereby constructing a sense of finality. The editor followed a strict policy of keeping the word suggested in the body of the poem or, when a word variant in the 'margin' was underlined, interpreted by Johnson as a representation of final authorial intention, that variant was chosen to stand as final. For rough drafts, Johnson kept to the word choice of the main body poem. Based on the editorial convention of critical conjecture, *Complete Poems of Emily Dickinson* is thus a more explicitly interpretive work than the variorum, revealing much more the editor's method and personal preferences. The editor allowed himself to choose that version or variant of a text that he deemed most likely to be the reflection of the writer's final intentions. The pretense was that a final intention was indeed intended and that the editor was in possession of enough knowledge to hypothesize that intention. The reader's edition is thus embedded in a hidden theoretical framework wholly determined by the conventions of the Book (in particular, the notion that a 'work' is a solid, unchanging entity) and the New Critical tenet of organic form. Johnson admitted that much of Dickinson's "irregularity" in lineation and stanza division suggests experimentation (*The Poems of Emily Dickinson* lxiii). Worries were thus articulated already in Johnson's editorial prefaces about Dickinson's practices. Assuming however that Dickinson conformed to certain visual-bibliographic conventions of poetic display, he nevertheless felt justified in standardizing her manuscripts. Strongly edited, the poems of the reader's edition are trademark Johnson-Dickinson products, the short and taut lyric poem presented as a minimalist black printed design on a white background that most post-1960 readers of Dickinson recognize quickly. Most critics concurred with Johnson, establishing thereby the canonical Dickinson poem even further.

Responses to Johnson's Editions

Contemporary Dickinson scholars reveal a deep interest in Emily Dickinson's versions and variants. Such interest has always been present, although guided by different ideological protocols. As an editor, Johnson certainly thought long and hard about these versions and variants. Rather than seeing such variation as constitutive of meaning in itself, Johnson, when discussing for example the variants of the poem beginning "A butterfly went out at noon," conflates the poet's 'chaotic' treatment of the poem and the resulting chaos in the workshop: "[L]ike the butterfly itself, the poet too was lost" (xxxvi). Besides revealing the sexist approach of the male editor, such paternalistic conflation of the female poet with the butterfly, of course, does not help much in exploring the poem's potential variant meanings: it presents a mere evaluation of the poet at work and the material results. For Johnson, such an abundance of versions and variants serves primarily as a "fascinating document of poetic creativeness in travail" (xxxvi). Contemporary critics interpret that "fascinating document" as a significant constitutive element of Emily Dickinson's workshop poetics. But, rather than appreciating variant versions of a poem as constitutive of extended social meanings, for example when a version was included in a letter, Johnson desired order.

Yet even in the most positive of reviews of Johnson's editions, reviews that praise that orderliness, it becomes clear that the idea of 'order' is relative and exceedingly difficult to precisely pinpoint. Newton Arvin, in a review in *American Literature*, first praises the editor for his "painstaking, responsible, and authoritative" edition as the long-sought answer to what he calls the "notoriously unsatisfactory and even exasperating" editorial state of Dickinson's work prior to 1955 (232). Even though Arvin argues that what "we" must have is "what Emily Dickinson wrote, whatever that was," he suggests that, although Johnson's edition is a boon for the study of the poet, there is a need for a reader's edition that does not attempt the kind of fidelity to the poet's manuscripts in terms of spelling, punctuation, word variants, and even line and stanza formation, that the Variorum does (234). Hence Arvin calls for the "perfect critical editor," preferably a "poet or critic" with the discerning mind of "Auden or Louise Bogan" to produce such an edition (235, 234). In Arvin's under-theorized response to editorial practice, the theoretical problematic inherent in asking the question of the possibility of an ordering or disciplining of Dickinson's texts inadvertently emerges as clearly subjective and reveals anxieties about the possibility of such 'order' surfaces in the very review of that final answer to the problem of disorder.

In an interesting review of Johnson's *Poems of Emily Dickinson*, Jay Leyda, in 1956, questions the foundations of Johnson's variorum edition. Even though generally satisfied with the editorial job, he questions the principles for selecting—or, rather creating—poems out of Dickinson's prose (that is, her letters) and the seemingly random inclusion of short two- and three-line long verses (245). In this review Leyda establishes the notion that Emily Dickinson, even though she did not print, did in fact publish. He makes clear that Emily Dickinson devised her own "publishing medium" and that the variorum edition describes a poet with an audience (242). Similarly to Smith, who in 1992 would refer to Dickinson's correspondences as 'books' (discussed at length in Chapter Two), Leyda refers to the sending out of copies of a poem to a circle of friends as "editions" (242). Even though Johnson's edition does not promise the 'definitive' aura that many readers had hoped for, Leyda concedes that it is the best edition thus far of Dickinson's work for the poems are "conveyed almost with the intimacy of the facsimile" (239). Basing his appraisal of the edition on his own perusal of authentic manuscripts, Leyda contributed to the establishing of the Johnson Variorum as trustworthy (239).

Inside parenthetical markers, Leyda inserts an interesting question: he asks "But will the familiarity of the previously printed versions prevent acceptance of the poet's versions?" (239) Such a problem of a radically different edition challenging the received knowledge and preferences of a generation of readers is, in fact, very much at stake at the present time. Again, we see a similarity between the critical environment of the 1950s and that at the turn of the twenty-first century. Dickinson's work was paradigmatically transformed by Johnson; is 'his' 'authentic' Dickinson, once more, then, being paradigmatically challenged, today? I will argue in the next chapter that the manuscript-oriented criticism that was the result, in part, of Franklin's facsimile edition which came out in 1981, is not simply undermining Johnson's editorial project but in fact, by radically questioning the received representation of the Dickinson text, has created a critical situation in which readers may find themselves in the kind of situation suggested by Leyda.

One of the first scholars to make use of Johnson's editions for a mapping and interpretation of Emily Dickinson's poetics, Charles Anderson, early on articulated the problems inherent in transmitting Dickinson's manuscripts to a larger audience through the print medium. In his *Emily Dickinson's Poetry: Stairway of Surprise* Anderson asked how such manuscripts could be "brought within the conventions of printing and made accessible to the modern reader" without suppressing their uniqueness (*ix*). While acknowledging the excellence of Johnson's 1955 three-volume edition, Anderson maintained a concern about whether Dickinson's manuscripts could be reproduced exactly in print or if that demand would have necessitated a facsimile edition (*x*). Thus in spite of the production of a scholarly edition, Dickinson's texts remained unstable, leaving editor Johnson to worry about her lineation and critic Anderson to ponder the status of her manuscript pages. Even though dwelling on the problems of lineation, however, Anderson contended that with the appearance of Johnson's editions, readers could feel sure that they had been given Dickinson's work "substantially" the way she wrote it (*x*).

In 1960, when Anderson's monograph was published, Johnson's edition was thus authorized by a scholar and Dickinson studies continued from there: the edition became the starting point of the business which is now an academic industry. Questions nevertheless continued, and continue, to be raised about the proper way to represent, interpret and understand Emily Dickinson's manuscripts, as will be seen throughout this dissertation.

What the critical attention to Johnson's editorial work reveals is not straightforward. On the one hand, many reviewers, subscribing to an ideology of finality, did feel that this edition was indeed 'definitive.' On the other hand, however, critics were still uneasy with the seeming impossibility of capturing Dickinson's work on paper. This uncertainty is important to capture because it reveals a *continual* critical difficulty with fixing Dickinson's text.

Raising the Stakes: Franklin's Reconsideration

Having studied the documents of Mabel Loomis Todd's editorial engagement with Dickinson's manuscripts, R. W. Franklin in 1967 articulated what he saw as problematic in Johnson's practice in his Variorum edition of 1955 and the subsequent one-volume *Complete Poems,* or reader's edition, of Dickinson's work, of 1960. Indeed, the problems he formulated in *The Editing of Emily Dickinson* are very similar to the problems raised by contemporary critics involved in the project of formulating Dickinson's 'manuscript poetics.' These problems are inherent in making sense of Dickinson's manuscripts in the first place. It is just that his opinions differ radically from much contemporary manuscript criticism. He writes, "printing is itself a misrepresentation of the texts as they exist in manuscript" (117). What was at stake for Franklin was the definition of what makes a Dickinson poem a Dickinson poem and how to represent that poem in print, believing as he did that print was, indeed, the best medium for the transmission of Dickinson's work. In order to understand Dickinson's manuscripts better, he inventoried the "mechanics' of her handwriting for any meaningful components, components that would be lost if translated into print. He discussed the poet's capitalization and punctuation, coming to the conclusion, in both cases, that the poet's practices were random.

As an example of Dickinson's random capitalization of words, seemingly not corresponding to any logic, Franklin uses the poem "Success is counted Sweetest." This poem exists in three versions (and one fourth, lost: this lost version was the basis for the poem's publication in *Brooklyn Daily Union* in 1864). The three versions that were known at the time of Johnson's publication (that is, excluding the lost copy of the published version, which was discovered in 1984 by Karen Dandurand) differ in many instances in the placing of capitalizations. For example, line one, in versions *A* and *C* runs "To comprehend a nectar" while in version *D* it runs "To Comprehend a Nectar." Line five is offered in three different forms: versions *A* and *C* run "Not one of all the purple Host," and line *D* runs "Not one of all the Purple Host." Similarly, line six provides a differing capitalization of the word "flag" (version *A*); as "Flag" (version *C* and *D*). These differences in capitalization to Franklin suggested randomness rather than a conscious artistic choice. Therefore he deemed capitalization to be an irrelevant marker of poetic significance in Dickinson's work.

Much of Franklin's hostility towards bibliographic meanings in Dickinson's dashes and capitalizations comes from his clear suspicion of reading Dickinson's letters as artistic texts (he argues that one reason that dashes and capitalizations may be deemed unrelated to Dickinson's poetic project is that they occur in letters as well, presumably in the same 'inconsistent' way), and from what must also be taken as sheer prejudice, namely his argument that because these characteristics occur also in Dickinson's writings on "domestic concerns," clearly the characteristics were "merely habits of handwriting" (121). Contemporary critics, quite contrary to Franklin, argue that the occurrence of such characteristics as dashes in recipes and shopping lists may in fact reveal how Dickinson blurred the lines between 'domestic' and 'public,' that is, between 'scribbling' and 'poetry.' To Franklin, in the 1960s, however, such occurrences could only boost his argument that such matters of the holographs were 'accidentals' rather than 'substantials.'

Nevertheless, Franklin devoted lengthy discussions to these matters, discussions that, if necessarily argumentative, also reveal the differences that existed, even then, of opinions regarding how to *read and see* Dickinson's holographs. This was a necessary move, since editors and critics had been long caught up in the problem of deciphering the writer's curious script and—for twentieth-century readers—her peculiar use of dashes for punctuation. Franklin attempted to contextualize Dickinson's handwriting historically, arguing that the use of dashes was common in nineteenth-century American handwriting and that the use of capitalization in more words than the beginning word of a sentence likewise would have been frequent among, in particular, women writers in the nineteenth century. Franklin's conclusion was that Dickinson's handwriting is conventional and representative of her time (if difficult to read), and thus does not contribute to the meaning of her work. Had Dickinson published, Franklin speculates, she would have changed dashes for other, more conventional, print punctuation, as did other writers (*Reconsideration* 124). Thus Franklin eliminates potential meaningful components of Dickinson's handwriting. The problem of transmitting this handwriting in print became, to him, one of legibility, or rather, illegibility: Dickinson's handwriting is difficult to decipher because of its variations in size and form and because of her inconsistent punctuation and capitalization rather than because of any calligraphic intentions.

Franklin's *Reconsideration* was published in 1967, the same year as Jacques Derrida's *De La Grammatologie* was published. The differences are obvious, and speak implicitly about the radical changes that were to take place in Anglo-American textual criticism in the subsequent decade. Derrida's insistence on the privileging of speech in Western philosophical tradition, and his subsequent play with 'text' and 'writing,' allow for critique of the de-privileging in Franklin's (and others) blunt rejection of the manuscript particulars. Writing about linguistics as the bastion of 'science' in the social sciences, Derrida asks "[. . .] does one not find efficaciously at work, in the very movement by which linguistics is instituted as a science, a metaphysical presupposition about the relationship between speech and writing? Would that presupposition not hinder the constitution of a general science of writing?" (28) However, such an apparent 'reversal' of the binary 'writing and speech' is not in itself the object of Derrida's critique. And so, it is not 'simply' a matter of 'privileging' writing in Dickinson's manuscripts, but rather of considering how 'writing' conditions our thinking about speech and of how 'language' is produced through writing (Goldberg 121). Such 'language' need not be, then, thought of in terms of 'originary' speech but rather as conditioned by 'writing.' In the decade after Franklin's critique of Johnson, textual criticism developed towards that moment when Jerome McGann would formulate the distinction between 'linguistic' and 'bibliographic' codes. Such a consideration of the 'bibliographic codes' of language influences contemporary criticism and editing of Emily Dickinson's work. But the question, which I will explore it in the following chapter, is how such an apparent privileging of 'writing' in its literal and material instantiation might be another instance of the 'metaphysical' that Derrida set out to critique in 1967.

We see, then, that a very important reason for returning to these mid-century debates is that the tensions expressed in them still shape Dickinson studies. But can these texts be engaged with 'positively' for our contemporary critical needs and demands? Robert McClure Smith's reading of male New Critics' analyses of Emily Dickinson suggests that, at least at the present moment, New Criticism may serve simply as that "entertaining," because politically suspicious, even ludicrous, background from which a more "self-conscious" criticism might develop its preferred editing/reading of Emily Dickinson. But, McClure Smith usefully continues,

> Rereading that criticism should not make the contemporary critic more complacent in his or her own self-congratulatory righteousness; the sexism of the postmodernist age, like all of its other manifestations of subjectivity, is merely more self-aware and, therefore, more covertly and carefully expressed. The value of reading the male New Critics is that they present us with a more honest portrait of Dickinson's male reader than their circumspect successors. ("Reading Seductions" 114)

Hence New Criticism, Johnson's edition and the debates that followed it, may all still serve as more than an antagonist to later criticisms.

CONCLUSION: EDITING A TEXT/EDITING A LIFE

Thomas Johnson's edition remains an important 'departure' for the Dickinson critic interested in the publication and dissemination history of the poet, but also for the critic interested in how 'Dickinson' has been shaped into being understood in a particular way in the twentieth century. But we must ask if this edition and the New Critical writing that preceded it can contribute positively to Dickinson studies or if it will increasingly serve as the 'negative' background to increasingly 'progressive' editions and readings of Emily Dickinson's work.[5] Recent Dickinson studies posits this period as precisely such a 'negative' background from which to produce new Dickinsons.

Roland Hagenbüchle points out that, if the New Critics were the first critics to theorize Dickinson, the seeming formalist approach of New Criticism was often, in fact, capsized by an "immoderate curiosity about the poet's private life" (359). In fact, much of the critical evaluation of Dickinson's work in the New Critical period depends to a high degree on such curiosity, in spite of the repeated insistence on the opposite. The New Critical period was the period when critical voices confidently formulated their contempt for the 'gossip' of the Dickinson lore that had permeated criticism of the poet until then. Such contempt for 'gossip' was also connected, as Lubbers suggests, with an elitist contempt for the "deplorable popularity of the poet" (175). This rejection of biography was, of course, part of the general program of New Criticism: "Honest criticism and sensitive appreciation is directed not upon the poet but upon the poetry," T. S. Eliot writes in "Tradition and the Individual Talent" (296). This kind of radical distinction between a poet and her work influenced much reception of Emily Dickinson of the early to mid nineteen-hundreds. Many critics insisted that personality would not yield information about a poem. A poem was not made out of a writer's personality, of her biography. Blackmur thus argued that it is in the words on the page that we will find any 'greatness' in Dickinson's art: it will not be found in biography or in any historically conditioned prejudice (209).

New Criticism attempted to steer clear from the notorious myth making that had suggested so many love stories for the reclusive and misunderstood 'poetess' of Amherst. Yet this prerogative to, as McClure Smith has put it, protect the author translated into a paternalistic and patriarchal approach that has since been scrutinized and thoroughly critiqued ("Reading Seductions" 116). The protection that New Critics offered Dickinson was shaped in the form of Tate's discussion of "our" modern prejudice that "no virgin can know enough to write poetry," a discussion meant to protect Dickinson, this "spinster," from such prejudices but that reveals more than anything else Tate's own prejudices against women writers (157). Indeed Tate could not help but insert seriously 'biographical' markers in his evaluation of the poet: the "moral image" that "we" have of "Miss Dickinson" is that of a "dominating spinster whose very sweetness must have been formidable" (157). The unselfconsciousness with which Tate formulates such a sentence immediately after having brushed off the biographers who searched for the poet's love affairs is of course only telling of the normative ("we") heterosexism saturating the critical vocabulary of Tate and his contemporaries, as McClure Smith has pointed out ("Reading Seductions" 114). In this chapter I have traced the 'authoring' of Emily Dickinson in the early twentieth century. We can describe the period after 1914 until 1955 as defined by New Critical readings of Emily Dickinson's work: it was the period when Dickinson became an academic subject, the beginnings of the industry of Dickinson studies. But it was also a period of confusing editorial ventures and, as Lubbers writes, "academic work [on Emily Dickinson] began late and hesitantly" (198). Lubbers suggests that the discrepancy in academic treatment of Whitman and Dickinson was largely the result of "the chaotic state" of the disarray that characterized Dickinson editing (199). Hence, although the period must be understood to have established Emily Dickinson as a serious object of study, between 1933 and 1948 no dissertation was published on Dickinson while, for example, Whitman was the subject of twenty-eight dissertations; and three dissertations dealt with Thomas Higginson, Dickinson's correspondent and first editor (Lubbers 199). Although the 'chaotic' state of the editing of Dickinson cannot fully explain what Lubbers describes as the remarkable absence of Dickinson in handbooks and histories of American literature even in the 1930s, it is striking how the editorial task of 'establishing' the poet and her work, a task so debated in the recent past, has always dominated—and always will?—the study of Emily Dickinson. It appears, then, that at the center of Dickinson studies is the struggle to edit the poet and her work. This struggle is continual and must be understood as an important or even key aspect of the production of 'Emily Dickinson' as an object of study. Appropriating the vocabulary of Bourdieu for the purposes of analyzing a critical field we might say that the 'struggle' to edit Emily Dickinson in ways 'better' or otherwise 'different' from earlier editions itself is a fundamental 'problem' that in fact generates and ascertains the continual editing and study of the poet.[6]

The most fruitful approach to New Critical readings of Emily Dickinson is to read them as palimpsests of the changes in American editorial theories and strategies, as palimpsests, furthermore, of changing critical formulations of the 'meaning' of literary texts.

To a historicizing project seeking to trace the various figures of Dickinson in the twentieth century, the kind of editorial 'censure' presented in pre-1955 editions, need not simply be denounced as ideologically repressive but rather serves as important markers of culturally specific values in literary study. Not the least, problematically no doubt, readings based on censured versions of a text have in this case proved to serve important canonizing functions, in the sense of bringing Emily Dickinson's poetry to the forefront of academic criticism. Such censured readings cannot be simply criticized for being flawed, but must rather be seen as important producers of Emily Dickinson.

Chapter Two
Material Dickinson: The Function of the Manuscript in Dickinson Studies

> To print a text differently is to print a different text.
> Stephen Orgel, "Margins of Truth"
>
> [. . .] the material of verse begins with the written word [. . .].
> Edith Wylder, *The Last Face: Emily Dickinson's Manuscripts*

Edith Wylder offered one of the first significant arguments about Emily Dickinson's manuscripts as bibliographically meaningful. Writing in 1971 she suggests that the manuscripts' punctuation in fact serves as logical rhetorical markers, with the function of directing the reading of the poem. With 'reading' Wylder does not mean 'declaiming' or even 'reading aloud' but rather the articulation of the 'tone' of the poem, in the reader's mind's ear. Such 'tone' is an abstraction of the mind's ear rather than a description of real, actual speech. Arguing that Emily Dickinson's punctuation should be understood to be part of the poet's "attempt to create in written form the precision of meaning inherent in the tone of the human voice" Wylder betrays a belief that a 'tone' can be ascribed a specific 'meaning' (4). However conditioned this argument is by an assumption that 'tone' is indeed easily deduced and classified, which we might want to question, Wylder offers an interesting theory of the manuscript punctuation as precisely a visual "poetic device" rather than a direction for the articulation of "actual speech" (5) [1] Wylder that is, hints at a method of reading Emily Dickinson's work silently, as written text (albeit conditioned by voice, human speech). This theoretical distinction between actual and 'abstract' speech is important: it directs the reader's attention to the visual surfaces of the text, and points in direct ways to the manuscript criticism which is the subject of this chapter. [2]

This chapter explores how the current scene of reading Emily Dickinson as experimental manuscript poet has developed by way of an analysis of the editorial debates that first spawned this particular construction of the poet. The perception of Emily Dickinson examined here depends on a formulation of her poetics as based in the handwritten word and a reconsideration of her relationship to 'publication.' The development of the idea of Emily Dickinson as manuscript poet grew out of the publication of R. W. Franklin's important facsimile edition of the poet's 'manuscript books' in 1981. This edition has triggered a serious 'editorial turn' in Dickinson studies. As an exclusive edition in itself, bound in sober brown and gold, this edition calls attention both to itself (as precisely exclusive) and to the texts it 'contains' as unique handwritten artifacts, indeed worthy of the high production costs involved in producing such a set of books. In intriguing ways, this edition spurred both a serious interest in Emily Dickinson's handwriting and a serious renewed interest in the editorial strategies of 'packaging,' which also means 'producing' (because it so blatantly does just that, package Dickinson as a commodity) this poet and her work.

The reception of *The Manuscript Books of Emily Dickinson* was informed by serious questions of 'editing,' questions that came to shape the construction of Dickinson as 'manuscript poet.'[3] Because 'this' 'Dickinson,' which depends so much on editorial questions, surfaced as 'the' Dickinson in the late twentieth century, I argue that the current 'scene of reading' Dickinson is conditioned by a serious negotiation of the roles of 'editors' and 'critics' in Dickinson studies. I will propose that tropes of editing inform this figure of Dickinson and the field of Dickinson studies to the extent that no critic can easily get 'beyond' questions of editing Dickinson. This metacritical analysis is important because, in fact, such manuscript-oriented criticism has challenged the very basis for reading Emily Dickinson's work since it suggests that any typographical print edition is problematic. 'Manuscript criticism' may be said to be but one of many 'directions' in Dickinson studies (Juhasz 427). But it remains clear that it has left one very important imprint on the academic reader of Dickinson's work: if it is taken seriously, it becomes impossible to read a Dickinson poem in a printed version and simply assume that this version is in fact 'reliable.' For pragmatic reasons, clearly, readers make this assumption all the time, but manuscript criticism offers a serious intervention in Dickinson scholarship and needs, in turn, to be taken seriously for the implications it not always makes explicit but that linger in their arguments.

On one level, this challenge, or questioning, of the 'foundations' for reading Dickinson, signifies an important realization of the often implicit fact (in literary study) that literary works are edited and hence always coded by a specific theory of editing that in some way will have an impact on the presentation of 'the work.' It thus makes explicit the fact that literary texts come to readers through the expediency of other, editing, readers. In this, the current interest in editorial questions in Dickinson studies reflects a more general tendency in textual criticism to produce 'inter-disciplinary' studies that reach into 'literary criticism' (thereby succinctly questioning the presumed separateness of the two 'tasks' of 'editing' and 'criticism').[4] On another level, this challenge, which I call an 'editorial turn' in Dickinson criticism, suggests something more radical: that, in fact, not only have Dickinson's texts not been satisfactorily edited in the past but that these texts cannot and should not be edited (typographically) for their meaning depends on a presumed 'immediacy' of the handwritten text as 'artifact' destined for specific readers at specific times. It is here that manuscript criticism becomes both interesting and problematic.[5]

Ellen Louise Hart writes "No editor can ever be 'objective' or 'disinterested,' no edition 'definitive' ("Editorial Scholarship" 94). She draws attention to Marta Werner's experimental edition of late drafts and fragments associated with Otis Phillips Lord, where Werner suggestively writes that 'Every reader is a bibliographer-poet finding his or her own way toward the future by striking out in a different direction through the past'" (94). The challenge, in the acknowledgement of this tempting *reader-as-writer* scenario, which is also a scenario of the *critic-as-editor*, is to remain, as a critic, critical of one's own imagination, one's own appropriations of 'the other's' writing, and in particular, to remain critical of one's own desires of exclusivity and originality, one's own desires to edit the 'perfect' Dickinson text. Because a desire for a more 'perfect' text is implicitly the aim of any editorial project, the problem, for a self-conscious criticism, becomes how to navigate an editing or criticism which is necessarily dogmatic, because precisely idealistic. For the purposes of an editorial/critical discourse meant to promote shared knowledge rather than individual epiphany, the task of the editor/ critic becomes one of combining interpretation with an acknowledgment of its temporality and its specific version of the edited/critiqued text.

Before I offer an outline of this chapter I wish here to comment on my selection and hence privileging of this 'manuscript poet' as representative of the late twentieth-century figuring of Emily Dickinson. In the context of an 'editorial biography' of Dickinson it is clearly the editorially inflected discourses about Emily Dickinson's work that concern me. Nevertheless, to choose the 'manuscript poet' as the central figure is necessarily a choice, and as such it reflects my conviction that such editorial debates indeed have had a paradigmatic effect on the way in which we see Emily Dickinson's work (and the poet *at work*), not simply for editorial but for critical and more general readerly purposes.

There are other important responses to the publication of Emily Dickinson's 'fascicles' and other important formulations of the 'visual' aspects of Emily Dickinson's work. Besides its implicit argument that Dickinson's aesthetics is book-bound, *The Manuscript Books* have had at least two direct effects on Dickinson studies: first, the representation of her gatherings of poems into little booklets has yielded thematic readings and intertextual studies of the poet's poetics. Second, the facsimile transmission of Dickinson's handwriting made the material aspects of her work known to a larger critical group; such public access to representations of her manuscripts has led to the growth of manuscript criticism. Cristanne Miller's chronological essay on critical formulations of "Emily Dickinson's Experiments in Language," sees such critical concern with the manuscripts' visual aspects rather than with the poems' linguistic form as a temporary effect of the "renewed [in the 1990s] critical uncertainty about the best edition of the poems to use" (250). In fact, the dilemma is serious: on a fundamental level it questions the possibility of editing Dickinson's work in the first place. Because I see the effects of the questions asked by manuscript critics as challenges not simply of the presumed paucity of 'best' editions of the poet's work but of the very basis for 'editing' and hence 'reading' Emily Dickinson's language/poetry, I believe it is crucial to consider further the implications of this return to the poet's script.[6]

This chapter begins with a discussion about the concept of 'materiality' in relation to Emily Dickinson's texts, which leads to a general discussion of Emily Dickinson's manuscripts as materially meaningful. I then outline in more detail the particulars of Emily Dickinson's handwriting and the documents on which that handwriting is inscribed. In the next section, "The Manuscript in/of Dickinson studies," I study the contemporary idea of the Dickinson manuscript-as-artifact as it has grown out of the publication of *The Manuscript Books* in 1981. I read Marta Werner's *Open Folios* and the work of Martha Nell Smith as a critical dialogue with Franklin's edition. The final section of the chapter, called "Print Editing in the Computer Age," engages Franklin's 1998 edition of *The Poems of Emily Dickinson*. Through engaging the ideas of 'ideal' and 'social' texts, this section discusses the numerous critical responses to this edition. Hence Franklin's editorial theory and method are evaluated, whereby theoretical and methodological editorial differences emerge and it becomes possible to historicize late twentieth-century debates regarding Dickinson's texts.

Hence the chapter explores the figure of Emily Dickinson as manuscript poet through the reading of Dickinson's manuscript page as it appeared in the 1980s and 1990s.

MATERIALITY AND MANUSCRIPTS

Emily Dickinson's assertion, in a letter to Thomas Higginson, that "I had told you I did not print" (L 316) is often taken as a sign of her antipathy towards print as a suitable medium for her work. Smith points out that Dickinson must have been "dissuaded" from conventional publication as she saw several of her poems in print with substantive changes (*Rowing* 11). Jerome McGann insists that Dickinson did not write for the print medium even though she lived in an age of print, and Werner theorizes a poet who "refused the limitations of a print existence" (McGann "Visible" 259; Werner 1). Emily Dickinson's own statement and the three critical formulations cited above locate the author in an opposition to and/or in antagonistic contest with the conventional means of materially producing literature in her time. I interpret Emily Dickinson's 'scene of writing' as a complex fashioning herself a poet through an engagement with print, the handwritten word, and poetic 'writing' in general. Such a tension in the textual corpus of Emily Dickinson's manuscripts needs to be considered in its complexity. I insist that a 'simple' return to the holographic 'productions' of the poet is not a satisfying response to this problem, as it tends towards an essentialist conception of the handwriting and the 'intentions' hidden in the hypothesized hand-based poetics. Instead we must see this problem of 'materiality' as a problem of editorial-critical construction and reception. Let us then consider in more detail the complex of 'materiality' as it is played out in the reception of Emily Dickinson's work in the latter part of the twentieth century. For we must consider the wider implications of such a construction of the poet's engagement with 'materiality' and its various inflections of 'material' and 'matter' before we move on to consider how Emily Dickinson's handwritten manuscripts have become, in the late twentieth- century, a privileged site (and problematic 'source') for the formulation of Emily Dickinson's art.

Marxist, cultural materialist and social theoretical orientations all focus on variations on a materialist conception of literature (Haslett 28). This means that there are many employments of the concept. The basic assumption of any materialist analysis of literature is that literary works are socially produced. Raymond Williams writes "meaning is always produced; it is never simply expressed" (166). Such 'production' of meaning is variously analyzed. Pierre Bourdieu insists that "the producer of the value of the work of art is not the artist but the field of production as a universe of belief which produces the value of the work of art as a *fetish* by producing the belief in the creative power of the artist" (*Rules of Art* 229). We can distinguish the employment of the concept of 'materiality' for the analysis of several and differing aspects of the literary work.

In the context of Emily Dickinson studies, it appears that the usage of the concept of materiality is more limited. Critics choose to consider the concept in the more limited usage of the 'physicality' of the documents of literary texts. Indeed, the critical concern with the more limited conception of the materiality of text as the 'physicality' of the text is well-established as an important field of investigation (Deppman et al. 1; Bornstein and Tinkle 1). It is in the interstices between textual criticism and literary criticism that important formulations of such theories of the materiality of text have emerged. McGann is an important figure to consider in this context.

McGann's theorization of the materiality of text is not easy to account for. What seems to be clear, however, is that for McGann the 'scene of writing' is at the heart of any textual analysis. For texts are "human acts" (4). It is this human labor with the textual condition that interests him, and he contrasts it with what he sees as approaches to literature that are based in an ideology of the 'mind' originating in the "Shelleyan lament: 'When composition begins, inspiration is already on the decline'" (5). Instead of such a logocentric lament of the 'corruption' of the written word, McGann insists that "the study of texts begins with readings of the texts" and that any such reading is "materially and socially defined" (8). There is, that is, no potential for 'discovering' an 'intrinsic' meaning in a text as meaning is always socially produced and constituted as such.

Yet it is in this privileging of the body of the text that McGann, in the context of Emily Dickinson's manuscripts, attaches a kind of essential subjectivity, indeed an ideality, to that body, the manuscript page: "Her surviving manuscripts take themselves at face value, and they urge us to treat all of her scriptural forms as potentially meaningful *at the aesthetic or expressive level*" (259). If we follow the logic of McGann's social theory of text, such meaning is socially constituted and the problem must then be: through what conventions do 'we' assign such 'aesthetic or expressive' meaning in Emily Dickinson's manuscripts? That is, how are those conventions, which are conventions of reception, material and social? If we are to refuse what McGann understands as the idealist thrust of various formalist theories of text, then, the privileging of 'matter' must in itself be theorized, in order that we do not simply exchange one form of valorizing reading with another by reversing the dichotomy of 'idealist' and 'materialist.'

Indeed McGann accentuates that the "only immutable law" of the textual condition is "the law of change" (9). In such a paradigm of reading text as 'change,' the task of the textual critic must be to somehow navigate the "mutability" of text not as a tragic loss (in the sense of 'corruption') but in a serious way 'simply' social, material, contingent. In this way we should understand editions of texts as socially constituted rather than ideal vessels of accurate representations of the author's intentions. The logic of this social model of textuality would seem to be an acceptance of change, which certainly should not mean an acceptance of 'bad' editions of texts but which must somehow engage all editions as readings, indeed writings, of the text in question. In the context of a discussion of 'authorial intentions' McGann writes that

> The indeterminacy of the textual situation (and the problem of 'intention') fluctuates in relation to the size and complexity of the surviving body of textual materials: the larger the archive, the greater the room for indeterminacy. And it must be understood that the archive includes not just original manuscripts, proofs, and editions, but all the subsequent textual constitutions which the work undergoes in its historical passages. (*The Textual Condition* 62)

It seems odd, then, that in the case of Emily Dickinson, McGann himself becomes such a staunch protector of the 'original' textual condition of the author inscribing her marks on the page and so exceedingly hostile in his critique of, in particular, Thomas Johnson's edition.[7]

McGann insists that texts—even 'the same' text—change through and within the sociohistorical conditions not only of their 'births' but also of their metaphorical re-births in re-productions and re-readings. But his insistence on that initial 'birth' in the context of Dickinson criticism means that the potentially radical implications of his theory are lost. I read his theory as a potential critique of the conventional textual critical formulation that the reproduction and historical dissemination of text necessarily involves 'corruption' of the original text. Indeed according to McGann's theory, it should be possible to investigate non-sentimentally the reproduction of texts and the social history of a literary work without immediately lamenting the 'corrupting' practices of editorial hands.

McGann, in his theorization of a distinction between 'linguistic' and 'bibliographic' codes, suggests a distinction between 'ideas' and 'matter;' but his insistence on the primacy of the 'aesthetic' means that his practice keeps him close to the text as artifact. George Bornstein and Teresa Tinkle take their cue from McGann's notions of linguistic and bibliographic codes for their argument that the theorization of a text's material features leads to a deeper understanding of how literary texts produce meaning and how readers receive those texts. In their accentuation of the materiality of text, Bornstein and Tinkle argue that the bibliographic code resembles Walter Benjamin's notion of 'aura.' In Benjamin's classic analysis, 'aura' is that which is lost in mechanical reproduction of an artifact; that is to say that the 'aura' suggests the historically situated uniqueness of an artifact. Such 'aura' disappears when an artifact is multiplied in copies (Benjamin 221–223). For Benjamin there is a radical political potential in new mass media that explicitly refuse/cancel the idea of the 'original' art work with its 'aura' (Haslett 109). But in Bornstein and Tinkle's version, criticism dealing with material textuality promises instead to *recuperate,* if ever so fleetingly, such lost 'aura' (2). Indeed, in his study of *Material Modernism* Bornstein argues that it is the 'aura' of the original presentation that is most important (for example in his analysis of Marianne Moore's poem "The Fish" and its various material instantiations because its first materialization is more political, more personal, less corrupt, less crudely capitalist(6–7). We should ask ourselves why a 'political' context is more 'historicist' than a 'deluxe' edition context: clearly such a division does not in a simple sense reflect intention in writer or editor but is a model for reading these 'intentions' in hindsight, the historicizing act is the critic's, not the editor's or artist's. What we do is to historicize the act of editing/reading. Bornstein privileges the original because of its 'aura:' hence for reasons of securing authenticity and authorial intentions, the original is important. Rather than completely vanishing, then, an artifact's 'aura' in Bornstein's version becomes a nostalgic lens, a construction, through which we can reconstruct the past—that is, the original—as somehow more ingenious, more political, more radical. Benjamin's essay presents a critique of elitist art, praising the shattering of aura as a "renewal of mankind," while at the same time portraying a despondent view of modern life: there is a tendency to nostalgically glance backwards in the face of crude mass-consumer culture (221–222, 240–241). I argue that it is important not to construct such nostalgic representations of the past, and that such relationship to a text needs to be queried. It is the critical thrust of Benjamin's notion of 'aura' that offers such a critical potential. This is not to deny the original work of art meaning, but rather to bring to light the critical risk of fetishizing the past through an untheorized privileging of that past as 'naturally' 'purer.' This is not, either, to deny Bornstein's critique of the anthologization of literary texts in textbook anthologies such as the *Norton* series, but rather to make visible the problem involved in choosing the authorially sanctioned version of a text as the necessarily most important or even 'best' one.

As can be seen in the discussion above, it is primarily materiality in the sense of the 'body' of the poem or text that has attracted critics to the use of the term for analytical purposes. As has been seen, too, such a privileging of the 'aesthetic' component of 'materiality' risks bringing the critical project into an idealist formulation of the original as nostalgically suffused with 'aura.' It is also in that sense that the most important Dickinson criticism of the late twentieth century has chosen to interpret 'materiality,' although such criticism, admittedly, also typically attempts to situate Dickinson, somehow, in one 'context' or another.

In the section entitled "New Directions in Dickinson Scholarship" of *The Emily Dickinson Handbook* only one essay is listed and this essay, Suzanne Juhasz's "Materiality and the Poet," suggests in fact only one major such direction in Dickinson studies: various interpretations of Dickinson through the not easily-defined concept of 'materiality.' In general it can be said that the concern with 'materiality' in Dickinson studies connotes a concern with the 'technologies' through which her work was initially produced and subsequently has been re-produced. In her essay, Juhasz defines the term as "the physicalness or corporeality" of Dickinson's writing (427). For the purposes of her discussion, she also uses the term to imply the "material contexts that surround and define the poet Dickinson and her writing" (427). In this wider sense of the term, it may be said to involve almost everything that is important to the study of a writer, from the concrete signs on the piece of paper (or other 'surface') to the social milieu in which the writer wrote.

We must consider the wider implications of employing the term 'materiality' here. For it is clearly not a 'neutral' term with which to approach a text. The concept's origins in Marxist thinking and its subsequent employment in various literary critical practices need to be made explicit. Because concerns with 'materiality' in Dickinson studies surfaced with the interest in Emily Dickinson's manuscripts, as handwritten and original art works, I will consider here in more detail the theoretical distinctions between such an 'original' work of art and its subsequent 'reproductions' in print (or through photographs or digital programming).

We must remember that the concept of 'materiality' is ideologically and indeed politically charged. In Benjamin's analyses of the materiality of the literary work of art in an age of mechanical reproduction, his formulation of the much-repeated concept of 'aura' has political implications: the loss of 'aura' in contemporary media such as film is not a sign of degeneration but of a renewed political potential for art.

We should not forget the critical potential of the concept of materiality. In the context of the present study, to employ Benjamin's notion of 'aura' to simply denote that which is lost with mechanical reproduction is to assign it ('aura') a merely nostalgic lens through which we can accuse mechanical reproduction for 'polluting' the presumably 'original' expressions of Emily Dickinson. Indeed, employing the term in such a way means that the potentially otherwise 'democratic' aspects of print dissemination of Emily Dickinson's work to a wider audience are erased, cancelled. To insist that Emily Dickinson's work is manuscript based does not mean that we must privilege the manuscript in an opposition to print (from a critical point of view, we should not reproduce Emily Dickinson's ideological position in our writing about her, thus simply re-inscribing a conservative ideology onto the present without reflection). Instead a thoroughly social theory of text, as McGann outlines it, helps us understand how the print editions of Emily Dickinson's work are part of 'her' textual condition and a necessary part of it, too (even though McGann himself seems to paradoxically prefer the original).

In fact a serious engagement with the 'materiality' of Emily Dickinson's texts must involve the realization that each critical act is part of that material history of 'reproducing' Dickinson. Moyra Haslett writes that the realization that literary works are "'re-produced' in their readings" leads to a formulation of literary criticism as one form of such reproduction. With such a realization, Haslett argues that "literary debates must shift from positions of 'intrinsic' meaning to considerations of their own modes of working" (34). This self-reflective aspect of a theory of materiality is not typically developed in Dickinson studies; instead, it is the more author-oriented aspects of the matter of text that concern critics.

If the point of manuscript criticism is to re-vision Emily Dickinson's manuscripts as exploring new means/forms of artistic expression, we must maintain that much of that re-vision is connected not with 'Emily Dickinson' but with tendencies in contemporary criticism. It is this 'confusion' that concerns me here.

EMILY DICKINSON, MANUSCRIPTS AND CRITICISM

In 1981 R. W. Franklin edited *The Manuscript Books,* a two-volume facsimile edition of the 'collections' of bound booklets (or, as Mabel Loomis Todd called them, 'fascicles') and unbound 'sets' of poems through which the poet had gathered around half of her poetic production. The edition quickly became an important tool for the exploration and formulation of 'Emily Dickinson' and her 'work.' Some critics seized on the potential for reading the various 'books' thematically or according to some other principle of organization. This was one way of critically maneuvering Dickinson's vast production, which in its very vastness (and with the lack of an explicit 'manifesto') is necessarily difficult to domesticate in any straightforward way. A second way to read these manuscript books was suggested by Sharon Cameron, who developed the thesis, in the context of a theoretical engagement with the conventional understanding of the lyric genre, that Emily Dickinson's fascicle poetry radically questions the idea of the lyric poem (in general) as 'bound' and 'closed.' This reading of Emily Dickinson's work questions the conventional notion of the lyric by asking "what if there are multiple ways of construing order, or what if there are multiple orders?" (*Choosing not Choosing* 17). Cameron reads the poems of particular fascicles as variants of each other, and she reads the word variants of specific poems; through both kinds of readings she explores the ways in which the conventional notion of 'unity' is precisely not achieved in these texts because the poems embody a problematization of the very notion of 'identity,' thereby radically questioning the concept of 'unity' as a possible achievement of a 'lyric' or other poem (*Choosing not Choosing* 4). Cameron's readings point in the same direction towards a theorization of Emily Dickinson's poetic experimentations (albeit in a different manner, because primarily engaged with questions based very much in the poems' linguistic codes) as those critics who, like McGann, see *The Manuscript Books* as a suggestive key to Dickinson's texts through what McGann called its "revelation" of the poet's handwritten practices (*Black Riders* 26). Susan Howe's reading of *The Manuscript Books*' 'revelation' is powerful. In *The Birth-mark* she writes:

> Words are only frames. No comfortable conclusion.
> Letters are scrawls,
> turnabouts, astonishments, strokes, cuts, masks.
> These poems are representations. These manuscripts should be under- stood as visual productions.
> The physical act of copying is a mysterious sensuous expression.
> Wrapped in the mirror of the word. (141)

This, a poetic criticism, can be read as a manifesto for manuscript criticism's engagement with Emily Dickinson's poetry. It gathers all those aspects of the manuscripts that fascinate critics and that have shaped the construction of this poet, Emily Dickinson, in the last decades of the twentieth century. In particular, Howe's accentuation and merging of the 'physical' and the 'mysterious' has become a key towards various projects of reading Dickinson's hand, intention, and poetic project. Howe, McGann and a number of other

Dickinson scholars seized on the opportunities afforded by this edition to turn critical attention to the poet's handwriting, her placing of words on the page and various formal aspects of those page designs. Hence McGann became one of the proponents of the thesis that we must read Emily Dickinson's manuscripts for their radical *intentions* and *implications,* a thesis that demands a formulation of Emily Dickinson's art as essentially handwritten. The various thematic approaches to *The Manuscript Books* are important, but it was the turn to the poet's 'scene of writing' that radically shifted the critical 'scene of reading' Dickinson.

Increasingly, then, Emily Dickinson's work has become theorized as radically based in a manuscript-bound poetics, and it is argued that critics, like Emily Dickinson, must refuse the 'commonsensical' approach of an ideology of reading literature coded by the 'machine of print.' I will argue that, through this privileging of the handwritten and its various implications, the ontological status of Emily Dickinson's texts has been seriously problematized in recent years with the effect of seriously undermining any critical project that bases its assumptions about Emily Dickinson's work in print editions of her 'poems' and 'letters.' This chapter is concerned with the general question of how we should approach Emily Dickinson's work; 'should' is used here because it will be argued that the question of 'how to read' Emily Dickinson has become increasingly polarized and indeed politicized. For the investments made in the various formulations of the poet's 'radical' handwritten poetics necessarily (if sometimes implicitly so) serve to polarize formulations of the poet's practices based in readings of the print editions of the poet's 'poems' and 'letters' as being equally 'conservative' or 'reactionary' as the assumptions implicit in those editions. But of course there is no 'natural' connector between 'print' as such and a conservative (editorial) practice, and there is no 'natural' connector between 'handwriting' as such and an exploration of an experimental poetics.[8] In fact, print can easily be seen to represent a 'democratization' of reading, and the handwritten production and private circulation of poetry can be understood as part of a legacy of an essentially elitist and conservative genteel poetry that shies away from print because of its improprieties (of class and gender). Hence, arguing the case of Emily Dickinson as radical experimenter with the visual word is not a straightforward task. This chapter engages with a number of important formulations of this manuscript poetics in order to challenge its foundation, which is, really, that of 'Emily Dickinson' as author of genius.

Through the poet's eye of Howe, Dickinson readers have learnt to see Emily Dickinson's handwriting as meaningful, carrying semantic import. Emily Dickinson dispersed her work in a fascinating array of letters, stitched-together 'books,' and on a variety of other surfaces. It was all written by hand, in pencil or ink. How can we ignore that original scene of writing? Even if that scene is forever 'lost' we can pretend to reconstruct it through making speculative connections between linguistic inscription and the

> backs of brown-paper bags or of discarded bills, programs, and invitations; on tiny scraps of stationery pinned together; on leaves torn from old notebooks (one such sheet dated '1824'); on soiled and mildewed subscription blanks, or on department- or drug-store bargain flyers from Amherst and surrounding towns. There are pink scraps, blue and yellow scraps, one of them a wrapper of *Chocolat Meunier;* poems on the reverse of recipes in her own writing, on household shopping lists, on the cut-off margins of newspapers, and on the inside of their brown-paper wrapping. (Millicent Todd Bingham, *Bolts of Melody* xii-xv)

The material base for Dickinson's manuscript production is laid bare in the introduction to *Bolts of Melody,* an introduction that reveals a fascination with but also an editorial discomfort with what to make of such a material and scriptural overflow: "Most of them [poems] were smothered with alternative words and phrases crowded into every available space—around the edges, upside down, wedged between the lines" (xii). For Todd Bingham, as for most other editors of Emily Dickinson's manuscripts, the specifics of Dickinson's manuscripts did not easily translate into print. Steeped in the convention of print and standard orthography, she hypothesizes that "Certain spellings had special meanings for Emily" but, she concludes, such meaning "evaporates" in print and may hence be 'standardized' (xi). While contemporary critics insist that it is because of this apparent 'evaporation' of meaning that occurs in the translation of manuscript orthography to print typography that we must read Dickinson in the holograph, Todd Bingham was tied to a convention of print and therefore saw fit to standardize spelling for the sake of legibility and conformity.

It is here, in the formulation of an 'evaporation' of meaning (which we must extend from the issue of spelling to the issue of the illegibility of the handwriting), that the dilemma of interpreting Emily Dickinson's work and hypothesizing her 'poetics' becomes apparent and really problematic. For Todd Bingham, the editorial translation from handwriting to print was 'natural' (because print was the naturalized means of representing 'poetry' for 'publication') and hence unproblematic. But what she formulated as the 'evaporation' of meaning remains a critical site where continual confusion and frustration are played out; it remains the 'location' of continually shifting responses to the question of how we formulate what is at stake in this apparent 'evaporation.'

Manuscript criticism's answer is that indeed such 'evaporation' occurs in print, and that therefore it is important to return to the original handwriting, in order to reverse such 'evaporation' of meaning.[9]

For the sake of opening up the field of reading Emily Dickinson's script, let us, by turning to the poem "In Ebon Box, when years have flown" (Fr180) unpack the implications of a turning towards the handwritten manuscript in recent Dickinson studies:

> In Ebon Box, when years have flown
> To reverently peer,
> Wiping away the velvet dust
> Summers have sprinkled there!
>
> To hold a letter to the light–
> Grown Tawny—now—with time—
> To con the faded syllables
> That quickened us like Wine!
>
> Perhaps a Flower's shriveled cheek
> Among it's stores to find—
> Plucked far away, some morning—
> By gallant—mouldering hand!
>
> A curl, perhaps, from foreheads
> Our constancy forgot—
> Perhaps, an antique trinket—
> In vanished fashions set!
>
> And then to lay them quiet back—
> And go about its care—
> As if the little Ebon Box
> Were none of our affair!

This poem provides a scene for interpreting Emily Dickinson's work as radically manuscript based. Boxed away for posterity, Dickinson's work can be understood, in analogy to the poem's 'Ebon Box' with its 'antique' contents, as the object of a disturbing editorial romance. The 'Ebon Box' brings to mind first of all that mythical chest-of-drawers in which Dickinson kept her manuscript books and other papers; the second box that looms rather large in Dickinson editing history is that camphor-wood box that Mabel Loomis Todd locked up for several decades, in some kind of defiance after her loss against Lavinia Dickinson in the court trial that symbolizes the 'war' between the 'houses,' thereby hiding a large portion of Dickinson's manuscripts from the world, one more time. In 1944, Todd Bingham's introduction to *Bolts of Melody,* an introduction which is basically a defense of her mother, echoed the poem's sentimental tone in the editor's description of her experience of first opening this box after having been given its key. This box, which contained a number of previously unpublished Dickinson texts, afforded Todd Bingham a minor shock: "I looked and caught my breath. For there, before my eyes, were quantities of Emily's poems. How could they have kept quiet so long? With such inherent vitality it seemed as if they must have shouted, lying there in the dark all those year!" (viii) Of course, Loomis Todd's possession of these documents for so many years is a travesty, a part of the romance which is the editorial history of Dickinson. This possessiveness restages, in the context of 'the war between the houses,' the sentimentality of the conventional notion of the box of memories of a deceased loved one—the 'antique trinkets, 'letter,' the 'curl.' More disturbingly, however, the 'mouldering' hand of this Gothicized family romance reveals that in the end, the meditation on such memories is not as nostalgically pleasurable as the convention tells: that 'mouldering hand' speaks of death as decay. Decay: because they grow more fragile for each year, Emily Dickinson's manuscripts are today coded 'access denied' by the libraries that archive them. This very literal 'access denied' means that only very few critics have accessed the holographic productions that we are assumed to turn to for critical reevaluation of their meaning. In the 'war' of competing critical voices, some seem to suggest that if a critic has not seen the original (or at the very least a photographic reproduction of the holograph), then she will not be qualified to comment on the text. "As if" the little box were "none of our affair" indeed.[10]

Dickinson produced, by writing about letters growing old in a box, an uncanny replica of her own poem: and one hundred years after her death, critics are engaged in "peering" into the materiality of her work, desiring an equation between those documents and the "mouldering hand" of Dickinson writing immortally: would we be able to, according to the romance, find in the crevices of the documents, Dickinson at work, would we be able to reverse the mouldering of that hand? Would 'it' reveal its writer's intentions (who is writing, anyway?)? And hence this question must be engaged: How exactly are the contents of the "Ebon Box"—the manuscripts that Emily Dickinson left behind—"our affair"? What are the implications of privileging the manuscript "Grown Tawny"?

Paradoxically it is here, in the return to the manuscript page (for the sake of revealing Dickinson's 'reader-response'), that Dickinson criticism turns away from a textual orientation, and cannot do anything but return, again and again, to the figure of the author (or the editor-as-author/writer, as the trope of editing in important ways has surfaced as the 'master trope' for engaging with Dickinson's texts) as the 'holder-together' of 'meanings' that are always on the brink of evaporation, always threatening to disintegrate (like the Tawny lettering of the poem's letter). For even in the handwriting, meaning is difficult to elucidate, as the poet's orthography is so idiosyncratic, so illegible.[11] Hence the continual and indeed inflected editorial desire to tame and to limit the text in various forms: standardization of typographic print rendition, 'manuscript book' facsimiles in solid hardcover, the 'book' of 'Susan and Emily,' and the 'flight' of the mind racing through the hand writing. For we must understand: academic discourse does not strive towards wavering or uncertainty, it cannot, clearly, be as 'blank' (illegible) as Dickinson's manuscripts, however filled with ink they are. Returning to the poem, we can see how the trope of the collector, or the editor, surfaces in the poem and becomes an analogy to the tendency in Dickinson criticism to treat the document as fetish and inflect the role of the collector-editor with precious power. After this excursus to the contents of the "Ebon Box," let us now move on to the purposes and *contents* of this chapter.

Since the publication of *The Manuscript Books* in 1981, Emily Dickinson critics have increasingly turned to the *materiality* of Dickinson's writing to study and elucidate the potential meanings of the poet's handwritten production. Her handwritten manuscripts, it is argued, disrupt conventional notions of poetic form, genre boundaries and 'publication.' Dickinson critics have always been aware of the difficulties of editing her work and have, as we saw in the previous chapter, continually challenged the reliability of any edition. The recent debates about the materiality of Dickinson's manuscripts tie in explicitly with such editorial concerns as the (general) practice of editing itself has become a self-consciously theoretical undertaking that is formulated as decisively interpretive, in effect conflating the practices of editing and literary criticism, seemingly erasing the boundary between the two practices. The tropes of 'editing' and 'editor' can, in such critical practice, be seen to replace the notions of 'reading' and 'critic' to an extent that 'editing' seems a more likely description of the act of 'reading' of Emily Dickinson.

ASPECTS OF DICKINSON'S TEXTS

For the purposes of clarifying the material details of Emily Dickinson's manuscripts, details that are central to the following discussions, I describe in the following the general properties of Emily Dickinson's *manuscripts*.[12]

Variants and Versions

The poem beginning with the line "It sifts from Leaden Sieves–" (Fr 291) exists in "five, variant, about 1862, 1863, 1865, 1871, and 1883" manuscripts. For simplicity's sake, I will here simply rehearse the format of the Franklin transcripts. The first two versions consist of five quatrains. The other three versions are twelve-line poems, the first of which is a two-stanza text and the other two divided into three stanzas. Among all five versions five lines are "common," of which two are variant. Hence, for example, line two, which is common to all versions, reads

> "It powders all the Wood." in the version of 1862
> "It powders all the Field—" in the version of 1863
> "It powders all the Wood" in the version of 1865
> "It powders all the Wood—" in the version of 1871
> "It powders all the Wood—" in the version of 1883

As we can see, in the second version "Wood" is replaced with "Field." Furthermore, only the first version ends with a full stop. And while the second, fourth, and fifth version end with a dash, the third version ends with "Wood" with no punctuation. What this brief rehearsal of one line of "one poem" reveals is that Dickinson worked with poems over a long period of time, leaving them aside for some time in order to later return to a text, cutting or adding stanzas, lines, words and punctuation marks.

With such a textual situation, readers and critics might wish to use different versions of a text for different projects. In order to make such choices, however, readers need to know all other versions of that work: these other versions may be equally 'authorized' or otherwise critically interesting but may, based on the informed choice, be left out of the particular analysis for one reason or another. To this point Domhnall Mitchell writes, in a discussion of "Safe in their alabaster chambers" that

> The truth, as Smith points out, is that P#124 (J#216) "Safe in their alabaster chambers" is more than a single remarkable poem; it is a series of them (Franklin thinks six or seven, one or two of which are lost), and any credible reading needs to take all of these into account, if not literally by offering an interpretation of each, at least by establishing the grounds for choosing one variant in front of the others. (*Monarch* 258)

We cannot retain the notion that 'a poem' consists of a final 'fair copy,' idealized and fixed, with one or several 'drafts' or 'rough copy' or otherwise non-finalized versions. All versions are potentially meaningful: sometimes the juxtaposition of all versions and variants of a text may be that meaning; sometimes the meaning that a reader interprets is based in one consciously chosen version or variant, but to make this choice, the reader must have studied all versions.

Lineation

In what Franklin, in *The Manuscript Books,* designates as 'Set 11,' a poem appears with the following line division:

> The Sea said
> "Come" to the Brook—
> The Brook said
> "Let me grow"—
> The Sea said
> "then you will
> be a Sea"—
> "I want a Brook—
> Come now"—
> The Sea said
> "Go" to the Sea—
> the Sea said
> "I am he
> You cherished"—
> "Learned Waters—
> Wisdom is stale
> To Me"—

Franklin determines the poem as number 1,275 and records its "three fair copies (one in part, lost)." The poem appears like this in Franklin's 1998 *Poems of Emily Dickinson:*

> The Sea said "Come" to the Brook—
> The Brook said "Let me grow"—
> The Sea said "then you will be a Sea"—
> "I want a Brook—Come now"—
> The Sea said "Go" to the Sea—
> The Sea said "I am he

You cherished"—"Learned Waters—
Wisdom is stale to Me"—

Dickinson sent a third version of the poem to Thomas Higginson. In this version, lines are divided even more. What Franklin deems to be one line 'The Sea said "Come" to the Brook–' in Dickinson's handwriting appears like

The Sea said
"Come" to the
Brook—

Not only does this rehearsal of the lineation of "one poem" show the precariousness of Franklin's judgment, it also problematizes the translation into print of Dickinson's holographs. It is for example not 'clear' that a print translation of this poem which follows the lineation of that poem actually renders more 'truly' the visual 'effect' of the handwritten page. By looking in *The Manuscript Books,* the poem appears not as the thin long poem (with plenty of 'white' space around it) that is represented above but in fact as occupying the entire page (although this might be a photographic effect). That is, the poem covers the entire page (at least as represented in the black and white facsimile), whereas in my translation it hardly takes up any space at all, while, in fact, the Franklin print translation, with its rather fat and chunky appearance on the page, looks more like the holographic production, in spite of its 'misrepresentation' of Dickinson's lineation according to some ideal metrical unit. Thus, while it is easy to see that Franklin's version in some sense 'misrepresents' Dickinson's lineation, it becomes clear that *all* editorial interventions are 'misrepresentations' in the sense that any representation will slightly differ in visual layout out of any particular text.

Of course it may be the case that we 'should not' read Emily Dickinson's poetry in printed form at all. If we choose to so adhere to the material page of her script, clearly, the above discussion becomes null. But such an adherence to the bibliographic code of Dickinson's script is not the only way of reading her work, for clearly its linguistic code is apparent, too. Recent years' critical concern with Dickinson's manuscripts has read the meaning of the manuscripts from a model of authorial intention. The problem then becomes one of choosing whether or not to demand that the holograph be virtually reproduced because Emily Dickinson's intentions so demand. But, in fact, the question is one of interpretation of that original layout, and there can be several valid answers to that question, all depending on the methodological framework the editor or critic works with. Of course, if we formulate an ideal 'intention' speaks from within the text, such a reader-oriented argument, or even the argument that literature is in fact a cultural production in which writers, editors and reader all partake, this perspective cannot be maintained.

Calligraphy

Perhaps the most influential critic of calligraphy is Susan Howe, who writes that "[i]n the long run, the best way to read Dickinson is to read the facsimiles, because her calligraphy influences her meaning" (*The Birth-mark* 153). But in the Dickinson studies marketplace have circulated, since the very first editions of her work came out in the 1890s, a number of strong and related discourses connected to Howe's argument. Thomas Wentworth Higginson wrote that Dickinson's handwriting "seemed as if the writer might have taken her first lessons by studying the famous fossil bird-tracks in the museum of that college town" ("Emily Dickinson's Letters" 446). All editors seem to have something to say about her handwriting. To this effect Mabel Loomis Todd writes

> The handwriting was at first somewhat like the delicate, running Italian hand of our elder gentlewomen; but as she advanced in breadth of thought, it grew bolder and more abrupt, until in her latest years each letter stood distinct and separate from its fellows. [. . .] The effect of a page of her more recent manuscript is exceedingly quaint and strong. ("Preface" 5–6)

Manuscript criticism's preference for the visuals of Dickinson's words thus stems from a long lineage of fascination with Emily Dickinson's handwriting. In *Rowing in Eden,* discussing the famous poem "Wild Nights, Wild Nights," Martha Nell Smith writes that "[e]rased from any typescript reproduction, which levels the effects of letters, is Dickinson's extraordinary, somewhat seductive, calligraphy—the wide-mouthed W, the triangular T at the beginning of the sixth line, and the stunning flourish that crosses both T's in 'Tonight'" (65). Yes, Dickinson's letters may be "seductive" and "stunning" but can there be a critical industry made out of such analysis? Of course, the answer to that question is, yes, there can be such industry spawned out of attention to calligraphy. To be sure, such analysis is loaded with ideological investment, something, again, that cannot be repudiated or critiqued. Smith writes about the editing for print of "Wild Nights, Wild Nights" that "Obviously, in their production Higginson and Loomis Todd regularize the minutiae of Dickinson's punctuation to 'correct' her ecstatic exclamation mark without a point and to even the long and short dashes by translating them into conventional, equally demarcated signs; then, by altering the lineation, they smooth out the lyric's rhythm, and, in doing so, mask the breathless sexuality conveyed by the holograph, tempering, therefore, her intemperance" (65).

The problem with theorizing Dickinson as radical is that it necessarily involves an idealization of her practices: this 'intemperate' poetic calligraphy is implicitly 'better' than the 'tempering' effect of a typographic rendition of this poem. Such idealization has always been part of the editorial projects on this poet's work. Even more problematic is a theory of Dickinson's script as intentionally radical when we recognize that the privileging of the holograph is conditioned by a trace of the typographic, as it is only after the typographic event that the holograph can be theorized as 'intemperate' in the first place. Dickinson's holographs, then, must be understood in a 'force field' of print and handwriting, in which 'print' becomes, in fact, one important 'shaper' of the handwriting that is constructed as original and expressive of the poet's desires.

It would be unwise to reject the critical formulation of Emily Dickinson as an experimental manuscript poet. But it is similarly precarious to engage her manuscripts as 'intentional' of anything in particular, with the purpose of producing any kind of 'libratory' (say, through queering the Dickinson text) argument. The crux is not to employ Emily Dickinson's text for the engagement of contemporary questions but to insert the concept of 'intention' in that engagement. 'We' can use 'the Emily Dickinson text' for anything 'we' want, but to attach an idealized 'intention' to such practice is bound to produce an idealist version of an author, an idealism that can only lead to the kinds of 'wars' which can be seen to be amply re-produced regarding the 'ownership' of the 'correct' Dickinson text. I do not suggest that we leave the question of the 'meaning' of the visuals of Emily Dickinson's manuscripts aside, but I do think that such 'meaning' should be located explicitly in the 'intentions' of critics, not in idealized authors.

THE MANUSCRIPT IN/OF DICKINSON STUDIES

As related in the previous chapter, critical reception of Dickinson's work was, from the beginning, concerned with the editorial transcription and dissemination of the poet's handwritten manuscripts. Dickinson's handwriting has always attracted attention and serious engagement with it is thus not new. As already noted, her correspondent and early editor Higginson compared her handwriting to the "famous fossil bird-tracks" in an Amherst museum ("Emily Dickinson's Letters" 444–456). Charles Anderson asked whether such manuscripts as Dickinson's could be reproduced in any other way than in facsimile (x) and Thomas Johnson describes the "Characteristics of the Handwriting" in a section of the introduction to his edition of The Poems of Emily Dickinson. Thus in 1981, Franklin met a real readerly demand with the publication of *The Manuscript Books*. This two-volume edition initiated a breakthrough in Dickinson studies. Critics, editors and readers rediscovered Dickinson's handwritten manuscripts and 'found' or 'created' a form and a poetics that had been quite removed by print representations. The manuscripts became central to the study of her work and have remained so. It may be argued that Franklin's facsimile edition is based in a conception of the manuscript page as simply a stage towards the final print object (Deppman, Ferrer, and Groden 5). Franklin himself seems to imply that such is his view, suggesting as he does that Dickinson "did not publish," an act with which he clearly associated printing (*Manuscript Books* x). Contrary to such a vision, recent criticism has formulated Dickinson's holographs as unique works of art, as artifacts that need to be understood as material objects aesthetically meaningful 'in their own right.' It is in such a light that Walter Benjamin's notion of 'aura' becomes a tool for critics concerned with the materiality of text: the artifact is a unique work of art that has been disseminated in reproductions, which cloud the origins, the uniqueness of the work of art.

Any kind of detailed knowledge of Dickinson's manuscripts was reserved for a very small group of reader-editors until the publication of the two-volume Manuscript Books. In these two volumes, readers encounter Dickinson's 'fascicles' and 'sets' in black and white photographic reproduction: readers, that is, encounter here those poems that Dickinson sewed together into booklets and leaflets and those poems that Franklin interprets as having been produced with a booklet context in mind. Franklin's rationale for representing these particular holographs is that it is important to represent Dickinson's practice of binding together fascicles, or little booklets: in other words, to represent the writer's drive towards the idea of the book. Dickinson left behind forty such finished fascicles and fifteen 'sets,' that is, unbound fair copy poems interpreted by Franklin as intended for fascicle inclusion. Left out are such texts as early editor Loomis Todd referred to as 'scraps,' that is 'drafts' of different kinds (x). The publication of The Manuscript Books is hence a select one: it chooses to represent that part of Dickinson's textual production that could be interpreted as bibliographic, as reflecting the idea of the book.

This is an expensive and exclusive edition, at some level the exquisite epitome of fine art book publishing, a bibliophile's crown jewel. The facsimile edition does not pretend to be a lay person's reader. In its very luxury, it enhances the privilege of the hardcover book reading scholar and the very literal gap between such readers and ordinary readers. The facsimile edition also shamelessly privileges a bookish aspect of Dickinson's art but also, like fine art books, exaggerates the visual quality of the documents. The bibliographic coding of *The Manuscript Books* accentuates the aesthetic pleasure of reading and seeing handwritten documents. As very expensive, solid tomes, and the results of scholarly effort, they represent the epitome of the Book which is also a return to the handwritten illuminated page of the Middle Ages or the expensive book productions of William Morris. To someone concerned with the literal 'freedom' of handwritten loose sheets, the edition functions literally as a dead end of representational capacity of the book format: it is only a shadow of the artifact. To critics concerned with arguing the importance of paying attention to the actual, empirical, physical materiality of Dickinson's manuscripts in and outside of the fascicles, *The Manuscript Books* function, paradoxically, like print editions, as a hindrance. By limiting its scope to those Dickinson texts that may be imagined as book-bound, *The Manuscript Books*, produced under the auspices of bookish thinking, shape Dickinson as a writer whose imagination was based in conventional typography and print publication. Also, the black and white photography fails to represent various kinds of details with apparent meaning, such as smudges and particular margin widths. It distorts the size of letters and paper. Hence, the radical demand for revealing the bare naked artifact, the document that some scholars so covet in the contemporary scene of reading-seeing Dickinson.

The Manuscript Books must be understood as one attempt to comprehend this poet's practices, and, certainly, the "Introduction" is a testimony to such speculative concern with Dickinson's intentions as an artist. It tells a particular story about Emily Dickinson's artistic life and practice in rather conventional terms, in which Emily Dickinson's production of the manuscript books is connected to her psychological state. In this narrative, the year 1861 is described as a "difficult" one in which she "faltered" in her fascicle making by using a mix of different papers (*xii*). The year 1862 is gloriously described as her *Annus Mirabilis* in which again her fascicle making was regularized. Generally, the years 1861–63 are referred to as years of crisis and drive, while towards the late 1860s, her "poetic drive" was "somewhat spent," a psychological state that eventually and accordingly led to a stop in her making fascicles (*xiii*). Apart from a hypothesized need to reduce disorder among her writings, Franklin reads the fascicles as a kind of self-publication, connected to a need to organize material both in terms of artistic 'bookish' gatherings of poems, and in terms of a repository from which poems for external letter-publication could be selected (*x*). The fascicles also increasingly, according to Franklin, functioned as a workshop where the poet would slip back into the poetic process of rewriting specific poems (*x*).

Franklin inscribes himself in a tradition that essentially argues that Dickinson was isolated and generally silent towards the external world (*ix*). At the same time he invites the interpretation of letter writing as a publication act and he argues that as her poems were never prepared by the author herself for print publication, critical judgment must "be informed by the manuscript conventions themselves" (*ix*). I argue that the facsimile edition is testimony to Franklin's sensitivity to critical discourse about the poet and her practices; the publication is a response to the continuing debate, in which Franklin himself has been a strong voice since the 1960s, of how to best interpret and make sense of Dickinson's handwriting and her punctuation, a lively debated issue. Franklin's fault, if one may judge it to be a fault, is that his imagination of what a poem is, is guided by an ideology of the book, or, generally, by an ideology of literature as essentially a public act structured by various *biblio*graphic codes such as titles, pagination, content-lists or "other apparatus to guide one's reading" (*xii*). Dickinson's poetry to a large extent lacks such codes and is hence difficult to understand under the auspices of conventional reading. That Dickinson did gather many of her poems together in booklets must, from such a perspective, be seen as representing a drive towards the book. Indeed, it is difficult not to think about books when encountering these leaves. At the same time, Franklin conscientiously records that many poems do not fit into the scheme set up by the book.

Two critics, Marta Werner and Martha Nell Smith stand out in the theorization of the Dickinson manuscript page, and I want to take the opportunity in the following to study their respective projects in detail.[13] First, the binary oppositions that structure the theorization of the manuscript as artifact need to be outlined. In the following the terms in the left hand column represent traditional concepts of thinking about Dickinson's texts, whereas the terms in the right hand column reflect critical preferences associated with 'the manuscript school:'

sound	visual forms
print	publishing—epistolary exchanges
linearity	variants/versions/hypertext/intertextuality
print	handwriting/digitized documents
the book	the holograph/the Internet
editing	unediting

Several ways of reading Dickinson as a visually oriented poet have been articulated in the past few decades. Judith Farr's intertextual reading of the sublime visual negotiations of 'love and death' in Dickinson's poetry, and various American (post) Romantic painters such as Tomas Cole stands out in this respect. Farr's reading of visuals is, however, very different from the kind of insistence on the materiality of text that impels a critic like Howe to formulate a visual 'reading' of Dickinson. Whereas Farr's reading is primarily thematic, Howe's is insisting on the visual aspects of language as material production.[14] Such critical insistence on the materiality of the Dickinson script has developed into a critique of print and its linear way of fashioning text: a call for the 'unediting' of the body of Dickinson's text. In the following I explore this idea of Emily Dickinson's writing.

Writing Dickinson's Manuscripts

Werner's editorial production of the late manuscripts of Emily Dickinson associated with Judge Otis Lord is based in an idea of 'loss,' as 'we' always arrive belatedly to the Dickinsonian 'scene of writing,' a scene of writing which then becomes a 'scene of reading' in order to attempt to gloss that 'loss.' Even if editing and reading is always a matter of such 'loss,' it is still based in the convention of assigning status to that which is written by somebody (an "author"), and more pertinently, and regardless of the theoretical disrepute of 'intention,' to that which was written in *the author's hand*. As David Greetham suggests, editing, in spite of theoretical constructions otherwise, typically associates the ontology of text(ual object) with "the original, the first, and the conceptual, rather than with the social, the derived, and the transmitted" (*Theories* 56). Discussing exhibits of famous paintings, Greetham reminds us that, in an age of mechanical reproduction, the 'original' painting (or text) only gains 'authenticity' in so far as it replicates the reproduction circulating in society, which is typically a viewer's first experience of that 'original.' The value of "A Matisse" is dependent on the circulation of its reproduction in society with the result that the more reproductions out there, the more valuable the 'original.' But the 'original' would be meaningless without its 'copies' (*Theories* 395). Greetham, rather like Bornstein, destabilizes the view of the "original" as more 'authentic' than the 'copy' by pondering the fact that an original only derives significance and value by the already-reproduced reproduction. It is through reproductions that one learns about the original. Therefore, the transmitted and socially derived text must destabilize the power of the 'original,' reducing it, at some level, to a belated status, only recoverable in archives and museums. This (being hidden from the social circuit of things) gives the original its coveted 'aura.' It is this aura that, I argue, Dickinson manuscript critics wish to prioritize. In the following I show how this is so.

I wish to situate Werner's work in the context of the theory and methodology of the French *critique génétique*. It seems to me that the manuscript criticism, as it is practiced by Werner in particular, owes much to, or at the very least, shares many ideas with such a general theory of the 'birth' of the literary work, a theory that leads to the study of a writer's workshop, all the writings that form part of that 'space of possibles' in which texts emerge (rather than focusing on the 'work,' which is nevertheless the logical outgrowth of this workshop). Genetic criticism insists that

> A work's manuscripts are clearly distinct from the text; although they lead to the text, they also keep reminding us that they are prior and external to it. To grasp the vast movement that, with increasing precision, produces the final text, without covering up the many divergences operating inside its transformation—such is the critical work of manuscript analysis. (de Biasi 38)

In this implicit dichotomization between 'draft' and 'final' work, genetic criticism differs from the tendency in Dickinson manuscript criticism to see the 'draft' as not 'simply' a temporal antecedent to a more 'final' text but in fact as an integral part of the 'entire' text that is 'the poem' in its various instantiations. Nevertheless, genetic criticism theorizes the manuscript as cultural object in ways important to consider in the context of Dickinson studies, a field of study, as we have seen, in which the manuscript page has increasingly come to serve as the conceptual frame for the idea of 'the poem' as the symbol for Emily Dickinson's 'intentions' and the meaning of her work, and hence our understanding of her work. Pierre-Marc de Biasi argues that genetic criticism removes the notion of the manuscript as 'fetish,' since it steers clear from the commodity oriented market in which collectors covet the manuscripts of famous authors. Instead of proclaiming an interest in the 'definitive' manuscript, that manuscript representing the 'final' work, genetic critics argue that it is "in the rough drafts, the handwritten documents of the writing process, that one concretely glimpses writing in the act of being born" (39).[15] But however 'close' to the documents of the 'genesis' of a 'work' a study stays, it remains difficult see how such 'glimpses' should be methodologically characterized: as somehow telling of the 'author's intentions' or of the critic's conception of the process of writing.

Nevertheless, it is in the interstices between the author writing and the author being critically constructed as 'writing' that Werner engages her 'glimpses' of the writing process about which Emily Dickinson's 'late scraps' tell us. In *Open Folios* Werner writes

> Like the transcripts, the facsimiles of Dickinson's manuscripts are only witnesses to a scene of original inscription. In even the finest

> photoreproductions both the materiality of the original documents and the three-dimensional nature of composition are lost: the colors, hefts, and textures of the various writing surfaces that Dickinson used are no longer discernible, watermarks and embossments are often difficult to decipher, and folding marks are nearly invisible. (57)

In this comment about the mechanical reproduction of the artist's manuscript, Werner fetishizes the always-absent original in a narrative of loss. While herself producing a facsimile edition of Dickinson's late 'scraps,' Werner notes how, in facsimile reproductions, readers miss all the little markers of 'authenticity' and 'presence' that the original carries. In particular, Werner's scholar-poet-reader misses "the colors, hefts, and textures of the various writing surfaces" and the "watermarks and embossments" that, when presented with the 'original,' a reader may experience and interpret (57). This experience of loss of the original document's idiosyncrasies or experiments is of course a condition of editorial practice generally. The reader of an edited text will, just like the editor, in an ever regressing lineage going all the way 'back' to the author herself-reading-her-own-writing, always be 'belated' as her aim is to present, as well as possible, the writings of an author: that presentation will always be a re-presentation.

Werner's editorial project, which is really a project of "unediting," is based in an explicit rejection of theory in the sense of "unified argument shored up by interlocking theses." In this way Werner formulates an alternative to the editorial tradition that has kept Emily Dickinson tightly within the bounds of books. Instead, Werner offers "only a series of speculative and fragmentary 'close-ups'" (*Open Folios* 2). Through this explicitly experimental method, Werner "[hopes] to discover something unknown but in which all 'proofs' remain provisional" (*Open Folios* 6). This experimental volume has, nevertheless, become quite influential, even dogmatic, through the process in which manuscript criticism has moved from radical critique to solidified convention. As such convention it cannot be analyzed as 'experiment' and 'speculation,' but must be analyzed as part of the power structures of the academic field (which, really, is what is at stake in Dickinson studies: it is not, primarily, a field where critics and editors work towards providing any sort of public readership with a 'better' Dickinson text). Werner's essay-edition is not a fragmentary scattering but in fact a coherent argument (such argument is part of the essay-edition's form rather than found in explicit theses). As an influential form of criticism and editing, *Open Folios* must thus be interpreted and engaged with as precisely a coherent argument, a critical narrative, as a set of interlocking theses. It, too, takes part in the 'economy' of a critical-editorial field, branding its very own 'Dickinson text.' I do not suggest that it does what it claims not to do, that is, present a "perfect return to a scene of writing." But it does represent the choice of a particular set of texts. These texts are the ones that have "(dis)appeared to us as the Lord letters," letters thus classified by "the scientific hands of the bibliographer and his assistants" (*Open Folios* 14). This is then the scene for reading Dickinson that Werner proposes. She realizes that we can never "master" Dickinson's texts. Such scientific mastery, Werner scolds.

Werner's general task in this "essay-edition" is to present a critique of the editorial tools of Thomas Johnson's New Bibliographic/New Critical practice (5). The concept of 'final authorial intention' that plagues Johnson's theorizing is rejected by Werner as part of such an idealist-nostalgic desire to present the 'original' text to the reader. Where Johnson discovers coherence (or constructs coherence out of chaos), Werner accentuates the "scattering" of poetic leaves (sheets, that is), the "risk" of such "estrangement" from order that Dickinson's late writings 'are'; she accentuates the reader-editor-scholar's implication in the meaning-making and this making of meaning is not about finding order but about "how to get lost" in the "enigmatically open code" that is Dickinson's orthography. Werner's aim is anti-establishment in the sense that she refuses a theory of editing and reading based in the instant-gratification (consumption) ideology of 'final authorial intentions' and the corresponding idea of text-as-closed-object. Werner symptomatically sketches an alternative to the conventional scholarly narrative that shapes both editing and literary criticism, a narrative, typically informed by "analytical methods and claims to comprehensiveness" (*Open Folios* 2). She writes, "our pursuit for 'Emily Dickinson' [. . .] only confirms her place outside the discursive economy: before and beyond any possible commentary the traces of a vision row in extremis and in antimony" (*Open Folios* 19–20).

Werner's critical writing narrates the Dickinson manuscript as an intangible physical object of which the reader cannot understand much, the 'original' meaning of which is gone, forever lost to the passing of time. But how can "Emily Dickinson" be outside the discursive economy? On the contrary, 'Emily Dickinson' belongs only in our "discursive economies." Unless, of course, we admit that there is a category 'beyond' what can be classified, seen, determined, and accounted for. As long as such a category remains impossible critically, 'Emily Dickinson' is a construction of our own critical imagination. Werner describes this 'beyond,' as a category of the 'unknown': "All editions are of unknown texts" for, as she explains

> The darkening of the manuscript pages, the smudges and tears, the bewildering of leaves, even the catalogue numbers written on them in a foreign hand, remind us of our distance from the original scene of inscription and the limits of interpretation. (*Open Folios* 41)

Werner thus relays the distance, historically and materially, between critic and scene of 'original inscription.' Werner expands to suggest that in the "drift of time" our "answers are also guesses, gone astray" (*Open Folios* 41). While Werner poetically and critically maintains a notion of the critical interpretive task being always subjective and historically limited, I would like to suggest that 'even' if we grant that Emily Dickinson's texts were composed in a historically distant time it is nevertheless in the 'present time' that these compositions are given the kind of sublime meanings that Werner implies are lost in the meandering of time. Werner herself gives these documents a 'negative' meaning in the sense that they spell 'loss.' For these documents never could mean anything but what she can produce out of them, at the present time. One such meaning is 'loss,' but such 'loss' is a socially constructed effect of reading the documents. Why does Werner, then, insist on situating the text and the author outside of the discursive economy? To do so is to make 'Emily Dickinson' and the Dickinson text mysterious; it is to inflect the *blank* with a suggestive unknown onto which we can produce meaning.[16]

As well as a critique of Johnson's editorial theory, Werner's work can be read and seen as a direct response to Franklin's *Manuscript Books*. The foundation for Franklin's edition is the idea of the Book. But Dickinson, Werner claims, clearly moved away from the form of the Book. That which Franklin interprets as 'unfinished,' Werner interprets as an explicit artistic strategy to overcome and move beyond the confines of the Book (which is also an artistic 'risk' because it challenges the consumer-ideology of the mass printed Book). That which Franklin thus chooses to omit and exclude is the very center for Werner's unediting. These texts do not 'belong' in the framework of the ideology of print and the Book, and hence need to be approached in a completely different critical manner. Instead, Dickinson turned, in the last decades of her life, to "explore a language as free in practice as in theory and to induce the unbinding of the scriptural economy" (*Open Folios* 3). The "scattered" leaves of Dickinson's 1870s and 80s do not simply reject linearity (the 'economy' of the Book), but are characterized by their "apprehension of multiple or contingent orders." Such loose leaves and scraps of paper, Werner claims, "are risked to still wilder forms of circulation" (3). The vicious "plot of 'pure scholarship'" that Werner equates with earlier Dickinson editing projects is always a "false witness" because it refuses to embrace in its confines scraps and unfinished writings (5). To edit Dickinson today, then, must mean to "unedit" her texts, to allow them, once again, to be seen as "*events* and phenomena of freedom" (5). Yet even the act of unediting, as much as it aspires to set texts free, is necessarily editorial, and consequently, the desire to liberate Dickinson's texts is, really, impossible to satisfy, unless we literally leave them alone. To edit is always to control, and the notion of the 'event' as 'freedom' is an impossible desire, which in turn creates a kind of critical *lacuna* from which we cannot articulate anything but a blank of 'absent presence.'

Therefore, if we believe in a purity of text (a thesis we cannot sustain) there cannot be anything but misrepresentations of Dickinson's texts. The paradox of desire and knowledge is the fight between yielding to imagination and remaining critical. While formulating a critique of idealism, Werner nevertheless yearns to behold, to access, Dickinson's mind at work, to know this writer through her surfaces. Inside the spines of a speculative editorial experiment (that in itself allows for a less 'scholarly' style or method), Werner can allow such yearnings for 'presence' and the vocabulary of *Open Folios* betrays such pretensions:

> The cometary pace of her thought determines her choice of materials—whatever lies close by—and is registered in the disturbance of the scribal hand: the script is small and angular, text is superimposed over text, fault lines interrupt the narrative, and, all along the margins, words and solitary letters appear sideways and upside down. By drafting within the drive of writing, Dickinson reached the torn and asymmetrical edge itself at which discursivity passes over into seizure and writing, against the (blue) rule, into risk and scattering. (21)[17]

Werner imagines Dickinson-at-work by an interpretation of her handwriting and choice of worksheet. This Dickinson is a figure whose body somehow works to produce, through a psychic overflow of inspiration, equally mystical documents: random pieces of paper that are flooded with the effect of a state of mind where "discursivity passes over into seizure." Contemplating the one daguerreotype of Dickinson, Werner reminds us that in this image her hands are not shown. The image of these hands, metonymic for the writer, Werner traces, instead, through Dickinson's handwriting itself:

> Their true progress toward liberation is traced on the pages of her manuscripts, on which Dickinson makes manifest, exterior, the desire of a

> pencil pressed upon paper, the intimate relation in her artistic process between conception and execution, or, more simply, the significance of touch to writing [. . .] On the slates of the 1870s and 1880s inscribing herself otherwise, autobiography, involved the transformation of the dead, restricting letter into a living letter of flame or spirit: autography. And if, as Walter Ong writes, 'control of position is everything in print,' these handwritten drafts record the alternative pleasures of driftwork and disorientation. (*Open Folios* 20)

Werner's work must be understood in the context of genetic criticism, a method or theory of textual criticism that has as its aim to understand the 'genesis' of a text, that is, how it is created. As such the ideal is lifted to a level of methodological inquiry into the 'matter' of textual production and we should, then, by studying Dickinson's writing, not only see words on a manuscript page but also be able to interpret a particular artistic process, Dickinson's process. We see, then, the autograph which is like living flame and/or spirit. If we cannot know the author, because of our inevitable belatedness we may still allow ourselves to excavate the traces of this author through her script. Werner rejects the dead, controlling, visage of print in favor of the apparent "alternative pleasures of driftwork and disorientation." But whose are those pleasures? Do they belong to Dickinson-the-scriptor or Werner-the-reader/editor? What can the materiality of text tell us about its writer? How much can a critical text allow itself to be poetic and imaginative? What are the rules of the game? Who can play by those rules? I argue that even if we 'do not know' how to classify these documents, they are nevertheless material documents, quite concrete pieces of paper, that can be handled. They need not necessarily be formulated as so very ambiguous. Yet, it is, of course, ambiguity that is a privileged 'image' for text in contemporary critical discourse. I suggest, however, that even in a critical discourse that refuses dogma and idealism, there needs to be an acknowledgement of the fact that every instance of editing a text is a taking-of-power, of the text and in relation to other readers. Werner writes that "Emily Dickinson refused the limitations of print" (*Open Folios* 1). But even as we move 'beyond' the Age of the Book into the Age of the Computer or, perhaps rather a 'Digital Age,' the ideology of 'limits' cannot be refused and scholarly writing remains within the bounds of linear development and argument. Editors and critics cannot, finally, 'refuse' the limits of print in the metaphorical senses of 'limits' and 'control' as these practices are the properties of academic discourse. Emily Dickinson, it seems, that is, cannot be 'free.'

Editorial practice (and theory; and literary criticism) can be characterized by a desire to control texts. Such control has been based in different theories of the text and of textual production. Since the 1970s, the theoretical formulation of 'text' has changed radically and with implications in textual criticism and editorial practice, as well as in the Humanities generally. With this reformulation of 'text' comes an ideological critique of the illusion of 'stability' in texts, a 'stability' which is shaped/controlled in print and its manifestation in the Book. It is from this theoretical position that Smith writes that "control has been the central issue for readers and editors of Dickinson" (*Rowing* 57). The authority with which print editorial projects have been invested (through the regulatory force of the Book) is not to be found in Dickinson's own manuscript pages, and hence any editorial project based in such a medium regularizes wrongfully Dickinson's free hand script (*Rowing* 57). In this theoretical construction of print (and the Book) as regulatory guardians of Logos, handwriting functions as the libratory antagonist which radically battles the oppressive forces of a capitalistic book industry (today, the hypertext serves a utopian space in which such a battle may be resolved). The surfacing of Dickinson's handwriting in recent decades is an effect of such a contemporary cultural climate, valorizing as it does the fragmentary and the 'unfinished.' Our present time sees Dickinson's handwriting as reflecting a radical dissatisfaction with print (because we, ourselves, are so dissatisfied with the effects of the Book and Print). Smith consequently calls for a new way to read Dickinson, and I quote in full:

> Following the call of her 'unfinished' texts and Dickinson's own actions as reader, we need not resign ourselves to a kind of hermeneutical stalemate, averring that techniques resisting print translation or found to be occasional are insignificant. What we should allow is a hermeneutics of 'Possibility' (F 22; P 657), a story of reading lending itself to a thousand and more interpretations, all of which may be faithful to Dickinson's poetic project. (*Rowing* 58)

This is the scene for reading Emily Dickinson today: her texts are 'open.' Of course, "possibility" is one of Dickinson's descriptions of poetry ("I dwell in possibility" F466). Poetry is, in Dickinson's version, that which, in contrast to the prosaic stuff of prose, provides the artist with the possibility to reach out towards the unknown ("the spreading wide my narrow hands"). That unknown, in Dickinson's case, is a querying relationship to "the sky," which is also 'Heaven' and therefore the symbolic place of 'God' (F466). Beyond the metapoetic commentary afforded by the poem, critics have appropriated "possibility" to refer to what they see as Dickinson's art of manifold meanings afforded by the variants and versions of her poetic texts, to refer, that is, to the many material possibilities of her texts.

These material 'possibilities' were once distributed by Dickinson among her coterie of readers, they were not scattered by the wind, to be randomly picked up by a surprised 'reader' who happens upon them accidentally. The variants of 'a poem' are the calculated missives to specific friends at specific times. As Smith proposes, such 'occasional' poetry should be interpreted as a kind of artistic production but, importantly, each such 'occasional poem' can be classified, for, I suspect, there is no way in which editorial projects can, at some basic level, reject the 'positivist' ideal establishing quite literally a 'better' or more 'correct' Dickinson text. And thus the manuscript and its 'possibility' are reigned in because edited. We are back at the problem that I began this chapter with: does the truly critical edition of a work exist? That is, is there an edition that remains skeptical about its own intentions, its own suppositions, its own practice? Or is every editorial project governed and limited by editors' determination to present a 'better' or 'more correct' or 'truer' version of that work? Why, if not to present what one thinks is a 'better' edition, would one edit already edited texts once again? What could otherwise be the 'rationale' of editing? If so, however, is it possible for an edition to be genuinely situated in its historical context, self-reflexively commenting on its own situatedness? What would such an edition look like? Perhaps it could look like the *Dickinson Electronic Archives* where reading is always editing; where, hence, there are not 'finished' versions of texts but only 'processes' of discovering/making meanings. But this requires that such reading-editing is continually qualified, continually acknowledged.

The 'scattering' of these documents seems, if we wish to maintain the concept of authors and authority as central in Dickinson studies, impossible: who would risk scattering Emily Dickinson's manuscripts anonymously into the world, onto the Web? I return in the third chapter in more detail to the question of editing Emily Dickinson's work editorially. Before we can engage that question, however, we need to study further the conflicts at stake in reading Dickinson in print.

Scriptural Poetics

The most important theorizer of the manuscript page beside Werner is Smith, who shaped Dickinson studies in the 1990s with what I call her 'scriptural poetics.' Before considering Smith's project I turn to a brief consideration of Jacques Derrida's reading of the concept of 'writing' and its usefulness for a rather literal employment in my own analysis of the critical scene of reading Emily Dickinson's manuscripts. Appropriating a poet's 'ideal intentions' through a reading of her '(divine/natural) script:' such a consideration is useful for the purpose of analyzing Smith's and other critics' return to Emily Dickinson's 'scene of writing' as 'natural:' 'natural writing' is connected to that 'ideal divinity' of the author's scriptural intention. Derrida outlines in *Of Grammatology* how, in Western thinking, the metaphors of 'the book' and of 'writing' have continually, paradoxically, been utilized to describe both an ideal divinity (which is also 'natural') assuming its presence in the world (the writing of truth in the soul, the book of nature) and 'bad writing'—human writing, literal writing 'in space' (which is always 'contrived' or 'artificial'). Writing is a metaphor that "systematically contrasts divine or natural writing and the human and laborious, finite, and artificial inscription." Divine writing is natural and universal, whereas human writing is always temporal and spatial. In this construct, the idea of the book refers to the idea of a divine, "natural totality." 'The book' as a metaphor of totality and closure symbolizes "the encyclopedic protection of theology and of logocentricism against the disruption of writing [. . .]" (18). In the doubling of the image of writing, the *metaphorical* writing is natural and universal (the Divine), whereas writing in the literal sense refers to "culture, technique, and artifice; a human procedure." The critique of logocentric thinking, however, cannot be sustained if the dichotomy of 'the book' and 'writing' are simply reversed, turned towards a privileging of writing. According to the 'logic' of Derrida's deconstructive method, 'the book' becomes 'writing:' and it is revealed that 'all is writing.' Similarly, I argue, it is not enough to write that "Emily Dickinson refused the limits of print" without elaborating on how Emily Dickinson's texts *are conditioned by print*. There can be no 'outside' of print, of writing, of books, an outside of 'culture.'

Smith critiques Franklin for transposing onto Emily Dickinson's manuscripts a vision of the poetic work as printed object: with *The Manuscript Books*, "His vision of the artist Dickinson is of a bookmaker who fashioned her art as if she were making objects for printed Book" ("Corporealizations" 197). She continues: "The primary form that Franklin asserts constitutes Dickinson's poetic image, and thus his scene of reading her, is the bibliographic image 'lurking in the mind' that he described to Howe, specifically that of the stanza visually and aurally regulated for print presentation" ("Corporealizations" 198). With this, what she believes is an ideologically corrupt vision of Dickinson, she contrasts the work of Werner: "Werner's scenes of reading Dickinson's writing, are the poetic images constituted in and by the poet's own holograph, choice of paper, writing instrument, alphabetic and punctuated design" ("Corporealizations" 198). According to this dichotomization, Werner's reading is somehow less socially mediated (because not shaped by the ideological machinery of the Book), decisively 'generous' in seeing in Dickinson's holographs nothing but that writing, a writing somehow visualizing meanings beyond the confines of print. But of course, Werner's decision to see Dickinson writing in this way is conditioned by a set of conventions, just as Franklin's 'image lurking in the mind' is. It is this insistence on an illusory 'purer' vision of Dickinson from the eye of manuscript critics, as if the manuscript itself could yield some kind of hidden message about Dickinson's poetic, that concerns me here.

Smith typically refers to Dickinson's writing as "scriptural."[18] She thus constructs a force field of the potential meanings offered by this word. The *OED* places "scriptural" in such a force field: the first meaning given is "Based upon, derived from, or depending upon Holy Scripture" while the second meaning is the more mundane "Of or pertaining to writing." According to this schema, Dickinson's text—her metaphorical body—becomes sacred. The privileging of Divine speech is only replaced by a privileging of the physical, of the material, of the text. In Smith's analysis of earlier editorial practices, it is thus only correct that Johnson and others have performed violent physical acts when translating Dickinson's manuscripts into print. Thus Smith's analysis of Johnson's editorial work forcefully condemns him for "surgically" separating poems from their contexts, thus producing a "dismembering" of the texts' organizational units (*Rowing* 87, 86). This embodying of the literary page/text accords with Smith's 'materialist' interpretation of literature where 'the body' of the physical text is contrasted to the idealism of final authorial intentions ("Corporealizations" 195–199). Ironically, however, the textual body, so material, in Smith and Werner's version, becomes another instance of [Biblical] *scripture,* of *ideal* document. Smith refers continually to Biblical sources in her book-length study of Dickinson *Rowing in Eden.* For example, she compares her imaginative construct of Dickinson's individual correspondences as "books" to the epistles of Paul, "which each make a book of the New Testament" (87). Dickinson's letters are constructed as scriptural, and Dickinson herself, by association, is constructed as a biblical apostle. The appearance of allusions to Biblical mythology reflects tendencies in Dickinson studies (and material studies) of making sacred, because primary, the handwritten page.

Mitchell provides an analysis of the problem inherent in the continual return to the manuscript. He brings up the common enough complaint that only very few people actually have access to archived documents. Yet, that complaint is more than simply the voice of one of those deprived of the touch and handling of such originals. It has analytical depth and is important because it reveals a serious gap between those in the 'know' and those who are expected to 'believe' in the democratization and liberation of Dickinson, yet not able to 'fully' be part of such 'democratization.' He writes, "at the same time as manuscript copies are being made more widely accessible in both textual and electronic versions, critics propose that the manuscript originals are the only sites that are fully indicative of Dickinson's actual practices: neither print nor pixels can capture all of the details that are deemed to be significant" and he argues that:

> this view gives the minority of scholars who have had, or continue to have, access to the originals a literary-critical equivalent of the nuclear deterrent: an interpretation can always be judged unsound or invalid if the interpreter does not refer to Dickinson's autograph version(s). ("Grammar" 494)

He qualifies this interpretation of the manuscript school's arguments:

> For instance, at the opening plenary of the 1999 EDIS conference at Mount Holyoke, Marjorie Perloff's understanding of Dickinson's poetry was subjected to criticism on the grounds that she had not looked at manuscript versions of the poems she discussed. ("Grammar" 494, note 39)

It is clear that "print and pixels" will always shape the objects they represent and thereby govern the kinds of knowledge that are possible to formulate and circulate. Given that the condition of literary study is that we deal, all the time, with reproductions, then why at all insist that the original is the only 'real' way of accessing Dickinson? Indeed, how can an 'original' at all be formulated as 'primary' in a context of post-structuralist deconstruction of apparently simple oppositions such as 'original' and 'copy'?

Manuscript criticism runs the risk, Mitchell argues, of the ultimate idealization of Dickinson's texts. When the original holograph is privileged as the only real source of meaning (lineation, margin widths, smudges, all things than cannot be 'seen' in a reproduction, because even a facsimile page will necessarily make a text appear smaller or bigger than it is in 'reality'), Dickinson studies turns both elitist and paradoxically circumscribed. As Mitchell points out, this kind of study privileges scholars-readers who have had or have access to the archives. It is, furthermore, this kind of criticism that accentuates the problem of a purist 'unediting' that implicitly rejects previous editorial work because of its improprieties.[19] Hence, while manuscript criticism typically pleads for "possibilities" of meaning, any tampering with the original document will be exactly an imposition (for example, a photographic representation will not reveal all the smudges of an artifact). Thus, "a Dickinson text must be left alone, with no decisions made at all: in order to be genuine, it must be frozen in a perpetual state of potential meaning" ("Grammar" 512, note 63). This is the extreme result of an elitist argument that bases all knowledge of a text in access to the archive, access to the artifact, which is access to the author's intentions (or, conversely, our only 'responsible' response when we cannot reproduce). When a text is reproduced facsimile wise in the electronic archive, for example, who, then, decides if it is a 'legitimate' source for knowledge and arguments about Dickinson's poetic practice? It would seem to be the manuscript critics-editors themselves. But can we trust them? If we cannot trust Johnson or Franklin, can we trust the Dickinson Editing Collective? Yet this is only a problem if, in fact, we assume that the original is the only source for reading Dickinson. It is only a problem if we accept the arguments of manuscript critics. The electronic archive seems democratic because the editors generously claim that they allow for 'general' readers to peruse documents with restricted access. But because those documents are already edited electronically and because the archive, like a bookish edition, carries editorial suppositions in the form of articles, it is of course not a 'pristine' original we see, and hence, readers of the archive can never be as certain as the editors are about a lineation choice, for example. Yet to fix our attention on the original's minute details, however rich in possibility they may be, may lead to a sense of paralysis:

> What drives manuscript criticism is a fear of being seen similarly [to Franklin] to choose, or to exclude. Rather than encouraging 'free play' in readers and critics, however, emphasizing the autograph poems has a paralyzing effect. ("Grammar" 506)

This is indeed an ironic paradox, as one of Smith's arguments against print editions is, precisely, that Dickinson's lineation implicitly critiques "the processes of poetic production and consumption that discourage individual production and, through automation, 'frieze' dynamic texts into static objects" ("Corporealizations" 206). Texts can be 'frozen' (and hence held in an idealist suspension) in different ways then, depending on how you approach them. The particular paralysis caused by manuscript critics is based in the belief that the holographs are "the only sites that are fully coincidental with Dickinson's meanings, with the result that even minor details haunt the reader with the potential of intent" ("Grammar" 506). In a critical scene where "Print is seen as blocking full access to the manuscripts, which is where the *real* work is situated and still ongoing" Mitchell's conclusion is that "[. . .] manuscript criticism has the effect of making manuscript *archives* an absolute precondition of scholarly discussion" ("Grammar" 506–510). Thus this privileging of the 'original' (that is, the holograph, the handwritten text, with all the smudges, fingerprints, calligraphic import that it carries) leads straight to the archive. But the 'archive' is in itself a problematic site, a problematic term. Chapter Two analyzes precisely the notion of the archive in relation to the editing of Emily Dickinson's texts.

Manuscript criticism merges textual criticism and literary criticism. Editing as a critical practice has thus come to occupy a central place in Dickinson studies. In this way Dickinson studies very strongly reflects and builds on trends in textual criticism that critique the conventional division between editing and criticism. Werner's editing of Dickinson's later texts is perhaps the most obvious example of the merging of editorial theory and literary criticism. *Open Folios* is both an edition and critical inquiry; it combines 'formal' textual apparatus with 'speculative,' inquiry into the 'meaning' of Dickinson's texts. The most obvious and also basic implication of Werner's work is that critics and readers must take part in not only the 'unediting' of Dickinson's texts but also in, as Smith calls it, "readerly strategies *un*bound" (*Rowing* 94). The two practices are connected: in order to envisage an (utopian) unedited Dickinson, the reader must learn to respond in unconventional non-*bookish* ("unbound," non-linear, open) fashion to the texts. The strategies of 'unediting' and unbinding imply a certain kind of choosing, a certain kind of meta-presumption: every reader must be an editor; must choose not only how to read Dickinson but also 'which' Dickinson (text) to read in the first place. Ironically, then, if Dickinson herself "chose not to choose" to paraphrase Cameron's argument, her readers find themselves implored to choose—in order to practice unbound strategies. Thus Smith and Werner, along with the other members of the Dickinson Editing Collective, choose to construct a very specific Emily Dickinson—in spite of their criticism of such hegemonic practices. This might be an inevitable effect of academic writing, which is necessarily based in an argumentative style, a style that requires definition and positioning. Critical discourse does not, finally, allow for endless multiplicity. For texts are not only 'open' scriptural forms but also contingent and hence to some extent limited.

PRINT-EDITING IN THE COMPUTER AGE

We can say that the formulation of Emily Dickinson's poetic project as a 'manuscript poetic' has challenged the limits or frames of our discursive construction of what writing can be: no longer limited by the confines of thinking her work through the notions of poetic stanzas, we can ask questions about these writings without the presuppositions that guide, for example, Thomas Johnson's 1955 edition and Franklin's *Manuscript Books*. In positive terms we can say that manuscript critics have explored the manuscript page to the extent of breaking that page away from the conventional binary of 'manuscript' and 'print,' a binary opposition in which the manuscript is merely part of the 'avant-texte' of genetic criticism, that is, the document which antecedes publication. This is McGann's point when he argues that Dickinson did not write for a print medium. This argument and this opening up of the discursive formation of the Emily Dickinson text leads to an important question: how is it possible to negotiate a print edition of this poet's work in this context?

In 1998, R.W. Franklin produced *The Poems of Emily Dickinson: Variorum Edition*. With its three volumes, the edition signals an attempt to be the scholarly edition of Dickinson's work for the twenty-first century, a conscious revision and improvement of Johnson's paradigmatic 1955 edition. At a time when editorial theory in general and Dickinson studies in particular think about texts through theoretical notions of bibliographic codes, at a time when the theorizing of Dickinson's 'manuscript poetics' governs our interpretations of this writer, Franklin's 'bookish' position seems idiosyncratic, if not radical. At a time when Dickinson's 'calligraphic orthography' is assumed by various critics to pertain to the meaning of Dickinson's work, it is striking to yet again produce a typographic Dickinson text distinctly book bound. Franklin's conceptualization of the literary work as an immaterial 'idea' which can be transmitted in different material guises cuts to the heart of recent decades' conceptualization of the Dickinson text. Once more, Franklin, through the material means of Harvard University Press, has produced an exclusive commodity of Emily Dickinson's texts. In the historical context of its publication, this edition, however obliquely, engages the reader to think through the implications of reading Emily Dickinson's texts in print.

The critical debate following the publication of *The Poems of Emily Dickinson* is instructive, as it can be read as a microcosm of the investments, developed in the 1980s and 1990s and discussed above, regarding the basic question of what a Dickinson text is. To Franklin himself, it is obvious that the literary work is something distinct from its material instantiations. In the Introduction to the edition, Franklin, certainly aware of the arguments both generally in textual studies and particularly, in the context of Dickinson studies, of the arguments of influential manuscript criticism, distinguishes clearly between what he sees as "multiple texts of poems" and "their documents or artifacts" (36). He assumes quite simply that a work of literary art is separable, at some fundamental level, from its material inscription. Such a work can be manifested in different media—for example the handwritten manuscript page—without altering its status as, first and foremost, a poem, a work. Franklin's ease with such a distinction between 'text' and 'work' is epitomized in his rearrangement into the ideal (typographic) metrical line Dickinson's manuscript lineation when it (as it often does) 'divides' into two or more lines (Franklin privileges an aural interpretation of Dickinson before a visual, calligraphic, one; his aural code for reading Dickinson is the tetrameter line). Hence the edition (if ever so implicitly, covertly, because it never really takes the step into a debate) critiques the assumptions of a generation of manuscript critics, a generation that has come to argue that the poetic conventions implied by print typography restrict our understanding of Dickinson's poetic practices, her poetics, and her texts. If Franklin privileges the abstract work, then many other Dickinson critics prefer the concrete texts, as left by Dickinson. Hence the critical situation circa 1998 was one in which disciplinary questions became primary. In spite of the desire expressed by manuscript-oriented critics to maintain an open Dickinson text, in the sense of not settling the question of what a Dickinson text 'is,' there is an urgency and importance to 'settling' texts at least to the extent that readers may interpret 'meaning' from both the linguistic and bibliographic codes of these texts.

I argue that it is impossible to actually discuss Emily Dickinson's poems in any other way than the meta-critical way if the text is not to some extent 'settled.' There are clearly serious meta-critical questions that need to be asked, and answered. And such questions do, of course, pertain to the dissemination of texts and the subsequent enjoyment of them by readers.

Franklin's edition can be seen as a questioning of manuscript criticism. In less 'vehement' terms, it can be seen as a 'complement' to the critical study of Emily Dickinson: we can make use of both print and facsimile (and, increasingly digital) resources for our study and understanding of Emily Dickinson's work. But in my insistence on the 'editorial turn' in Dickinson studies I wish to maintain the more 'vehement' opposition which this edition sets up versus a manuscript-oriented editorial-critical perspective; more is at stake than simply an expansion of a harmonic co-habitation of various editorial forms. For what we see, if we take manuscript criticism seriously (and we do), is the clash of theoretical formulations of what a text is, what a literary work is, and how to categorize (if we can and want) Emily Dickinson's texts as 'poems' and 'letters' or 'letter-poems.' Such theoretical considerations clearly need to be taken seriously as they have direct impact on the kind of Dickinson text that is disseminated through editions. The editor, that is, powerfully wields her prerogative of being the archiving editor, the 'first' reader of Dickinson who 'offers' this text to readers.

Franklin's edition needs to be considered for its ontological claims about what kind of 'object' he engages as a Dickinson poem. Such considerations were voiced in the debates after the publication of this edition. As it has developed, this debate must be said to be dwelling on the 'disciplinary' aspects of editorial and critical discourses. Increasingly, in Dickinson studies, the central disciplinary question has become 'what is a Dickinson poem'? As Shira Wolosky writes, Franklin's edition "highlights" this conundrum ("Manuscript Body" 87). We return here to the fact that the underlying, and fundamental, question is what constitutes the Dickinson text as an object of study (86). Developing this idea of the disciplinary, Mary Loeffelholz comments that Franklin's edition, in the context of manuscript criticism, contributes to the foundational question of what the 'literary' is. For, she argues, the editorial choice to represent Dickinson's work in print or in the handwritten form has bearings on how we, as critics, constitute the literary object—what kinds of objects do we see and read as 'literary'? ("Corollas of Autumn" 56)

Smith and Hart praise Franklin for raising "astute" and "generative" questions regarding the Dickinson text ("Gifts and Ghosts" 25). They question, however, the covert interpretive stance of the edition. For example, they note that Franklin has edited, as in shortened, the famous correspondence between Dickinson and Susan Dickinson regarding the poem "Safe in their alabaster chambers," in effect de-emphasizing the 'domestic' aspects of the correspondence. Smith and Hart read this as a privileging of the high cultural (public) work before the low cultural (domestic) text (30). But clearly Franklin's edition does make it amply clear to the reader that Dickinson did exchange versions of this poem with Susan Dickinson. Smith and Hart's critique in this light seems somewhat deflated and indeed seems to consciously silence the 'fact' that Franklin does extensively provide a textual history of 'collaboration' regarding this poem. According to Smith and Hart, Franklin's work is anachronistically fixated on "the image of a writer who was an isolato," but since there is ample evidence in Franklin's discussion of "Safe" that Dickinson worked with an audience, Smith and Hart choose to silence the text of Franklin's edition for the promotion of their own battle to imprint their image of the poet onto others ("Gifts and Ghosts" 34). In fact, we can read Franklin's editing of "Safe" as an ultimately social reading of the text, as it situates the poem/s in its various contexts of three sets of readers: Susan Dickinson, Thomas Higginson, and the readership of *The Springfield Republican*. I return to a more detailed commentary on the "Safe in their Alabaster Chambers" sequence of poems in the context of electronic editing in the next chapter.

There is no easy answer to the questions of the status of the Dickinson text. Editorial projects are necessarily based in different theoretical and methodological choices, all of which may be 'legitimate' but which will produce different versions of the 'artist' and her 'work.'[20] Timothy Morris touches on this when he concludes that, in the end, the matter of Dickinson's lineation may be a matter of "taste"—with all the implications of personal, social, theoretical and methodological assumptions that such "taste" signifies ("Is That All There Is?" 7). At the same time as Morris might have a point, and that various methodologies of editing and reading may be equally legitimate, the question of 'intention' remains as a vexed foundational issue in the reception and construction of Emily Dickinson and this points to a theoretical problematic of the construction of a poet's 'intentions' and how one should relate to such intentions. And it is in the context of such 'intention,' necessarily biographically based, that the clash between Franklin's perspective and that of Smith and Hart makes itself felt and becomes more than a matter of 'taste,' for it extends to the problematic question of the relationship between the question of 'what' Emily Dickinson did and 'how' critics can formulate answers to that question. The problem extends, that is, to how we define a work of art and how we legitimize an editing or reading of that work.

Franklin's edition puts this question into play on both the level of 'who' can be the producer of such a work of art: it not that which is written by an author? Can such authorship be collaborative?; and on a textual level: Can Dickinson's work—her oeuvre—be said to incorporate everything that she left behind, or is it viable to achieve the kind of tentative closure that a Variorum edition such as Franklin's does? On the level of 'who' is the producer of the literary work, we need to consider the role of the editor as producer and what assumptions about the material text the editor bases her edition on: how the editor chooses to 'control' the text. While commending Franklin for his reliance on the holograph original rather than on the photostats that Johnson had to rely on for part of the editorial task, Smith and Hart point out the risks of Johnson's choice. Because Franklin clearly did have access to the 'originals,' their point must be made polemically not against Franklin but as a 'warning' meant to have bearing on anyone's encounter with Dickinson's texts through reproductions.

Crucial for readers is an awareness that a limited, possibly distorted analysis is produced when working with only the information conveyed by the photostats. Photostats may or may not be the actual size of the manuscript being reproduced, but more importantly, paper patterns and marks on the manuscripts cannot be determined via Photostat (an ink mark might look like a pinhole or vice versa, and pen and pencil are not necessarily distinguishable). (24)

This is a description of a reading which is always fearful of what it might 'miss' in the inscriptive crevices of the original handwriting's tracing of a text on a page. Such a 'fear' can be productive, in the theorization of what 'writing' and 'reading' as practices may be, but in the context of Dickinson editing and study, this insistence on literal dependence on the original's smallest bruise turns reading into an impossible aporia of potential mistakes and definite loss.

It appears, in the debate about Franklin's edition, that the question of 'control' is not, furthermore, simply a matter of how 'Emily Dickinson' formulated a poetics of control or freedom, but is radically a debate about how editors and critics appropriate the Dickinson text for various theoretical and practical purposes. And we return here to the question raised by Wolosky and Loeffelholz regarding the disciplinary boundaries of 'a poem' and 'an author.' Inevitably such boundaries shift. Recently this has become increasingly obvious in Dickinson studies, not simply because of re-considerations of how literary history is shaped through cultural negotiations (through, to mention the most obvious in this context, considerations of the female author in literary history), but because quite literally the 'body' of Emily Dickinson's texts has become the site of such contests: manuscript critics reveal how patriarchal (print) culture has inscribed itself into Dickinson's texts. In this way, manuscript criticism tells us about how critical practice is ultimately an inscription of ourselves in our histories of the past. In this light, the inscription of our own privileges 'in' the body of Dickinson's poems stands out, to tell us very literally about these powerful interrelations between criticism and its objects of study. The privilege to read Emily Dickinson in the holograph manuscript is a rare one; it still constitutes a hierarchy among Dickinson scholars and decisively serves as a locus from which to challenge those unfortunate enough not to have the same privilege. This is one aspect of manuscript criticism which clearly needs to be articulated and challenged by asking how such a privilege is a control of texts, even in the name of 'freedom' of the constraints of print (or editing in general).

We control the past even when we desire to locate in Emily Dickinson's texts an open-ended textual production. In their return to the manuscript page, and in the face of the literal aporias of the inscribed marks, critics appear obsessed precisely with marks of intentional control, to the point of enforcing a perpetual uncertainty in any reader regarding 'what' indeed is a Dickinson text. It is a paradoxical insistence on controlling the 'free' marks of a dead author.

CONCLUSION: A MATTER OF CONTROL?

Authorial intention has always been a particularly disturbing trope in Dickinson studies. It is clear that the idea of authorial intention is crucial in Dickinson studies: in the debates about representing her work, such intention is typically implied by the critical text. The kind of metaphorical death of the author theorized by Roland Barthes in the 1960s, with its privileging of the 'reader' as 'writer,' is radically challenged by the insistence, in the general study of literature and, in particular, in the case of Emily Dickinson. Hers is a special case of an author who did not 'print' but did 'publish' her work to a select world of friends and family. Her texts are then radically 'unauthorized' in any large scale edition. We cannot know anything about 'her' 'intentions' and 'desires' regarding such mass publication. What is clear, however, is that from the moment that Emily Dickinson's work appeared in printed form, her work and name must be understood within the context of the copyright authoring of the work: it is impossible to socialize these texts by simply assuming that these are "unauthorized" texts. We cannot 'scatter' them to the wind anonymously. Werner writes that every edition is of "unknown" texts, but even her work is colored by a dependence on the notion of the author as the ultimate source of textual intent.

In the previous chapter I established how 'Emily Dickinson' was first formulated and theorized as a canonical author. In this chapter I moved on to study how the 'texts' of this 'author' in turn have been established and, in the past twenty years or so, been increasingly de-established, de-centered, but nevertheless thoroughly authorized (in a conscious move towards the inscription of Emily Dickinson's hand). We find ourselves with an author-figure that holds together all the discrepant papers, an inveterate reviser whose work cannot easily be categorized into those seemingly old-fashioned notions of 'rough drafts' and 'fair copies' that Thomas Johnson's edition employed as a heuristic towards cataloguing and representing the poems of Emily Dickinson. But such a refusal to categorize Emily Dickinson's work according to a linear and rational progression towards the 'fair copy' does not emanate in a radical chaotic dispersal of meaning, the scattering of Dickinson's texts to the wind that one could theoretically expect from manuscript criticism's critique of the conventional imprint of Dickinson in typographical bookish form. This testifies to the strong hold that the concept of the author has on criticism and editing. Rather, it leads to an exploration of the 'purer' because less 'corrupted' body of the manuscript poem. I see this as a territorial mapping of the ultimate space or the last bastion of 'pure' text, pure Dickinson body, not tainted (if sometimes marauded by some unknown intruder) by the ravages of print. In this sense manuscript critics must be seen as appropriating the Dickinson text, its manuscript body.

Each edition of Emily Dickinson's writings is a representation. As such it is also the result of a critical choice reflecting the critical mood of the time. To this effect, Johnson's 1955 *Variorum* is the most explicit. He entitles one section of his introduction "Creating the poems." This title reveals Johnson's realization that his edition is not somehow pure Dickinson (that transcendental, metaphysical unknown), but in fact a social construct, of the here and now. It also, however, alludes to a certain sense of editorial prerogative of 'wrapping up' or 'finishing' Dickinson's texts: here they are, in their perfect form. Manuscript criticism has problematized such assumptions by emphasizing the variant, the version, the fragment, in short, the flux in which texts exist.

In recent editorial history, however, this critical-editorial choice has been dichotomized into the traditional and the contemporary choice. The first choice represents a view of the literary work as primarily an abstract category which can be manifested in different material media, print being the most convenient such medium. The second choice represents the contemporary view that Dickinson is an avant-garde artist whose poetics radically changes the way in which literature may be conceived. The first choice depends on New Bibliography and New Criticism, the second on poststructuralist notions of text and authorship. Whereas former editions conform to set standards about poetic form and typeface, Werner, Smith and Hart attempt to 'unedit' and 'undo' such editorial constructions (Werner, *Open Folios* 13). These editors emphasize Dickinson's calligraphic orthography and thus the aesthetic significance of the writer's 'script' (Werner, *Open Folios* 21; Smith, "Corporealizations 196). Thus Dickinson's handwriting takes on significance and meaning: thus it becomes essential that critics address the visual materiality of her manuscripts when analyzing her texts. Today's manuscript critics argue that Dickinson's poetic practice radically questions such divisions as Franklin makes between form and content, between matter and idea. Dickinson's handwriting itself, it is argued, manifests such a critique. Her handwriting is her form, and it signifies on both an ideological, critical, level (as it functions as a critique of capitalist print industry) and on a 'semantic' level in that it corresponds to the mood of the thematic contents of the script's lexical signs.

Smith writes that "control has been the central issue for readers and editors of Dickinson" (*Rowing* 57). She bases this argument in an understanding of print (and as an extension, the Book, generally) as regulatory, and hence speaks of oppressive authority. The authority with which print editorial projects have thus been invested is not to be found in Dickinson's own manuscript pages, and hence any editorial project based in such a medium regularizes wrongfully Dickinson's free hand script (*Rowing* 57). In this theoretical construction of print (and the Book) as regulatory guardians of Logos, handwriting functions as the libratory antagonist that radically battles the oppressive forces of a capitalistic book industry. In recent decades, Dickinson's handwriting has once again been allowed to surface.

This is the scene for reading Emily Dickinson today: her texts are 'open.' They are not, of course, scattered by the wind, to be randomly picked up by a surprised 'reader' who happens upon them accidentally. That would, one imagines, be too radical a step in the 'liberation' of Dickinson's manuscripts from the archive. Smith's poetics of reading is, as has been shown above, constructed as a response, and as a critique of those editors and critics that shaped Dickinson long into the late twentieth century. For these editors, she claims, control has been the central issue. Editions have been invested with editorial authority, of which one effect has been to make Dickinson's poetic form seem inflexible. One consequence has been that the horizon of expectation in Dickinson's readers has been governed by a Dickinson text that is not the flexible 'original' one (57–58). In this light, 'possibility' is an attractive alternative:

> Eschewing stasis, readers will want, like Dickinson, to assert 'I am Eve' (L9) and avail themselves of the ecstasy of eating fruits forbidden by print reproductions and notions of final authorial intention about finishing a literary product. (Smith, *Rowing* 58)

To "allow" readers the pleasures of infinite interpretation, especially those "forbidden" by a medium (it could be print, as Smith suggests, but any medium is 'disciplining' and 'limiting'), requires a sophisticated editorial framework: it certainly always implies a position from which an editor "allows" difference. Editing is always an interpretive project and therefore a limit on the reader's interpretive range is always constructed before that reader encounters the text. The representation of Dickinson's art in mass-produced form is difficult but it is not a newly realized problem. It has been a concrete problem from the beginning. Versions and variants; calligraphic signs and choice of paper and pen; all these aspects of Dickinson's manuscripts contribute to their complexity. Editorial choices, such as how to represent these texts typographically in printed books or by photographic facsimile, either black and white in a book context or in full color pictures in an electronic file, determine the range of interpretation that a reader may work with. A print edition such as Franklin's *Poems* depends on verbal description rather than on the 'literal' display of digitized photographs that an electronic archive can offer. While Dickinson disseminated her work in handwritten manuscript/letter form, Franklin asks readers to agree on the presupposition that to print these texts in typographic form is not a reduction of their artistic value or importance. Such a decision necessarily denies a certain access to the original 'scene' of production and, perhaps, to conscious aesthetic choices. Smith writes that The *Dickinson Electronic Archives,* while not a solution to the problem of "data mediation" subjectivity, by representing all extant versions of a text in its history of manuscript through print to electronic document, at least offers readers a chance to decide for themselves the accuracy of different critical claims ("Computing" 839). The story of Dickinson editing is very much the story of elite scholars perusing manuscripts in sealed-off archives, manuscripts for "experts-only" ("Computing" 837). In the following chapter I analyze the latest major editorial project concerning Dickinson texts—the *Dickinson Electronic Archives* and continue such querying of 'expert-only' positions.

Chapter Three
Digital Dickinson: From Editions to Archives

> [Photography's] documentary function masks its character as edited translation. Since [photographic representations of the Sistine Frescos] are so much more widely known than their Sistine subject, supposedly reproductive images actually displace the original and become, themselves, a new, constantly growing and changing pictorial text. We must learn and think more about how to edit it.
>
> Kathleen Weil-Garris Brandt, "The Grime of the Centuries"

Literature and art are different kinds of artistic objects and the academy provides different methodologies with which to engage their specific forms. A work of art is usually thought of as original in a different sense as a poem or a novel is. A novel comes to the reader in an edition and the reader may not typically think about the potential differences between this edition and the manuscript supplied by the author for publication; a work of art as received through its representation maintains a certain 'originality'—there is an original version to be encountered in a museum somewhere beyond the representation. The question of 'the original' is not usually relevant to literature whereas for the interpretation of works of art it is a guiding principle.[1] Yet, as Kathleen Weil-Garris reminds us in her discussion of the Sistine Frescos, a work of art is often received through pictorial mediation. We read a book about the Sistine Frescos rather than making the trip to Rome. So Weil-Garris argues that the reproduction becomes primary—that the original loses a particular function, perhaps what Walter Benjamin refers to as the aura of the work of art. How can we go about interpreting those pictures, those reproductions and where does that interpretation leave the original? What is the difference between an original artwork and its representation or reproduction? Does that difference matter? Weil-Garris Brandt suggests that the reproduction or re-presentation takes on a life of its own. Representations of Emily Dickinson's work in typographic print editions, facsimile book editions and in digital images in electronic productions, like the photographs of the Sistine Frescos, in Weil-Garris Brandt's words "displace the original" holographic production: they invert the 'scene of reading' Dickinson so that the 'original' holograph in fact is mediated by the print edition through which we encounter Dickinson's work: the representation becomes primary, the original secondary. It seems, then, that we cannot in any easy way speak of originals and copies. The 'original' holographic production can never be in any sense purely appreciated, even if we were actually to behold it or hold it in our hand, touch it and smell it. For we have come to appreciate it through an entire system of representing Emily Dickinson's *hand writing.* The work of art or the manuscript holograph becomes a part of a wider text. This must be the starting point for thinking about Emily Dickinson's work and the ways in which it is edited, archived, and read. The emphasis on the aura of the original must be questioned, for it represents a desire for an immediacy that is not attainable. And yet editorial projects that aim to represent the poems of Emily Dickinson or the writings of Emily Dickinson maintain a desire for the holograph. This desire is, as we saw in the last chapter, connected to a desire to figure the author, to better posit Emily Dickinson. But we cannot return to the site of production.

The complex relationship between original and copy has resurfaced as a source for discussion with the development of increasingly sophisticated electronic archives of literary texts. In this chapter I discuss the latest versions of Dickinson as produced digitally. The properties of electronic media help to accentuate the longing for a return to the writer-at-work which informs recent projects to edit Dickinson on-line. For, on the computer screen it is as if Dickinson's manuscripts and *hand* spring to life, glowing or radiating in electronic space. This effect can be said to be achieved by the process of remediation which will be discussed below. Electronic editing accentuates the difference between an original and a representation, perhaps precisely because of the electronic medium's sometimes uncanny ability to remediate or incorporate other media into itself.

Dickinson is represented digitally in a number of venues. In "The Flights of A821: dearchiving the proceedings of a birdsong" Marta Werner offers a 'dearchiving' of the manuscript, which is actually two fragments, pinned together, labeled A821 and A821a. It is written by Emily Dickinson. Werner describes the manuscript as "outside the reach of conventional classificatory gestures."[2] "[A]nnexed" as a footnote in Thomas Johnson's edition of *Letters,* Werner found the document first by accident, in the Amherst

College Library, when it "fell (rose?) out of an acid-free envelope, out of the space of claustration." This is the confessions of an archivist who, holding the document "lightly" in her hand can appreciate its "brevity and immediacy." Werner's aim is to dearchive this manuscript, these fragments, to "liberate" them from the confines of the claustrophobic archives. But is it possible to 'liberate' such documents, to return them to a free space of non-intervention? This is the crux for the un-archivist whose desire is for objects non-tampered—the archival intervention is precisely the reason why the document is available at the present time and we cannot know it as anything but a version of the representation.

Instead of aiming for an impossible 'raw' Dickinson object, un-archived, one way of coming to terms with the Dickinson objects that have been handed down through the years is to analyze that tradition of archiving and editing Dickinson's texts, to unread those forms through which her work has been received. This further leads to a de-tangling of Emily Dickinson as she has been archived, edited, formulated; for, in Dickinson studies the manuscript and the author with her pen and pencil are one. The precious lightness of the fragment in one's hand, the heaviness of 'Emily Dickinson' in critical tradition: can she be 'unread'? The edited forms in which readers encounter Dickinson's texts continually change. For some time the printed typographical and facsimile forms of the poet's work have caused much controversy and debate in Dickinson studies. What then could be a more encompassing form for the editing of the poems, letters and whatever else she produced? That is, how can Dickinson's manuscripts be more generously relayed to readers? The Dickinson Editing Collective is a group of scholars who, as already mentioned in the previous chapter, have taken it as their task to reform Dickinson editing, study and appreciation through the use of electronic and digital media (Smith, "Because the Plunge" 2).[3] This move towards digitizing Dickinson has led to a website, *The Dickinson Electronic Archives,* which promises to comprise transcriptions and digital images of all of Emily Dickinson's writings.[4]

As we have seen, Dickinson criticism has continually been concerned with the question of how to disseminate her writings. In the 1990s and the early 21st century many critics have formulated an understanding of Dickinson's writing that depends on the study of her handwritten manuscripts. Some focus on the visual aesthetics of the surfaces of these manuscripts. Others argue the significance of the fact that the lineation of these manuscripts is different from the lineation readers know from typographic printed editions. Still others read the manuscripts as historical documents that tell us much about both Emily Dickinson's personal relationships and her poetic practices.⁵ These critics all agree on one point. The transmission of Dickinson's work in conventional printed scholarly editions is misrepresentative. As an answer to this problem a few critics in the mid-1990s took the initiative to launch an electronic archive for the study of this writer. In the following analysis of this archive as a new kind of editorial project, I consider its implications for our relationship to this writer's texts and its potential implications for critical study of Dickinson's work and the formulation of the figure of the author, 'Emily Dickinson.'

Here the electronic archive will be interpreted as a kind of *scholarly* edition. Sections of the *DEA* are indeed described as scholarly editions, a phrase associated with the discipline of textual criticism and editorial theory.⁶

This chapter explores how 'manuscript Dickinson' moves to 'digital Dickinson.' In doing so, this chapter continues the analysis of how 'the Dickinson text' and 'Emily Dickinson' are constructed in the context of Emily Dickinson studies. The general focus of this study on how editors and critics figure Emily Dickinson through discussions of how her texts are presented in edited form is here directed to the electronic archiving of the poet's writings. In the previous chapter I analyzed how a 'manuscript poet' was shaped in the wake of *The Manuscript Books*. In this chapter the focus is on the connections between the development of electronic media and the theorization, by manuscript critics, of Dickinson's work as visually meaningful. The electronic archive of Emily Dickinson's work has been in progress/process since 1995, but little critical attention has been given to it beyond various analyses, which read more like manifestos, of the editors of the project.⁷ That is, in Dickinson studies the serious employment of electronic media for the editing of her texts has not until now been considered in terms of its usage and effect: in fact, as an 'edition' the *Dickinson Electronic Archives* maintains a marginalized position. This marginalized position of the editing of Dickinson electronically needs to be remedied, and this chapter contributes to such remedy by offering a meta-critical consideration of how the archive/edition shapes 'Emily Dickinson.'⁸

Recently some critics outside of the electronic editing collective have begun to engage critically with the electronic editorial projects. Virginia Jackson asks a key question in her study of Dickinson and genre, *Dickinson's Misery*: do changes in the dissemination of Dickinson that the electronic medium allows for in fact challenge and change the way in which readers understand Dickinson's work, generically and otherwise? For example, will access to the "visual archive" of Emily Dickinson's work will make "each of us a historian or a viewer?" And when viewing these objects, "what kind of readers of those images do we become?" (52) The ambition of the editors of the *DEA* is to challenge the way 'we' read. The habit of reading Dickinson as lyrical poet is strong as is the habit of thinking about lyrical poetry as self-contained objects. The editors of the DEA generally maintain Dickinson within the boundaries of the lyric. So Jackson asks if the shift in media does not radically alter our generic reading of Dickinson, how might it otherwise affect our reading? Does the fact that we can view manuscript holographs radically alter our perception of Dickinson as writer of poetic texts? While Dickinson's work is not pictorially oriented like, say, the work of William Blake is, her manuscript holographs nevertheless contain visual cues, manuscript critics argue. How do these cues affect our reading?

In this chapter I study this digitization of Emily Dickinson's texts. The aim of this chapter is to explore the significance of digital editorial practices in the context of Dickinson studies by asking how such practice shapes the poems and other writings of Emily Dickinson. Such digital editing not only represents a radical shift in the dissemination of Dickinson's work but is part of a much larger shift in scholarly editing and criticism, a shift that is important to document. The introduction introduces the notion of 'archiving' and emphasizes the importance of critically evaluating the current changes in editorial and archival 'storage' that the surge in electronic and digital scholarship brings with it. It will be argued in this chapter that the notion of 'archiving' is important to consider in relation to recent debates in Dickinson studies regarding the 'best' means of representing the poet's work (and life).[9]

Closely connected with the notion of 'archiving' are the various projects under the rubric of 'genetic criticism,' as the very basis for such criticism is 'the archive' in the sense of the collected avant-textes and other material that shape the work's 'birth.' I discuss genetic criticism here to connect archiving with such an ambition to map and analyze the literary text/s. The notion of archiving is furthermore increasingly connected with electronic and digital scholarly projects: scholars of various disciplines turn to these new media because they provide such ample storage space and suggestive visual representation of important visual documents. I introduce the notion of 'remediation' as a methodological tool with which to approach these new media. I outline the development of electronic text and media and their increasing significance for the production, archiving and editing of literary 'texts.'

In the second section of the chapter I introduce the concept of electronic text and media in more detail, in the context of early humanities hypertext theory, which self-consciously posited a literal link between post-structuralist theories of text and hypertext. In the third section I analyze the *DEA*, an ongoing editorial-archival project that aims to represent all of Emily Dickinson's writings as well as the writings of her family. I consider this as a new form of editing Dickinson's work and therefore as a significant tool in the future dissemination of her work as well as, potentially, an important critical resource. In the fourth section I analyze the editing of one particular Dickinson text, or sequence of texts, "Safe in their alabaster chambers." Because the sequence of writings associated with the 'work' "Safe in their alabaster chambers" is the best example of electronically editing Dickinson's work, I engage with this poem and its recent critical reception. The poem has in fact come to play a significant role in the construction of Dickinson as manuscript poet, and it has become a commonplace to cite the poem's variants as offering, as Jane Donahue Eberwein writes, a "revealing insight into the poet's artistic workshop and the editorial advice she received" ("Safe in their alabaster Chambers—" 256). The chapter concludes with a discussion of the potential of the 'archive' for purposes of 'editing.'

ARCHIVING AN AUTHOR

Emily Dickinson's work is archived in two locations: the Houghton Library of Harvard University and the Amherst College Library. Book editions of Dickinson's work can be understood as the mass-mediation of such archived material. Currently these editions are challenged by the editing, or *archiving*, of these texts electronically. It is in this light that a consideration of the notions of the archive and of archiving becomes important.

ARKHONS, ARCHIVES, ARCHIVING

The archives that store Dickinson's poems are inaccessible to the general reader and researcher: the manuscripts are too fragile to be exposed to the touch and otherwise handling of too many readers. In a period of Dickinson scholarship that has come to privilege the handwritten document, it then becomes increasingly important to develop means by which ordinary readers and researchers may gain access to scholarly edited facsimile editions. The risk is clearly that a few critics may make large claims regarding documents that only those few critics have actually seen. This is a clearly anti-democratic tendency in Dickinson studies, at least if the notion of the primacy of the 'original' is accepted, left un-theorized, as it has, for the most part, been thus far in Dickinson studies. The phrase 'anti-democratic' is used consciously here as a comment upon the usage of the word 'democratization' by critic Martha Nell Smith. She argues that electronic media promote a democratization of access of literary texts ("Computing" 836). Domhnall Mitchell has also commented upon the exclusionary implications of manuscript study

("Grammar" 494). Regarding this question of access, Alfred Habegger notes "Few things can be so dangerous for biographical objectivity as the sense of privileged access" (456). Although this study does not agree with Habegger's insistence on 'objectivity' it, too, critiques the assuredness of such critics with a "sense of privileged access." Such access creates a discrepancy in the argumentative logic between those with access and those without. But, furthermore, such an insistence on the import of the 'original' betrays an assumption lodged precisely in the traditional textual criticism which manuscript criticism purports to critique: for the 'original' is indeed that coveted document which the textual critic goes in search of in her formulation of an author's intentions and the production of a textual stemma from which to produce the 'work.' I return further down to the potential problems of this ambition to remediate transparently one medium (here, the handwritten manuscript) in another (here, the computer). What can be said for now is that the question of limited access certainly contributes to the enigmatic status that the original holograph certainly has in Dickinson criticism.

In order to alleviate this kind of problem of access, Franklin published *The Manuscript Books* and Werner experimented with typographic rendition of handwriting in *Open Folios*. It is with the development of increasingly sophisticated electronic/digital tools, however, that the representation of rare handwritten manuscripts in mass-reaching media has become possible. The possibilities of editing Dickinson's texts electronically, then, seem a boon. Peter Shillingsburg describes the tendency of a shift from the book to the electronic text as a "vision of the scholarly edition" that "begins to resemble an *archive of editions* with annotations, contexts, parallel texts, reviews, criticism, and bibliographies of reception and criticism. In effect it is really a library we want" ("Principles for Electronic Archives, Scholarly Editions, and Tutorials" 24). Such a "vision" is in fact currently translated into real archival editions. This is witnessed by the ever-increasing availability of critically edited electronic archives of literary texts, as noted by Kathryn Sutherland (9). One effect of the increasing use of electronic media for the production and dissemination of literary texts is hence the development of electronic archives. These archives are increasingly, if not replacing, then at least supplementing the printed scholarly editions of a wide range of texts.

The meaning of the notion of the archive spans a wide continuum from the literal to the figurative. Marlene Manoff surveys the status of the term in the human sciences and finds a tension in this literal and figurative dichotomy. She finds a resistance, among 'traditional' archival researchers, to the theorization of the notion of the archive and the practice of 'archiving' (17–18). What is at stake in such theorization of the archive is a questioning of the 'common sense' interpretation of the archive as a mere repository, presumably 'objective.'

Jacques Derrida's specific application of the term to analyze the history of psychoanalysis through Freud's 'personal' history, or 'personal' archive guides the usage of the term in the present study. In a typical turn Derrida scrutinizes the word's apparent straightforwardness by probing the etymology of the word when he theorizes the term, or 'notion,' in *Archive Fever*. The 'arkheion' (Greek) is the house, domicile, address, with an *arkhon* as its guarder. Derrida writes, "It is thus, in this domiciliation, in this house arrest, that archives take place" (2). In the context of the Greek etymology of the word, the 'archive' "has the force of a law, of a law which is the law of the house ('oikos'), of the house as place, domicile, family, lineage, or institution. Having become a museum, Freud's house takes in all these powers of economy" (*Archive Fever* 7). Etymologically, archives thus originate in private homes that are in the process turned public. Derrida finds himself, and brings his reader, to the door steps of the Greek private house turned government house. It is here, at the gate, guarded by the *arkhon* that the dichotomous pairs of inside and outside, secret and non-secret, private and public, and interior and exterior, are constructed and begin a legalistic and governmental tradition of the archive. It is from this complex of 'inside and outside' that the contemporary interest in theorizing the notion of the archive stems. On the one hand, there is the notion of the archive as a place where the researcher gains insider access and information about an archived past; on the other hand, there is the problematization of such access, begging the questions of how the past is archived in the first place and subsequently of who gains access to that privileged past. The tension between the literal and the figurative sense of the word 'archive' appears as an important component in such theorization.

The tension between 'inside' and 'outside' (inclusion/exclusion) is consequently crucial to any discussion of the 'archive.' David Greetham draws on Derrida's question of how to draw the line between the outside and the inside of the archive (see *Archive Fever* 8). Greetham asks, "Who are the guardians, protectors, of the documents but also, and importantly, who is given the power to interpret the archive?" These questions are political and crucial for any analysis of the dissemination of cultural texts. Greetham writes about a "clerisy" of critics and editors that have the culturally legitimized right to play the role of 'arkhons' or guardians of specific shared cultural heritages, implicitly critiquing such figures. This 'clerisy' of critics-editors is in control of the archive and hence also of how material is archived and, as a consequence, of what is archivable. The archive determines what is possible to archive and how that material is organized and made accessible. Derrida writes:

> [. . .] the technical structure of the archiving archive also determines the structure of the *archivable* content even in its very coming into existence and in its relationship to the future. The *archivization* produces as much as it records the event (*Archive Fever* 17).

Such a description of the archive calls for critical attention and reflection. With the profusion of electronic archives of texts in current Humanities study, critical narratives in the intersection between textual criticism and literary theory explore the notion of the archive. Meta-archival reflection and study is needed, as argued by Terry Cook and Joan M. Schwartz. They write that "very little notice is still paid by non-archivists to how the record is chosen and shaped, privileged or marginalized, by archivists' intervention" (174). Still, is it possible for an 'outsider' to speak about 'archives' outside the context of archival research in the conventional sense of 'going to the archives'? Without the experience of the physical archive, typically housed in a library, at a university, or other official, often government-related, address? When one hasn't shifted papers, fragile from age and wear? As already suggested above, the tension between 'inside' and 'outside' is obvious in any discussion of the 'archive.' It suggests at least two questions, both related to power and legitimacy: Who shapes the archive? What is included in the archive? This study is written from 'outside' both the archives that hold Emily Dickinson's work and the 'disciplinary' boundary of editorial theory or textual criticism: yet it is my contention that it is important to analyze the ways in which the texts that literary critics study are shaped by both archivists and editors. Such analysis hopes to break down such power and such disciplinary boundaries.

The editors of the *DEA* desire an inclusive editorial environment that represents more rather than fewer of Dickinson's texts' features. Yet, such an open-minded project has its limits, too. Greetham suggests that the risk of editorial-archival *exclusion* is the greatest when a shift from one mode of representation to another is taking place, as for example "from epigraphic inscription to papyrus rolls, from papyrus to parchment, from rolls to codex, from manuscript to print, from print to digitization" ("Who's In, Who's Out" 1). This observation is pertinent to this study, examining as it does the different media representations of Emily Dickinson's poetry and prose. In particular, it is pertinent because the shift from print to digital media is occurring at the present time. It will guide the following chapter's analysis of 'Digital Dickinson.'

A paradox of the contemporary editorial task, influenced by post-structuralist theories of the fragmentary and infinite text, is that it cannot help being selective and hence exclusionary. That is, editorial and archival practice remains a matter of choosing what kind of information is displayed. Critical practice must acknowledge this contingency, this subjectivity, this blindness which always results in exclusion. In the context of an editorial theory and practice of the fragment, the version, the variant, this task must explicitly be theorized. If not, the project risks falling into the trap of totalizing a textual 'product.' Or, rather, the editor needs to acknowledge this totalizing drive, for as Greetham writes about the notion of the archive (which is really a kind of edition; or, the edition is a kind of archive), "all conservational decisions are contingent, temporary, and culturally self-referential, even self-laudatory: we want to preserve the best of ourselves for those who follow" ("Who's In, Who's Out" 2). This notion of the 'self-laudatory' is related to a certain kind of blindness. It is, to put it differently, and according to Foucault's analysis, impossible to somehow step outside of one's own cultural discursive structures. Foucault writes in *Archaeology of Knowledge,* "it is from within these rules that we speak, since it is that which gives to what we can say—and to itself, the object of our discourse—its mode of appearance, its forms of existence and coexistence, its system of accumulation, historicity and disappearance" (130). In this respect, this thesis is written under the horizon of manuscript criticism and its privileging of the holographic page and it can only attempt to discuss this horizon by acknowledging such blindness.

Genetic Criticism and Electronic Editing of Emily Dickinson

In the previous chapter I introduced genetic criticism as an intertext to Werner's project of unediting Emily Dickinson's 'late scraps' in *Open Folios.* I wish here to further consider the potential of such a connection between Dickinson studies and this French method of analyzing the texts of the literary 'work.' By tracing the potential problems in the genetic method, I am able to articulate the problems in manuscript criticism and its inflection in the electronic archiving of digital images of manuscripts.

Genetic criticism seeks to answer the question how a literary work is created. It strives to figure out a work's 'avant-texte' which is nevertheless not to be understood as a work's 'origins' but rather as part of the work, as a "halo" emanating from the final product but also as part of it, surrounding it (Jean Bellemin-Noël, 31). To work with the notion of 'avant-texte' is then to *"read, continuously with the text and without any presuppositions, the totality of formulations that, as previous possibilities, have become part of a given work of writing"* (Bellemin-Noël 31, author's italics). Although Bellemin-Noël coined the term 'avant-texte' to get away from the problematic notion of 'rough draft,' a notion that implies that there is indeed an ideal goal (in practice, the final draft) that the writer continually strives to meet, rather than the more fluid conception of the literary text as always, in the process of writing, even the term 'avant-texte' suggests something of a temporal conception of the text. In spite of Bellemin-Noël's theorization of this avant-texte as the psycho-analytical 'other' of the final text rather than the final text's 'origin,' paradoxically genetic criticism must valorize this background because it tells us about the process of the composition of a work. As such, it implicitly assumes that literary works indeed reach a kind of 'finished status' which is the work. At least this must be one implication of the logic of the question of 'how' a literary work is composed and created, how it is 'born.' Or, to put it differently, genetic criticism depends on a dichotomy between what Laurent Jenny calls the 'consecrated text' (that is, the finished work as a market commodity, 'consecrated' by a public) and the origin to be traced through the composition process for its meaning, for its purpose, for its value, in the first place. The implication is, as Jenny points out, that there would be no task for genetic criticism without the finished work. At the same time the paradox is that the "birth of the pre-text is at the expense of the text" (23).

For if traditional textual criticism sought to establish texts as in a textual hierarchy progressing towards the final draft, genetic criticism in fact seeks to disrupt such establishment by "destabilizing" the notion of text—to the extent that it could be asked if genetic criticism in fact is concerned with text and not rather with the writing process (Deppman et al. 11). Nevertheless, in spite of its interest in the process of writing, such interest is always based in concrete material objects. This basis sometimes seems to take an empiricist note, returning literary criticism to the domain of the 'real,' to the palpable materiality of texts. At the very same time, this 'reality' is used to figure out the "very origin of meaning, pure creation"—something which seems to negate such a 'real' (Jenny 23). In Bellemin-Noël's version, the task of the genetic critic becomes a version of psycho-analytic criticism. The idea is not to pursue the text's 'symptom' but rather he envisages the 'avant-texte' as a kind of return of the repressed. It is in such repressed words, such blotted or cancelled out variants that the genetic critic may extrapolate a hidden, a lost, clue for the appreciation of the creation of a particular work. Such a 'missing link' then apparently makes the reader's interpretation of the meaning of a work less fantastic and more based in the real, in the sense of the materiality of texts left behind (even if it cannot completely explain a work because such explanation is impossible) (Bellemin-Noël 34). In spite of such aspirations to somehow reveal the lost meaning (or the thought that went into it) of the work, "there is nothing mystical in the activities of genetic criticism, which pursues an immaterial object (a process) through the concrete analysis of material traces left by the process" (Deppman et al. 11)

I have introduced genetic criticism because we can understand the *DEA* as an implicit genetic study of the author in the sense that it offers the reader/user 'Emily Dickinson' as writer, in her workshop and in her various correspondences; and it offers the reader the role of 'archivist.' But, can, in fact, the 'creation' of a work be analyzed? Werner's exploration of Dickinson's later writings constitutes such an attempt to search out the poet at work, a scene of creativity and creation that equals that trajectory of the poem's birth. She describes the manuscripts as scenes of "original inscription" (*Open Folios* 57) but also, sublimely, describes this inscription as always already lost to the passing of time (*Open Folios* 41). Her project thus seems to complicate the positivistic determination of genetic critics to discover the moment of birth; but in fact, Werner's project shares with genetic criticism a desire towards the receding availability of the process that constituted a particular text, that is the process of a specific writing.

Genetic criticism sees electronic media as a useful methodological potentiality (Deppman et al. 11–12; Jenny 23–24). Like recent Dickinson editorial theorization is conditioned by a critical investigation of the manuscript, the pre-print, pre-published authorization of the 'work,' so it is in the desire to represent these hypothesized moments of creation that electronic media prove useful for genetic criticism and editing based on such a philosophy of text(ual creation). For electronic media prove much more flexible than traditional book formats for the representation of the multitude of documents that comprise the genesis of a work: electronic media provide both more space and systems of logical links between the various texts. This is, then, as I see it, where the perspective of genetic criticism and the aims of manuscript critics merge. For just as genetic criticism is concerned with the 'real' of literature (Jenny 21: as in the constitution of the physical matter of documents as the 'real' or 'reality'), so manuscript critics are concerned with contemplating the material objects left by Emily Dickinson, by considering them both as artifacts in their own right and as compositional processes. Just as a genetic critic "[handles] the boxes where the documents are kept, dusts off the manuscripts, scrutinizes ink blotches, compares the texture of different types of paper or the bindings of notebooks, classifies scattered pages left in inextricable disorder by negligent heirs," so the manuscript critic pursues the details of manuscript pages, thereby constructing a poetics of the holograph (Jenny 23). The risk is obvious in this allocation of the 'real' to an irreducible materiality or reality that can be easily appropriated and understood by the critic (Jenny 20). It is this critical risk that Dickinson criticism must continually question in order to prevent the manuscripts in the various libraries from becoming sacred objects that somehow, in their concrete materiality, empirically would offer an answer to this kind of dream of a revelation of the past.

Genetic criticism is poised between what is conventionally divided into literary criticism and textual criticism. Typically, literary criticism concerns itself with illusions of stability, even in its most deconstructive readings of texts. For such texts are usually treated as 'stable' in the sense that the edited text is, in its material form, seen as authoritative and 'final.' The typographical signs on the page are treated, that is, as solid 'signifiers' to be put into play. Genetic criticism shares, with the general recent interest in the materiality of text, an implicit critique of such a narrow definition of 'text.' Hence, Jonathan Goldberg writes that "Derridean impulses to break up the text have [...] remained rooted in a restricted sense of the text" (ix). From a materialist point of view and according to a geneticist program, any edition of a work is necessarily only one version of a larger text, only one potential outcome of the many potentials of the 'avant-texte.' Such a theory of literature fits well into the paradigm of electronic media, media that in their very form privilege the version and variant, as a document may be linked into a potentially endless chain of documents.

Jenny theorizes that in the face of the destruction of the documents that genetic critics work on (considering the material fragility of manuscripts), electronic media may appear as a rather too-messianic solution. In what he sees as the 'immaterial' space of the electronic library or archive, the 'materiality' of the document may be preserved (23). In such an electronic environment the distinction between 'reality' and 'unreality' becomes complicated. He writes:

> Reality and unreality never stop fighting over the originary archive which, first conceived of as the true site of the 'real,' should soon metamorphose into its own hyperreal simulacrum, endowed with ubiquity and infinite reproducibility. The technique would effectively allow the subversion of the opposition between the original and the copy, between the materiality and the immateriality of the archive. (23)

In this subversion of the notions of 'originals' and 'copies' lies a potential for a critique of the fetishizing appropriation of the coveted 'original' holograph: if anyone can download a copy of this document, then what purpose does the original serve? At the same time, the risk is that technology itself becomes the object of a metaphysic: "Technology appears here as the instrument of an archival Pentecost that manifests its luminous presence everywhere at the same time and offers the always renewed miracle of its material reincarnation" (Jenny 24)

Is the electronic editing of Emily Dickinson's writings, then, a simple 'incarnation,' an apparent fulfillment of discovering original documents, in the reassuringly 'scientific' "background of advanced technology"? (Jenny 24)

The editors of the *DEA* maintain that the archive is another way of editing and representing Dickinson's work. As such the electronic archival pages are simply another instance of representing the poet's work in a form that allows an auspice of 'archival presence.' Yet the force of electronic media in the Humanities parallels the force of electronic media in general and because of the electronic medias' powerful ability to remediate, as theorized by Jay Bolter and Richard Grusin, 'old' (or 'other') media, with the implications of the play of the two logics of 'immediacy' and 'hypermediacy,' we need to consider in more detail the effects of archiving Dickinson electronically.

Genetic criticism is a precarious undertaking wavering between the assertion of a positivist discovery of 'facts' in the outlining of the birth of the literary work and the subsequent cancellation of that 'work' itself once 'discovered.' Manuscript criticism, too, maintains an unsteady balance between, on the one hand, the desire to behold not only the original document but the hand that traced the figures of that document, at work; and on the other, the refutation of a 'fixed' Dickinson text.

ELECTRONIC TEXT

An analysis of the *DEA,* by which I mean the analysis of electronic publication of Emily Dickinson's writings and the production of the figure 'electronic or digital Dickinson,' requires a general introduction to the rapidly growing field of digital studies. This section begins with a consideration of the notion of 'remediation' as developed by Jay Bolter and Richard Grusin as an important concept and tool in the study of these media. In particular it helps to conceptualize the growing employment of the computer medium to exhibit and present works of art as transparently as possible, with the aim of simulating transparency (45). I then consider how electronic text, the concepts of hypertext, and hypermedia have been understood in comparison to the theories of 'intertext' and 'text' developed by critics like Julia Kristeva and Roland Barthes in the 1960s.[10]

'Remediation' as Analytical Tool

In the following section I wish to consider how the strategies of electronic media generally beg such complex queries to be pursued. I begin by considering the notion of 'remediation.' Bolter and Grusin formulate this to describe the process by which one medium 'absorbs' another. Such remediation is a crucial aspect of cultural production. Remediation operates under two logics: the logic of transparent immediacy and the logic of hypermediacy. Whereas the first downplays the differences between the two media, "as if the contents of the older media could simply be poured into the new one," the second emphasizes the differences, exploiting the 'differences' for the purposes of remediating or refashioning the old (45). Whereas transparent immediacy strives for the erasure of 'mediation,' hypermediacy exploits the effects of 'mediation,' so that, for example, the user of an electronic encyclopedia will recognize the form and usage of the encyclopedia, all the while enjoying the added features such as sound and film, which the electronic encyclopedia can offer. Transparent immediacy is, clearly, not attainable: it represents a utopian desire. There is, of course no unmediated presentation (30). But the operations of remediation are two-sided and a project like the *DEA* employs aspects of both the 'naïve' desire for immediacy and the self-conscious theorization of remediation as representation and mediation.

Bolter and Grusin write, "At one extreme [of remediation], an older medium is highlighted and represented in digital form without apparent irony or critique" (45). Using the metaphor of a vessel, they continue, "the computer is offered as a new means of gaining access to these older materials, as if the content of the older media could simply be poured into the new one" (45). In the *DEA,* the computer is not seen as a simple 'vessel,' but, very much as in the case of the electronic encyclopedia, it is employed to remediate means of representing knowledge, in this case images of manuscripts, in new ways. In particular, the ambition is to offer users digital images of Emily Dickinson's manuscripts, as one of the cornerstones of its philosophy is that Dickinson's poetics is based in handwriting. In the *DEA,* then, the editors emphasize the 'original' document's status as unique document by simulating its 'virtuality' in the reader-user's encounter with a digital image of it. The desire is to offer the user an experience of 'immediacy' however self-consciously framed that experience is. Employing tools like the *Versioning Machine,* an electronic version of the book-bound Variorum edition, with added electronic media-specific applications, through which for example users can move various digital documents within the same window, the *DEA* depends on the presumption that readers or users in fact 'want' to experience a simulation of an unmediated authenticity of the 'original.' The editors exploit tools like the *Versioning Machine,* which is to employ the logic of hypermediacy to bring users 'closer' to Emily Dickinson's workshop. And it is here that it becomes clear that the DEA operates under both logics of remediation. This is not to say that the practice of the editors of the *DEA* is naïve, striving for 'transparent immediacy,' but that a project like *DEA* operates under two logics, of which transparent immediacy is one part and hypermediacy the other

Electronic Text and Poststructuralist Theory

It is not primarily in Dickinson's poetry's potential hypertextuality (in its versioned and variant state, it would seem to incarnate the logic of hypertext) that Dickinson scholars have found fruitful connections to the digital medium. It is rather the digital medium's capacity to represent the visual aspects of her work that has proved useful for the editors of the *DEA*. Yet, some preliminary comments on hypertext and its theorization need to be presented here. Theodor H. Nelson coined the term hypertext in the 1960s (Landow 4). To Nelson it means "nonsequential writing—text that branches and allows choices to the reader, best read at an interactive screen. As popularly conceived this is a series of text chunks connected by links which offer the reader different pathways" (Nelson, quoted in Landow 4). In Nelson's definition, hypertext is suggested to work best in the electronic medium but is not restricted to it. George Landow chooses to expand the term to include hypermedia, that is, to include visual information, sound, animation and other forms of non-linguistic data. Thus, the terms hypermedia and hypertext merge to denote an information medium that links verbal and nonverbal information (4). For the purposes of his own work, Landow defines hypertext as blocks of text—including "visual information, sound, animation and other forms of data"—and the links that join them. Landow offers the conventional scholarly article as a prime example of how hypertexts work. Reading such an article, we encounter footnotes. These notes guide us to the end of the article where we find more information about the issue at hand. A note may give us further suggestions for reading—thereby further linking the reader away from the article text. But we can also choose to return to the article in question, reading on. The transitions between different links is smoother in the electronic environment as it may link us directly (ideally) to other articles, books, reviews, and so forth. We don't need to go to the library, only click on the link on the screen.

Landow argues that such a hypertextual network is, in fact, a material and literal proof of the intertextuality theorized by Kristeva and others. This network structure parallels poststructuralist theories of text, narrative and the role of the reader to the extent that Landow argues that similar paradigmatic changes are taking place in the work of such hypertext theorists as Nelson and critical theorists such as Barthes and Derrida. The common denominator is an insistence on "multilinearity, nodes, links and networks" as an alternative to traditional conceptions of "center, margin, hierarchy, and linearity" in our thinking about texts (2). Landow insists that literary theory, since Roland Barthes, in fact theorizes what the electronic medium promises to literally fulfill. Theories of textuality and the role of the reader may thus be tested, Landow suggests, in and through the electronic medium (3).

The Web has hence been formulated as the ultimate postmodern site of literary construction, as a space of freedom and multiplicity. Instead of walking into the confinement of the library and its closed books, the web provides the surfer with many choices and no limits. However, the Web is an edited space, just as much as the book is one. Each Web page and Web link is an editorial construction that allows only certain readerly strategies. The Web is thus not a place for unlimited writerly (in Barthes' ideal/utopian sense) production. It does, however, demand that the reader, or user, is active in his choices and in this way it problematizes the traditional view of literature as a container of meaning that simply is there, ready to be found by the reader. Instead the reader, by making choices, has to actively take part in that production of meaning. Similarly, in order to make sense of Emily Dickinson's vast manuscript production readers need to navigate versions and variants and make the kind of choices that confront the user of a hypertextual 'document' or 'space.' Nevertheless, growing out of Roland Barthes' notions of the readerly/writerly text, through which the reader becomes the writer, the Internet is often formulated as a liberating reader-oriented medium. Discussing hypertext, Landow writes "All hypertext systems permit the individual reader to choose his or her own center of investigation and experience. What this principle means in practice is that the reader is not locked into any kind of particular organization or hierarchy (13).

The privileging of the reader in hypertext theory, as an essentially liberating practice of the reader who, in "an infinitely re-centerable system" "becomes a truly active reader in yet another sense," reads like a parallel to Smith's articulation of Emily Dickinson's texts as reader-oriented, demanding an 'active' reader. Rather than producing organic, sealed artworks in the mode of "a Pound or Eliot," Emily Dickinson

> [s]eems more concerned to involve even the most common of readers by offering a different kind of field for perusal and play, one which privileges reader participation and hard work by which 'each and all' may acquire knowledge rather than elitist keys to understanding held by those already 'properly educated' (*Rowing* 54).

Difficult as it may be to define what constitutes 'common readers' as opposed to those 'properly educated,' Dickinson's variant, versioned and sometimes to the point of illegible calligraphy demands time to be appreciated and the navigation and employment of electronic space for the purpose of acquiring 'knowledge' rather than 'information' is afforded only those readers with a privileged position as reader, precisely the academic reader who is indeed paid to read. The democratic 'self-made' reader of Smith's "even the most common reader" is necessarily determined by access to and by having the time for such perusal of reading as "play" (54).

Early writing on hypertext thus tended to make enthusiastic claims about its literalization of poststructuralist theoretical models of 'text.' Both Landow and Johan Svedjedal borrow formulations of Barthes to describe the properties of hypertext. Landow makes use of the phrase "galaxy of signifiers" from Barthes' *S/Z* to describe the ideality of hypertext: a galaxy with no beginnings but several entrances of which none is the main one (4). Svedjedal refers to the same text when he compares hypertext to Barthes' notion of the 'writerly' text:

> Hypertexts offer readers many paths and have no fixed structure. They may be called non-linear, multilinear, nonsequential, multisequential, or multicursal, the point always being that traditional literary works are nearly always linear or monosequential. Such multisequential hypertexts may be said to be 'writerly' rather than 'readerly' in Roland Barthes's sense of the word. Freed from the restraint of the author's way of structuring the work, the reader can make his or her own choices. ("A Note on the Concept of 'Hypertext'" 3)

Hypertextual structures are interpreted as representing a concrete opposition to notions of center, margin, hierarchy and linearity by offering networks, links, nodes and multi-linearity, thereby concretizing the poststructuralist theorizations of 'text.' Barthes' ideal textuality shares similarities with the above descriptions of hypertext. To Barthes, the 'text' is the experience of the transcendental object we call 'work' (in a complete reversal of textual criticism's conception of 'text' as the material object and 'work' as the abstract ideality) and this experience is never finished, never absolutely defined, is always in flux. With this definition of text, which assumes that the reader is a producer rather than an observer or consumer, Barthes constructs a critique of the institutions of his contemporary society that define the author as the owner and producer of works and the reader as customer and consumer of the same (*S/Z* 4). If traditionally literary criticism sees the words on a page as the representation of an abstract 'work,' the meaning of which the author has somehow intentionally nestled in to the text, there to be discovered by a clever scholar, Barthes calls instead for a practice of interpretation that allows for multiplicity of meaning, for a dispersal of meaning. The traditional notion of an author who produces works of literature is revised as the text becomes a process rather than a ready-made product. The reader becomes a producer of the text she 'enters.' Instead of searching for the ultimate meaning of a work (as assigned by the author and the tradition; by canonizing institutions), the act of reading should allow for plural meaning, which is not to say that there is no meaning:

> The more plural the text, the less it is written before I read it; I do not make it undergo a predicative operation, consequent upon its being, an operation known as reading, and I is not an innocent subject, anterior to the text, one which will subsequently deal with the text as it would an object to dismantle or a site to occupy. This "I" which approaches the text is already itself a plurality of other texts, of codes which are infinite or, more precisely, lost (whose origin is lost). (*S/Z* 10)

Critical readers do not get 'lost' in such plurality of texts, for they make choices and while embracing a vision of a textual universe, the editors of the *DEA*, as will be developed later on, nevertheless adhere to a 'realistic' version of Dickinson, securely based in biography and in the limited number of her poetic versions and variants.

It is typically argued that electronic editing will allow for a broader and more inclusive dissemination and appreciation of literary texts. As the work can be situated in a network of linked texts, it will be understood in the context that is always there but made more or less invisible in the confines of the book medium. A binary opposition is set up between the 'book' and the 'hypertexual' environment that is characteristic of the electronic edition or archive. As we have seen, Barthes' theory of the 'readerly' and the 'writerly' text is often called forth as a founding text in hypertext theory: this binary is a theoretical inflection of the practical distinction between book and hypertext (it is worth keeping in mind that Barthes' notions are indeed theoretical rather than practical). With this distinction as a basis for hypertext discussions, the field becomes inflected with the ideological critique implicit in Barthes' attempt to radically challenge the consumer model of the reader by introducing the reader as writer, that is to say, the reader as producer. We must then consider any usage of Barthes' theory in the light of such a political challenge (which is also part of his metaphorical 'death of the author'). In *S/Z* Barthes conveys his notion of the 'writerly' text in the following manner:

> The writerly text is ourselves writing, before the infinite play of the world (the world as function) is traversed, intersected, stopped, plasticized by

some singular system (Ideology, Genus, Criticism) which reduces the plurality of entrances, the openings of networks, the infinity of languages (5).

"Plurality of entrances, the openings of networks:" the critical-poetic prose of Barthes in such pieces as *S/Z* was jubilantly read by the early critics of hypertext. Barthes' theorization of the reader as writer, a political overthrowing of the thralldom of reading as 'consumption' to a utopian practice of productive 'writing' is part of his general project of theorizing intertextuality as a condition of cultural production. But Barthes realizes the limitations of the 'freedom' offered by the 'writerly' production of the 'writerly text:' in fact such a writerly text has never been read in the normal sense for, once read, a text becomes, relentlessly, a 'work' that we can reach for in the bookcase, purchase in the bookstore. Such is the condition of the "world" that through "Ideology, Genus, Criticism" (or other "singular system") "reduces" the networks, the plurality, the infinity. With such a realization of the social contingency of reading comes an obligation, for the "interpretation demanded by a specific text, in its plurality, is not liberal: it is not a question of conceding some meanings, of magnanimously acknowledging that each one has its share of truth; it is a question, against all in-difference, of asserting the very existence of plurality, which is not that of the true, the probable, or even the possible" (6). Such an obligation to assert "the very existence of plurality," that is, depends on the first realization that reading is contingent. In early hypertext theory, the usage of a hypertext appears to be ahistorically disconnected from such contingencies. Readers, as ideal figures, are hence theorized to

> [. . .] move through a web or network of texts, they continually shift the center—and hence the focus or organizing principle—of their investigation and experience. Hypertext, in other words, provides an infinitely re-centerable system whose provisional point of focus depends upon the reader, who becomes a truly active reader in yet another sense" (Landow 15).

I would like to argue a different, less utopian version of electronic text. In the following I wish to situate the early, now classic, criticism of hypertext in the context of that 'reader' who such early criticism tends to formulate as utopian producer. Many critics have sought to problematize these early utopian models of the electronic text and the apparent 'liberation' it yields for readers.

Electronic Text: Democratic Dickinson?
Katherine Sutherland situates her discussion of electronic text in such a political binary as it is conjured up in much discussion and critical investment/

investigation into 'electronic text.' She sees a rift, ideological, between those who see electronic text as a democratic opening up of access to once-rare texts, in the vein of the Barthesian text, and those who see the electronic world of the Internet as a brutal reduction of knowledge (of the book) to a cacophony of 'information' (1–2). But as Sutherland points out, we need to remind ourselves that the electronic medium is not autonomous and as precisely socially contingent on interpretation (and production), cannot denote either democratization or reduction of knowledge 'in itself.' (2)

Clearly the technology in which a text is disseminated contributes to the meaning of that text; but the 'vessel' is not a pure form: the 'codes' of the medium are *woven* with meanings, textured for particular purposes. It is in the meanings that are attached to the 'codes' of the medium that we may be able to trace an answer to Sutherland's question, "why do we assume such powerful agency in this particular technology? Or, to ask the question another way—what is it that we believe texts should give us access to and how does their electronic representation enhance, compromise, or betray this? (3)

The communal 'we' of Sutherland's question seems to seek a certain kind of access to that which is otherwise far away, in various dimensions: spatially, temporally, or simply 'access denied' in the archival policing of a cultural memory. Michael Heim suggests that "the computer network appears as a godsend in providing forums for people to gather in surprisingly personal proximity—especially considering today's limited bandwidths—without the physical limitations of geography, time zones, or conspicuous social status" (73: quoted in *Remediation* 182). But as Bolter and Grusin write

> precisely the opposite is true. The people are not in personal proximity; furthermore, geography, time zones, and social status are indeed limitations or rather characteristics of computer networks. Where we are located on earth (in what kind of urban or rural setting, in an industrialized or developing country) will determine how and whether we can connect to the Internet at all." (182)

In a global perspective, it is of course true that electronic media serve only particular communities.[11] Such a realization of the material conditions governing both the production of electronic text (who gets to produce electronic text) and the access to such text offers a sobering commentary to the enthusiastic comments about the 'democratization' of access to literary texts: such comments are clearly limited to specific audiences.

The tendency to read the Web as a democratic liberation of the reader, with 'democratic' access for readers to literary texts, is reflected in Smith's arguments for "democratizing access to primary materials" which have typically been "viewed by Experts-Only" ("Computing" 837). Her argument that it is crucial for critics to have access to some kind of visual representation of Emily Dickinson's manuscripts to be able to (democratically) be able to partake in the critical debate, is made in the name of this democratizing of access. But even if we entertain Smith's argument, that 'our' histories of "authorship, textual play, and literary experimentation" depend on access to the 'authentic' source of a literary text (on archival research), it is a rather dramatic usage of the notion of 'democracy' and a radical inflation of the import of 'electronic media' to use the word 'democratizing' in this context. This kind of problematization of the usage of a word may seem facetious. There are certainly powerful gains to be made by digitizing manuscripts for public perusal on the Web, but it is not primarily a 'democratic' process that leads to the publication of that manuscript page on the Web: and the access to such materials is not necessarily 'democratic.'

The title of Cristanne Miller's article, which is also a question, "Whose Dickinson?," is loaded with all the questions of ownership and property rights that, as we have seen, have conditioned the reception of Emily Dickinson from the first edition in 1890 to the present. If we apply this question to the question of access—who has access to 'Dickinson,' following the argument of Smith regarding the latest, electronic edition of her work, the answer would be that the digital Dickinson is 'everybody's Dickinson. But in fact, the answer to the question is clearly more limited. I wish here to comment briefly on how a 'democratic' medium like the Internet is in fact a decisively edited space. Smith compares the poetics of the *DEA* to what she assumes were Dickinson's practices:

> This ongoing collective thinking about the identities and meanings of documents is, informed as it is by different sensibilities, different talents, different opinions, akin to the long-term collaboration of Susan and Emily: At heart it is a generative, capacious poetics accommodating different sensibilities, different talents, different readers. ("Because the Plunge" 2)

While articulating a postmodern erasing of categories such as poetic and critical (so that we conflate the poetics of the editing collective with the poetics of Emily Dickinson and Susan Dickinson), this statement also articulates a nostalgia, a kind of longing to be present at that creative moment of production where Dickinson's texts were originally written: we, the editors and the edited authors, are the same. The web has often been formulated as the ultimate postmodern site of literary construction, as a space of freedom and multiplicity. Instead of walking into the confinement of the library and its closed books, the web provides the surfer with many choices and no limits. However, it is also true that the web is an extremely edited space, and that behind each page and each link are choices just as strictly editorial as behind the book page. The web is not a utopian Barthesian writerly space. The *DEA* is a critical space, constructed by a Collective who claims to be involved in the same kind of practice as "Emily and Susan." In such a way, in fact, the *DEA* becomes a partial, select and limited site.

Landow notes this, when he acknowledges that the potential democratic effect of the Internet depends on the potential user-reader's access to such media (Allen 206). But in the next breath he envisages the French Academic Dictionary as an example of how a new medium—in that case print—may "sponsor" "nationalism, the vernacular, and relative democratization." Such growth of nationalism is at the expense of marginalized groups in society but "also permits the eventual homogenization of language and a corollary, if long-in-coming, possibility of democratization" (Landow *Hyper/Text/Theory* 175 quoted in Allen 207). Critics have noted the rather too enthusiastic comparisons to French poststructuralist thought, in early critical writing on hypertext (Sutherland 7, Allen 206). The electronic medium is, of course, in spite of the rather romantic idealism of such theorists of electronic text as Landow, as much a site for ideological and aesthetic choices as the printed book is. The electronic medium affects the form of Dickinson's poetics as much as the book medium does. It needs to be critically scrutinized. Electronic media are also conditioned by a capitalism which is essentially exclusive and excluding. Surfing the Internet, everyone is a consumer. As Allen writes, the emergence of electronic media cannot easily be seen as either an analogue for the 'active' reader or as an indicator of increasing 'democratization' of the flow of information (206). The publication of digitized images of Emily Dickinson's manuscripts must be seen in a larger, even global, perspective, and the discussion of such publication must refuse the kind of rhetoric that suggests a veritable 'democracy' of readership: such readership can never be democratic (or equal).

DIGITAL DICKINSON: SHAPING AN AUTHOR

In this section I describe the digital editing of Emily Dickinson's work along with that of the writings of select members of her family in the *Dickinson Electronic Archives*. Smith points out how the "cool screen" only simulates the 'real' documents ("Corporealizations" 203). Yet, according to the logic of 'remediation,' she also cites user experiences as "testifying to the near sensate experience of viewing photographic representations of the manuscripts in color and in close-up." It is, hence, the "near" experience of the 'real' thing that Smith wants to convey in the archive. Documents displayed on the screen can neither "be held, eaten, drunk, nor breathed, yet in their luminosity they make the manuscript object more palpable to the imagination" (203). Similarly, while the book facsimile, in its black-and-white state, flattens the richness of Dickinson's manuscripts by blurring the distinction between strokes of pen and pencil and flattening smudges, the electronic medium promises a much better delivery. Smith argues persuasively that electronic media help formulate questions about Dickinson's texts not possible, for most readers, to ask before. That is to suggest that the electronic medium restructures the way we think about text. She hence touches on the effects on interpretation that the new media may have.

The apparent 'naturalness' of seeing Emily Dickinson's manuscripts 'incarnated' on the screen emanates from the process that Bolter and Grusin refer to as 'remediation.' Remediation is the process by which one medium absorbs another (273). Emily Dickinson's manuscripts are presented 'virtually' on the Internet, as they were in *The Manuscript Books;* the metaphor of the desktop environment is exploited to promote the tactile handling of remediated versions of Dickinson's manuscripts on the screen (by way of clicking the mouse, by looking and hence experiencing the graphics images as they appear on the screen, one or several windows open at the same time).

As we have seen, one of the strongest arguments for electronic archiving is the potential for both a larger audience and a more reader-friendly or -oriented procedure for disseminating cultural forms. The electronic archive allows for the dissemination of rare documents to many, many more users. This is understood to encourage thinking that would not otherwise have been possible. The electronic archive organizes and indeed constructs its contents differently than the physical archive does (just as the 'physical' archive archives its material in particular, structuring ways). And, the material is forever changed: "[what] is no longer archived in the same way is no longer lived in the same way. Archivable meaning is also and in advance codetermined by the structure that archives" (Derrida, *Archive Fever* 18). This means that the *DEA* has forever changed our thinking about Dickinson, what is possible, and also, importantly, what is *impossible,* to say about this poet and her work. In this sense, the archive is both radical and conservative, as Derrida points out: "What is at issue here starting with the exergue, is the violence of the archive itself, as archive, as archival violence (7). Every archive is both institutive (*shapes* what is possible to say) and conservative (*determines* what is impossible to say). The archive is revolutionary and traditional and makes the law or makes people respect the law. (*Archive Fever* 7). Because of their powerful and conflicting roles, as both conservative and constructive at the same time, archives need to be critically engaged with. There is always a certain sense of 'secrecy' about an archive, and because such secrecy is not always a correlative to 'democratic' openness, it needs to be addressed. Even an electronic archive is necessarily protected by 'the arkhon,' or the guarder of the house ('arkheion') (*Archive Fever* 2). This guardianship may be revealed in the shape of a 'site licensing' fee, a particular structuring of links within the network that is the web site, and indeed comes from the very choices made of what (and how to) incorporate into the archive.

Emily Dickinson Digitally Edited: An Idealist Notion of the Electronic Archive?

To study the *DEA* is to study a work-in-progress, a continual labor to encode text and images. I begin by surveying the "entrances" to the archive, that is, the "introductions" to the archive and its various sections. How do we enter this archive and how do we unfold it? Already in the first section of "About the Archives" we learn that this is a collaborative venture, dependent on the work of four editors who "work collaboratively with one another and with numerous coeditors, staff and users." We learn that the archive is plural: it is not the 'Emily Dickinson' archives but notably 'Dickinson' archives, as the writings of other family members are included; the archives are several, rather than one devoted singularly to Emily Dickinson.

The appearance of a digital edition of Emily Dickinson's work is not in itself a sign of the decline of the importance of the book as a primary medium for reading her poems and letters. Yet like other hypertext theorists, the editors of the archive tend to privilege the potential of the digital environment, embracing the networking structure of hypertext as a kind of liberation from the constraints of linear bookish text and in fact a materialization of the reader-oriented utopian textual writing theorized by Barthes and others. Dickinson editor Smith makes a simple correlation between 'print' and the authoritatively closed text, arguing that "hypermedia urges readers beyond the closures and certainties of print and beyond the possessiveness of definitude that would fix and settle the questions raised by such dynamic writing" ("Corporealizations" 214). Disagreeing with Jackson who sees the *DEA* as a perpetuation of the formation of Dickinson as lyrical poet, I suggest that when Emily Dickinson's work is represented in electronic media, its status (genre, form) changes: this means that to edit Dickinson's texts for such media means to participate in the (radical) "settling" of 'what' a Dickinson poem is. I hence argue that Smith and the other editors of the *DEA* do "settle" if ever so cautiously, the study object 'Dickinson poem.' Editing is a material practice with material implications—and any editorial project, including the electronic, "settles" a particular Dickinson text. Clearly hypermedia editing, in the Dickinson case, implies an ideological stance against the "machine of the book." Many critics have responded to such apparent critique of the book. Philip Horne writes

> The politicizing of the printed page as in itself a capitalist machinery of oppression, "erasing" and "flattening" the individual marks of creativity, excessively flattens the variety possible within print itself, used after all by all sorts of people for all sorts of purposes, certainly, which print's fixities can painfully insist on, but including also inspiring purposes of liberation, education, spiritual, social, political, and imaginative. (736)

Clearly, the printed page is not in itself a "capitalist machinery of oppression" (just as the electronic page is not in itself 'liberating'). But, maintaining a materialist methodology, it must also be maintained that no 'page' can be transparent.

The *DEA* is one of various projects that aim to unedit Emily Dickinson's writings in such a dismantling of print as the necessarily 'best' medium of transmission and the dismantling of conventional categorization of texts into poems and letters. Dickinson studies is an interdisciplinary field of editorial and literary study because the current questions about her and her work are so basic. Even the controversy even about what a Dickinson poem *is* demands that each critic becomes an editor, deciding which version/s of a work to base her reading on. General readers and critics, however, do not usually have access to archives where Dickinson's documents are stored, and even the existence of a facsimile book edition of a number of her manuscripts does not satisfy such demands because it is much too expensive to appeal to a general readership—perhaps even too expensive to appeal to certain university libraries. Therefore even today, when critics argue that Dickinson must be read in manuscript, very few readers can actually do so. There is thus a gap between those with access and money and those without either. The editors of the *DEA* suggest that the electronic archive may fill a very practical function in this respect: admittedly it is much less expensive to scan manuscripts and publish them on the web; and for an increasing number of readers, the access to the Internet is better value than purchasing the Harvard editions.

But, like any other editorial-archival project, the editing of Dickinson electronically also suggests certain choices. These choices connote a certain 'possessiveness' and 'definitude' regarding Dickinson's practices and manuscripts: manuscript critics do make choices and these choices have implications, clearly, for how readers will interpret Dickinson in the future. The documents, in the electronic form, are icons, fixed to be moved around as complete text segments (in an hypothesized endless possibility) but not to be manipulated on a lexical level (presumably because of copyright and a notion that the words on the page/screen belong to the 'author').

ARCHIVING A POEM: SAFE IN THEIR ALABASTER CHAMBERS?

> Until the year of her death, Emily regularly sent poems to Sue, and the total of some two hundred seventy thus transmitted is vastly greater than that sent to others. In 1861 Emily still turned to Sue for criticism and advice. In that year she sent Sue a copy of her 'Alabaster' poem, evidently with the intent of grooming it to some purpose, perhaps for *The Republican*. (Johnson xxvii)

In a letter of 1855, Emily Dickinson writes to her friend Elizabeth Holland about her visit to Mount Vernon, the home of George Washington and the site of his tomb. She relates the tomb as a "marble story," a story which she contrasts with her narrative of visiting the city of Washington, and "the elegance, the grandeur" of its wealthy inhabitants' material display. Richard Sewall references this letter as an example of "a sense of history she is seldom credited with," but nevertheless simply references the poet's description of George Washington's tomb as the narrative of a "beautiful and moving" experience (445). But Sewall modifies his articulation of Dickinson's sense of history by continuing to concede that "It is true that she was never discursive on historical matters; her imagination was more prophetic, or apocalyptic." In his description of the poet's letter as an instance of her "being caught in the spell of the past," he conflates the two apparently opposite positions of the discursively narrative and the prophetic: history as a "spell" to be caught in. Nevertheless, Betsy Erkkila polemically finds precisely, if obliquely, a sense of history in the letter.

Erkkila employs this letter to propose a reading of Emily Dickinson consciously situated in her culture: more precisely, in a lineage of criticism reaching back at least to Allen Tate, Erkkila here sees the poet as conservatively upholding a nostalgic notion of a pre-capitalist rural New England of inherited wealth; critical of the ostentatious manner of the new urban industrial money makers ("Art of Politics" 134–35). In such a context, the letter with its referencing of a "marble story" becomes an interesting intertext for the poem that I will now discuss, the much explored poem beginning (in all its versions) with the line "Safe in their alabaster chambers" (Fr 124). For this poem, too, with its "alabaster chambers" and its suggestive alliterative images of "diadems" and "doges," produces an interesting "marble story."[12] This poem has surfaced as a particularly 'political' poem in recent critical debates: for the production of Emily Dickinson as manuscript poet; and of that manuscript poetic as based in a collaborative mode of production, is based in reading this poem.

To Smith, the eponymous beginning line of "Safe in their alabaster chambers" becomes emblematic of what she and others refer to as Dickinson's manuscript poetic. She suggests "the Alabaster Chamber of Dickinson's poem might be the printed page itself, a page which seems to put words 'safely' out of touch from change" ("Corporealizations" 206). The "alabaster chambers" become synonymous with print—in particular with the print editions that have, literally and metaphorically, buried Dickinson's manuscript texts in inappropriate bibliographic codes.[13]

Smith has seized on this constellation of texts in order to argue the thesis that Emily Dickinson work-shopped her poetry with Susan Dickinson (Smith, *Rowing* 180–197, "Musings" 2, and "Corporealizations" 204–211). This poem is in fact the only extant example of the two women 'working' together on particular texts. Noting, but leaving aside for now the potential critical problem of generalizing from one particular example, this section focuses on how a poem becomes a source of cultural critique, a site of contestation of contemporary problems. The object of the following analysis is hence to analyze how this poem served as an emblem of the notion of the collaborative handwritten production of poetry that became so privileged in the 1990s. Smith outlines the effect on criticism as an extension of "critical inquiry beyond the horizon of the book" that "makes possible higher, broader, deeper, greater powers of analytical consciousness" ("Corporealizations" 215). In the following a few suggestions are made for a better reading of a digital Dickinson. The aim is to reach a better critical understanding of the shaping of Emily Dickinson as manuscript poet and of the idea of the poet as participating in the workshop that Smith theorizes as crucial for our understanding of Emily Dickinson.

I explore this general query by asking how to adequately read an Emily Dickinson 'page.'[14] I thus study the particular instances of "Safe in their alabaster chambers" in its typographic, bookish facsimile and electronic forms. It is obvious that the Dickinson text changes depending on the media through which it is disseminated: as it is remediated, new avenues of inquiring into her texts open up. How, then, does the specific medium affect the meaning of the Dickinson documents that it encapsulates, represents and simulates for the reader's benefit? The following section studies how the set of texts that we refer to as "Safe in their alabaster chambers" has come to appear differently, and what such difference has signified, editorially, in terms of defining the Dickinson text. This sequence of texts has been chosen because it allows an analysis of all the arguments of manuscript critics, arguments that govern the editing of Dickinson electronically, relating to versions and variants; collaboration; fascicle form, letter form and collaboration style, as well as the notion that the visual surfaces of texts carry meanings. In the following I read this poem, in its variants and versions, as an archive of contemporary editorial theory.[15]

On March 1, 1862 a poem entitled "The Sleeping" appeared anonymously in *The Springfield Republican*. The poem is today known as "Safe in their alabaster chambers." In her initial letter to Thomas Wentworth Higginson, dated April 15, 1862, Emily Dickinson included four poems: a version of "Safe in their alabaster chambers" was one of them (Franklin names this version *F* in *Poems of Emily Dickinson*). This poem is also the subject of an epistolary exchange between Emily Dickinson and Susan Dickinson—with Susan acting as critic to Dickinson's 'revisions' of the second stanza. During Dickinson's life, the poem was thus published once in the sense of 'printed' and, furthermore, it was 'published' at least twice, in the medium that manuscript critics argue constitutes Dickinson's private publication form, in epistolary form—to her two perhaps most important correspondents. Dickinson also copied two different versions of the poem in her handmade booklets, in fascicles 6 and 10 respectively. Because of the contemporary publication of "Safe" and because it is twice inscribed into the fascicles, we can say that the poem is at least partly imagined with a print / book environment in mind. The fascicle texts allow for an interpretation of the texts as 'bookish' as they resemble the leaves of a published book. However, as we have seen, the poem is also part of a major epistolary exchange between Dickinson and Susan, and it was sent in a letter to Higginson. The poem's various material contexts thus appeal to both 'bookish' and epistolary interpretation. The poem, in all its variants, hence modifies extreme arguments about Dickinson's intentions regarding print and publication. For, the poem had a double status of both print and handwritten object, as part of both a private book making enterprise; the poems serves both a private gesture of intimacy with Susan Dickinson and a public gesture towards critic Higginson. "Safe in their alabaster chambers" thus belongs and functions both inside of the 'fascicles' and outside of them, in both print and epistolary handwritten environments. In this sense, the employment of the poem for the promotion of a particular kind of biographical interpretation of Emily Dickinson's poetic practices, as proposed by Smith, seems, if brilliant, also forced.[16] Existing in such a wealth of material instantiations, the "Safe" sequence serves to modify claims of both manuscript critics and of earlier editorial conventional 'knowledge' about Dickinson's text production. It seems to me that these texts conform to several genres at the same time, without quite breaking away in any one direction. The sequence is both poem and letter.

Editing the Poem

The poem is one of Dickinson's most edited and anthologized. Recent editorial history provides at least four significant sites where a reader may encounter this poem. As part of two of the fascicles it is presented in facsimile in Franklin's *Manuscript Books;* Franklin's 1998 edition of *The Poems of Emily Dickinson* allows the poem six pages. In Smith and Hart's *Open Me Carefully* it is presented as part of the epistolary exchange between Emily and Susan. Finally, *The DEA* features an article, "Emily Dickinson Writing a Poem," which represents the poem's different textual variants and elaborates how it came about through the Emily-Susan correspondence. The article, by utilizing two different kinds of interactive software, functions as an edition or archive of the various extant variants of "Safe" while at the same time making a critical argument about those texts. All these editions are clearly interpretive. *The Manuscript Books,* as already discussed in the previous chapter, sells the idea of a poet working towards a bookish existence; shaped by the editor's Introductory notes where he suggests that the fascicles served in the poet's "isolation and poetic silence" as "a personal enactment" of the public act of publication. Such a restricted interpretation of the poet's relationship to 'the world' has, of course, been thoroughly repudiated since the year of the edition's publication: but the prejudice of its remarks serves as a powerful antipode to Smith and Hart's insistence on a radical re-editing of Dickinson's work as not private at all but essentially driven towards various audiences; their select audience is Susan. This is also the motivation of the editing of the poem electronically. The presentation of the Safe sequence in The *DEA* is explicitly argumentative. Smith uses the sequence of texts that make up "Safe in their alabaster chambers" as the most important context for arguing her thesis that Dickinson and Susan were serious collaborators. Her project is to revise radically the understanding of these two women's relationship, which in such works as Sewall's *The Life of Emily Dickinson* is described as plagued by Susan Dickinson's unpleasant character (Sewall makes much of Sue's "cruelties" and "scars" her person left on Dickinson but admits that "terms of endearment persist[ed] to the end." To his credit, he also considers Susan as "a mentor of some standing" in his reading of the two women's correspondence on the "Safe" sequence. See Sewall 197–214). Rather than a marginal example of 'collaboration, in the *DEA,* Smith presents "Safe in their alabaster chambers" as a paradigmatic example of Emily Dickinson's writing practices. She argues that the correspondence through which it was re-worked problematizes the conventional view of Dickinson as a writer reclusive from the world, working in complete isolation. These texts also problematize how we understand "the identity" of Dickinson's work. How many stanzas does the poem have? Are these texts perhaps several different poems? What kind of texts are they, anyway?[17]

Dickinson through the Versioning Machine and Lightbox: Remediating the 'Original'

Discussing *The Blake Archive,* Katherine Hayles notes how its application of technologies for allowing the screen to display several documents at the same time precisely aims to remediate, transparently, the visual codes of the 'original' texts. The insistence on the accuracy of visual details, such as size of document and shade of color, however, reveals how bound in that 'original' text the remediation is—it is precisely the original that is desired. The editors of the *DEA* bring attention to the differences between the media. Hence Smith writes that the simulation of the manuscript pages does not offer touch and smell or scent (I return to this comment further down). Clearly, as Hayles notes archives such as the *DEA, The Blake Archive* and *The D. G. Rossetti Hypermedia Archive* are important means of relaying the visual components of handwritten and print textuality (271).

But such remediation, or simulation of one medium in another, is problematic precisely because of its insistence on offering readers a radical pathway into the rare books room. But in fact the reader is probably further removed from that rare books room than she has ever been before, considering for example how Emily Dickinson's manuscripts are becoming more and more fragile. If this realization was articulated by the editors/archivists, it could lead to a reformulation of how Emily Dickinson's texts serve as visual [art] objects in digital space, but the editors keep returning to the 'aura' of the manuscript which cannot be 'reproduced' or even 'simulated,' therefore privileging the model of the rare books room, which in itself is saturated with notions of the original and rare document. This aura maintains the status of the original (and the status of those with access to it). That is to say that the difference between the original and the simulation is in a paradoxical way made to be exactly the important difference between scholars with access and readers without.

Therefore, the potential offered by the electronic medium for critique of our inherited classificatory and evaluative systems of approaching art is bypassed. It is here that manuscript criticism, through the *DEA*, leads straight back into the mythical Amherst bedroom and its chest-of-drawers. We need to consider this move in more detail because the electronic archive, in the process, risks producing an imaginary 'authentic' Emily Dickinson, a poet understood as belonging in her Amherst bedroom.

As Hayles writes, the editors of *The Blake Archive* know that they do not offer the 'original' to the reader, and so do the editors of the *DEA*, but this is merely to emphasize their implicit privileging of that absent original in the first place: their employment of the digital environment for the remediation of the handwritten manuscript. The problem of the 'original' is left unproblematic as the electronic archiving of rare manuscripts such as Emily Dickinson is based on the logic of the original as privileged. Again, this is not to suggest that the *DEA* operates under a logic of transparent immediacy but that this logic is, as it were, put into play in the ambition to strive for the user-reader's experience of 'immediacy,' in her encounter with the Safe sequence.

I wish to consider how the "Safe" sequence is presented to users of the *DEA*, to consider how its pages are remediated in the electronic medium. The *DEA* offers a rare opportunity to study Dickinson's manuscripts. In contrast to black-and-white facsimile reproduction, the digital images provide color representation that helps readers appreciate details of both paper and writing. Two software programs, *Versioning Machine* and *Lightbox*, create an editor-reader space. The technology of the *Versioning Machine* builds on bibliographic thinking: the very rationale behind it is to make that kind of research which requires access to documents of a 'work' that exists in variant versions easier. The ambition inscribed into the tool is, that is, based in that kind of critical study that depends on access to manuscripts and books. The effect of the tool is to bring readers to the rare-books department without having to physically be there: to allow the reader to browse the pages of a manuscript or book without having to actually bring the document from the repository to the reading desk. The *Versioning Machine* is a tool which is engaged for remediation as transparency.

These software programs are developed by teams of scholars at the Maryland Institute for Technology in the Humanities for the purpose of taking advantage of the flexible form of digital media. With these tools, editors may construct a flexible representation of variants and versions, allowing the user to handle various documents 'at the same time:' these tools are, then extensions of traditional editions.[18] Here several texts are displayed at the same time, in the same window, with the possibility for the editor-reader to move the different items around within that window, hence simulating virtually, on the user's computer screen, a 'real' desktop with a number of documents on it. Presently these tools are used to present the documents that make up the "Safe" sequence and hence are relevant to this study.

Leah Marcus notes that poststructuralist theories of text have made 'text' "more malleable, less fixed" than previously conceived. Merging such thought with the growing uses of electronic media for the storage and dissemination of literary texts, she suggests that "the idea of the 'original' loses much of its charisma: how can we reliably differentiate 'originals' from 'copies'? (*Unediting* 26) The editors of the *DEA* readily to point out that they do not in some ideal fashion "pretend to return readers to Emily Dickinson's site and moment of composition, for this digitized presentation is a mediation and translation of her originary practices" ("About the archive"). But it is here that we locate a foundational problem, for that statement does privilege the original: for why, if the notion of the 'original' did not shape our reception of Emily Dickinson, would the "representation" and "mediation" of such an "original" need to be pointed out? The *DEA* privileges the remediating goal of achieving transparency that the computer screen merge with the 'original,' the fragile and illuminated manuscript, making it present, tangible. This effect of remediation is based in an initial privileging of the original. Such is the ambition of the *Versioning Machine*: to offer "without apparent irony or critique" the manuscript to be held, metaphorically, by the reader/user (Bolter and Grusin 45).

Smith writes that user responses to her digital 'samplers' "testify to the near sensate experience of viewing photographic representations of the manuscripts in color and in close up." She contrasts this feeling with how the "Halftone representation in books smothers" the text's materiality ("Corporealizations" 203). Because she makes such a clear evaluative binary between the computer screen's "*near*," 'live' sensation and the 'smothering' effect of the book page, there is a sense that the one experience closer to the original is to be preferred. The question remains, for an editor who so radically argues the importance of studying the physical codes of the original page, can such 'near' sensations serve as valid base for a critical analysis of the poem? Smith once more restricts the effect of the computer screen by inserting the qualifying *yet* and *more*: "Screen images cannot be held, eaten, drunk, nor breathed, yet in their luminosity they do make the manuscript object more palpable to the imagination." ("Corporealizations" 203)

Because the critical environment is still based in the notion of basing research of original documents in the 'real' libraries or archives where they may be found, it is perhaps difficult to legitimize such editor-reader tools as the basis for scholarly research. This seems to be the effect even of manuscript criticism's arguments for an electronic environment to study Dickinson's texts in: the process of 'remediation' does not offer 'the same thing' as reading the manuscript in the original but precisely a virtual simulation of such reading. Mitchell has noted that the extreme interpretation of manuscript criticism's arguments is that only the manuscripts will do: "one of the implications of manuscript criticism is that only manuscripts suffice: we may choose to use standard print or photographic editions, but then we run the danger of missing a graphic aspect of the poem's inscription that is absolutely germane to its meaning ("Grammar" 510). It is in this way that manuscript study maintains the impossible dichotomy between 'original' and 'copy.' In the following, I take advantage of the virtual versions of Dickinson's texts that are available in *Versioning Machine* and *Lightbox* form, as I develop my analysis of this dichotomy and explore how Dickinson's texts can be read without yearning for the lost original.

Above I described how electronic text is often received as the literalization of post-structuralism's celebration of plurality/deferral of meaning and its critique of the Author as solid origin of meaning. In particular, those who argue for such an analogy use Barthes' theories of text to make their points. I also pointed out that this analogy between hypertext and post-structuralist thought is perhaps simplistic. Graham Allen warns, for example, that technological change may neither easily change readers' habits nor create a more democratic information environment than the Book (206). Much celebration of hypertext claims that it will make readers 'active' and hence less 'passive' in their consumption (they will, indeed, not consume but produce texts) (Landow 5–7). Let us for the moment accept the idea of the 'author-reader' who embodies poststructuralism's points about the death of the 'Author' as sole authority of meaning and the accompanying birth of the reader as 'scriptor' (Allen 202). For this is the kind of reader that the editors of the *DEA* envision: "In the spirit of the article, which explores a collaborative mode of Dickinson's compositional process, we invite users to become participants in Emily Dickinson's poetry workshop."[19] Such a "participant" becomes, then, in a sense, a reader-writer. But, of course the reader-writer can manipulate neither the linguistic codes of the documents nor the computer code that makes it materialize on the screen: it is the documents as documents that are moveable and possible to manipulate in size and shade of color (although size and shade is decided by the computer code). The linguistic meanings remain 'fixed,' then, however 'variant' they may be between the respective documents. The user, hence, becomes not so much a 'participant' in the workshop as an onlooker, someone who can browse among paper rather than produce linguistic responses to the texts (in the space of the 'workshop' that is).

The digital object is executed through an applet: on the screen the user can not only see but also move the objects around, hence simulating the way the viewer would, by way of touch move the paper document. In the *Versioning Machine,* as in print facsimile editions and 'static' web browser images, the Dickinson manuscript becomes something else altogether. The idea of the 'original' can no longer hold any theoretical value in this digital environment. Therefore, it is important to consider just how, in insidious ways, it is precisely the 'original' that is 'conjured up' as the effect of the employment of the *Versioning Machine.* In radical, if unarticulated ways, the electronic archiving of Emily Dickinson's work breaks, ruptures, the discourse of the 'original' and 'handwritten' manuscript as artifact with a privileged analytical thrust. Paradoxically—seemingly against its own aim—the editorial project that articulates 'origins' the most is in fact the edition that materially questions the division between original and copy the most. Electronic editing thus could serve to radically theorize Emily Dickinson's work as precisely "more malleable" and "less fixed" in Marcus' words. But instead, the archive conforms to an inherited and untheorized notion of the original as the site of ultimate meaning and revelation—that which can be 'really' touched and, if not breathed, then at least smelled: and that smell is of the archive, the hidden repositories where the manuscript of Emily Dickinson's work reside, in sacred solitude.

"Emily Dickinson Writing a Poem" is an interpretive article (exploring Dickinson's collaboration with Susan Dickinson) and should therefore not be analyzed in the same way as other parts of the *DEA*. Nevertheless, this article is also presented as a first example of more to come, a first example of how to make use of the material being compiled on the vast site. It claims to be an interpretive article but is also an edition. For it is by accessing this article that users of the *DEA* actually access the 'hands-on' experience of using the Versioning Machine and Lightbox tools to see and read the "Safe sequence." Because this edition of "Safe" is embedded in the article, it must be assumed that the article, to some extent, is not an 'interpretation' but rather an 'edition.'

The model reader in "Emily Dickinson Writing an Poem" is someone aware of the possibilities of a multi-linked, multi-pathed network of textual variants and versions, and hence someone aware and capable of manipulating such links and paths, and of making sense of the result. This multi-linked and multi-pathed textuality is radically different from the textuality the same reader would encounter sitting down in the Houghton Library, artifacts in hand. It is important to stress this simple point, I think: the documents that we study in the *Versioning Machine* are not handwritten documents but electronically and digitally reproduced documents. They may be triggered to simulate our reception of a paper document but this can never be the case. Therefore, to say that we are studying, primarily, "Emily Dickinson Writing a Poem" may be an editorial desire but not necessarily what happens in a reader's interaction. Rather, the reader-user-editor (I am not quite sure what to call this *figure*) takes part in a virtual reality, ever more ambitious, advanced and complex. The *DEA* is a site primarily for its editors to argue a critical position: it is a testing ground for hypotheses about Dickinson's creative processes. As the editors persuasively argue, their object is not to represent 'fixed' objects but rather a process.

The editing of Dickinson electronically is part of a general change in the media landscape generally and, in particular, such archives are part of a general change in academic practice. Such changes include the ways in which academics communicate with each other, how courses are managed, how students and faculty alike search for information and critical materials. Libraries (and in conjunction, archives) have been among the first institutions to accommodate their practices to an electronic paradigm. There are so many advantages with regard to the handling of information that this seems only logical. Needless to say, the *DEA* is a splendid resource for readers, but the Internet also comes with its own set of rigid structures to conform to, if admittedly more 'open' than the Book, for reasons discussed above. Less is written about how the electronic medium may inflect its own ideologies on those documents.

Does the electronic edition of "Safe in their alabaster chambers" change its reception? The 'near-sensate' feeling of the radiant digitized documents that some readers testify to in relation to the *DEA* is perhaps a testimony to the desire, as Walter Benjamin describes it, to "get hold of an object by way of its likeness, its reproduction," a desire that Benjamin, in the 1930s analyzed as "growing stronger" every day (223). With increasing means of reproduction, the desire for the object de-reproduced intensifies. Yet, it must be the task of the critic to think about the quality of that 'near-sensate' feeling. This 'nearness' to experiencing an 'original' is perhaps what constitutes the radicality of the electronic medium, with respect to the dissemination of rare objects of art such as handwritten documents. But the digitized image carries with it also something else: it is, in itself, also a produced object, (that is, it is not a transparent looking glass through which reader-users may glance into the Dickinson archive) functioning as such. It is decidedly an electronic-Smith-Vetter-Dickinson object. While the ambition hinted at in the name of the Dickinson Electronic Archives is to provide precisely an archive of Dickinson, the website remains a particular rendition of the artist just like any other edition or archive. It directs our use of the material on the site in particular ways. The site negotiates a specific "settlement" of who Dickinson was and how we should read her.

The electronic medium offers programmers and editors the opportunity to experiment with the act of representation by negotiating the logics of transparency and hypermediacy. Can the electronic archive stand in for or replace the physical archive? Is the difference between these two 'institutions' similar to the difference between 'copy' and 'original'? How, that is, can we understand the representation of documents in electronic space? We cannot simply view and read the *Dickinson Electronic Archives* as an archive in the conventional sense of repository of Dickinson's manuscripts. It is, in fact, something else. This 'something else,' needs to be traced in the gap between 'original' (the holograph document) and 'copy,' (electronic facsimile) in a consideration of the process of remediation in a period where things appear to appear in the likeness of the 'authentic.' But it also needs to be traced in the way in which authorship is formulated in and through this medium.

CONCLUSION: DICKINSON IN THE 'ALABASTER CHAMBER' OF EDITING

In this chapter I have established that critics have seen parallels between post-structuralist theory and electronic text: the links of the vast network we refer to as the Internet can be read as a kind of simplified literalization of notions of intertextuality. Rather than 'opening' texts, however, these theoretical investigations into hypertext lead back to very concrete desires of mastering a text. Landow writes of producing an electronic version of Joyce's *Ulysses* that would link all the intertexts of that novel. A user of this e-text would simply click on a link and be given the pertinent intertextual reference (201). Such an encompassing intertextuality is, however, theoretically non-attainable (in the Barthesian conceptualization of the term), as there is no way in which the 'number' of intertexts can be captured by hyperlinks: the notion of intertextuality is built on an ideological rejection of the utopian 'complete' text as precisely a construct to tame cultural practices.

At the same time, there is clearly a limitedness (however ephemeral: each time we 'visit' an electronic text it is 'new' as it is activated by the command to execute a specific string (Sutherland 12). A cited hyperlink in my bibliography will perhaps not be accessible a week or a year after I have made that hyperlink 'present' in print, or the contents of that hyperlink may have changed.

There is a paradoxical play on the binary axis of absence/presence as there are hypothetically endless links to be created and executed, but the hypertext environment that we encounter each time we log onto the computer and access the specific site and text will be limited (even if only temporally so). Therefore, it becomes clear that electronic media contain and limit texts in similar ways as books do. At the same time as the text is constructed 'anew' each time a user enters the website link, so that website is temporally controlled by a name and an aim. Emily Dickinson gathers together the links, the links lead to the user's appreciation of 'Emily Dickinson.' Emily Dickinson is not dispersed, even as her texts may be theorized as dispersed. Rather than offering, in Landow's version, a utopian Barthesian space of 'writing,' the Internet, as part of a consumer culture, which is also dictated by the powers that produce commodities, in fact offers the final 'death blow' to Barthes' theory of the death of the author: authorship, as it is bound by the copyright, which according to Foucault's analysis of the modern author-function governs the construction of 'authorship,' is not shattered by Internet editing and archiving.

Just like the medium does not necessarily change the genre we read Dickinson through (genre, as a grid or model through which we de-code a text) so the medium does not change or even challenge our notion of authorship—Emily Dickinson remains a stable and solid *figure*—a readerly classic in Barthes' terms.

The editing of texts electronically demands a reader not simply competent to read a single text but able to keep several narratives together at once, linking back and forth between texts, having several images in front of her at the same time. Genetic criticism points in the same direction:

> According to Jean-Michel Rabate, a new kind of reader has started to emerge in this multifaceted genetic activity: an 'ideal genetic reader' or 'genreader.' This reader is not merely a decoder of textual signals, a detached consciousness, or an emotional being, but rather a kind of 'textual agent' who reads texts 'in the context of an expanding archive' in order to see both how they are written and how they are read. (Deppman et al. 12)

A final comparison with Barthes' theorization of the difference between 'readerly' and 'writerly' texts is inevitable here. It is in the context of such readers, readers with access to networks of texts, that the development of electronic archives makes sense. The utopian suggestion of such readership is palpable, even in contemporary digitized communities.

The *DEA* radically unedits the assumption that Emily Dickinson wrote poems; in its emphasis on correspondences, the website does not appear to be about 'poetry' although, embedded in the texture of the website, Dickinson's poetry appears. The archive also successfully unedits the assumption that authorship is a lonely business, important, in particular, for the reconstruction of Emily Dickinson as precisely not a lonely *isolato*.

In this chapter I have shown that the *DEA* can be understood as one instance of a burgeoning new academic field of 'humanities computing.' This kind of computerization of culture promises a tempting access in many ways. Internet courses make students' and instructors' presences on a 'real' campus unnecessary as virtual classrooms grow more and more abundant. Networks promise a virtual accomplishment of the idea of the total library. But as shown above, such a library is, naturally, an illusion, wishful thinking. This thesis queries such a vision, as it demands a questioning of the perpetuation of the institutionalizing as radical, a particular elitist canon, transposed onto a postmodern scene, with the help of electronic media, media that in themselves represent Western power. If manuscript critics wish to critique patriarchal, patronizing, New Critical, Idealist, tendencies in the representation of Dickinson's life and texts, it seems rather unfortunate that they, themselves, do not question their own profoundly privileged position.

By claiming that their ambition is to transmit Dickinson's writings "with as little interpretive noise as possible" the editors seem to hark back to the bookish editions that they denounce as 'closing' meanings rather than opening the text up ("Introduction" to *Emily Dickinson's Correspondences*). Thereby they seek an authoritative voice that is associated with the traditional scholarly edition. In this desire for authority the editors paradoxically fall back into the same hierarchical framework that they appear to challenge.

The aim of this chapter was to explore the significance of digital editorial practices in the context of Dickinson studies by asking how such practices shape the poems and other writings of Emily Dickinson. How is the archival record chosen and shaped, privileged or marginalized? Who is in, who is out? Archives can generally be described as (typically legitimate, copyrighted) collections of texts. But archives also house materials, personal and intimate: the objects-turned-artifacts of a person's life, that, because that person is now a famous figure, are taken to be significant, important, essential to that character, and, in particular, of course, essential to our interpretation of that figure's *oeuvre*. Sometimes an entire house, a real dwelling of the archived person, becomes a giant meta-artifact of that person's oeuvre. Emily

Dickinson's home, the *Homestead,* is indeed a museum, as is Susan Dickinson's dwelling, the *Evergreens.* In the garden of the Homestead, a visitor can wander and wonder among the 'same' flowers that Dickinson cultivated. Visitors are shepherded around the Dickinson home, to reach, ultimately, Dickinson's bedroom. Even though this house-museum is dedicated to the personal space of Dickinson's life rather than her texts, it serves as a kind of metaphorical entrance to her, as a source, of sorts, of this woman's creativity. Focusing on a different, more obviously important aspect of Dickinson, the *DEA* attempts to function similarly as a virtual meta-archive, of the poet's texts, personal and textual contexts. Such an archive has its legitimacy.

As long as there is a desire to remember, to not miss, not lose, there will be a place for archival-editorial projects about the Emily Dickinson text. It is important to acknowledge this subjective desperation that is a reason for archives in the first place. At the same time, the desire to remember is intimately connected with aggression, possession, and destruction. In each archiving practice, there is exclusion and loss. Yet, such loss needs to be balanced with the accomplishments of a widened knowledge of Dickinson's texts. In that balancing act editorial projects must negotiate the desire to totalize, to gain knowledge and power over a text (and a field, a readership) at the risk of exclusion, loss, destruction. Such loss is inevitable, but so is the desire to archive, to complete, and to understand. As Barthes writes, the 'writerly' text is utopian, an imaginary pointer, it is

> ourselves writing, before the infinite play of the world (the world as function) is traversed, intersected, stopped, plasticized by some singular system (Ideology, Genus, Criticism) which reduces the plurality of entrances, the openings of networks, the infinity of languages. (S/Z 5)

That is, to 'live' in this 'world'—to be situated materially—means to be "reduce[d]" to "Ideology, Genus, Criticism [and so on]. This means that the infinity of the text, in order to be understood and critiqued, needs to be "reduced:" such is the logic of academic discourse. Hence, the Dickinson text as 'writerly' text may serve as an idealistic heuristic but it must be balanced by the sobering realization that each editorial act, each critical act, will necessarily express that text as "readerly," as a "classic."

The figure of the author, of the 'digital Dickinson,' who emerges in the electronic environment of the *DEA* is not a radically digital poet. The experience of seeing a manuscript simulated digitally on the screen is not appreciably different from seeing that manuscript in a printed facsimile. The 'difference' between reading a poem of Emily Dickinson in a print book and

Digital Dickinson

in the *DEA* is based in a usage of the electronic space as a replacement for the monograph, the print typographic edition and the facsimile edition: even if the *DEA* produces Dickinson as a writer in an environment, it does not let go of the author, Emily Dickinson, as the producer of *Writings of Emily Dickinson*. In all this, the archive is useful, but it does not offer a challenge to book editions, and it decisively offers the 'original' as the source of the authentic Dickinson and thus leads us back to the 'archive' of Derrida's etymology: this is a guardian of a cultural heritage to be preserved rather than radically produced. In this is built on, in Timothy Morris' phrase, a critical 'poetics of presence.' And so the figure of digital Dickinson takes us back to the beginnings of this study and to the beginnings of the study of Emily Dickinson: to the image of the author as genius, the proper name signaling origin and authenticity.

The 'Digital Dickinson' that emerges on the World Wide Web is produced as reader-oriented. But to archive is always, as Derrida argues, to engage in a metaphorical battle between a death-drive and a pleasure principle. Choices are made to literally negotiate this battle. Archival projects always spell out such choices, implicitly or explicitly.

It is through the concept of the 'archive,' then, that a final difficulty with the *DEA* emerges. The archive implies limits, implies an ideology that encompasses the book, the very medium that the *DEA* positions itself against: paradoxically, the rationale behind both the printed editions and the electronic archiving of Dickinson's work is the same: to achieve better and fuller accuracy in representing the author's texts.

In "The Flights of A821: dearchiving the proceedings of a birdsong" Werner engages the usage of the word 'liberator' in the study of birds:

> in order to determine whether or not certain kinds of birds possess homing instincts a person known as a 'liberator' throws several up into the air, then turns and turns again, each time releasing more birds in different directions. The birds are then watched out of sight and the points at which they disappear from view recorded. When a significant number of vanishing points has been noted, a scatter-diagram is drawn up for study. At times, for reasons that are not yet fully understood, large numbers of birds returning to the original release point lose their way and drift widely across the migration axis. These drifts, sometimes called 'radical scatters,' both solicit and resist definitive interpretation. (326)

From manuscript Dickinson to digital Dickinson: is it possible to literalize Werner's reading of the documents as metaphorical birds and imagine these documents, these birds, take flight (into electronic space, or other space) without the reassurance that they will 'come back' to us, at all, or in the 'same form'? Without, that is, the reassurance that 'Emily Dickinson' will never come back to us 'the same.' Do we dare permit the flight of these imaginary birds, and risk the "radical scattering" of those birds that do not come back to the point of departure?

Are we ready for a radical unediting of Emily Dickinson and her manuscripts, to the point of dispersing her and them, as the "liberator" releases her birds to the risks of them not coming back 'home' again? A completely and literally liberated Dickinson, dispersed in cyberspace, would mean a radical dispersal of the proper name, a literalization of the death-drive, a shattering of the specific cultural heritages that 'we' designate through that name 'Emily Dickinson.' In a period that still pays heed to the modern notion of authorship as analyzed by Foucault, even an archive in cyberspace, as exemplified by the *Dickinson Electronic Archives,* must maintain limits, must organize the material in hierarchical structures. The archive cannot, because of its role as 'arkhon' of cultural heritage and because we require works to have authors, be an archive of anonymous texts.

Conclusion

> We must resolve to admit that each period invents its imaginary and always provisionary library, because of the urgency of the questions it seeks to ask of it.
>
> Laurent Jenny, "Genetic Criticism and its Myths"

In this book I have studied the negotiation of Emily Dickinson in scholarly editing and criticism. By considering a number of discussions regarding the 'correct' way of editing Dickinson's manuscripts I have argued that the negotiations over the correct means of editing her work can be seen as a continual editing of her biography, of 'Emily Dickinson' as a literary construct. In the recent past, editing has been reformulated as a historicizing practice through which readers receive not objective works but indeed socially and historically conditioned texts. "[H]ow can one define a work amid the millions of traces left by someone after his death?" Michel Foucault's asked his question in 1970 but it is still pertinent (199). It would seem that the answer, remains, within literary discourse, the same as it has been since that shift in the dissemination of literary works that took place in the seventeenth or eighteenth century whereby literary texts came to depend on the validation on authorship. While we have become used to assertions of the death of the author in more or less polemical forms, authorship seems to remain that final category in which a work originates. But a work is the product of many hands, as contemporary textual criticism reveals. Authorship, just like the work, is always derived, always conferred upon, always a construction. Emily Dickinson is such a construction of editorial and critical investigation into her texts.

This study began with a consideration of a name—Emily Dickinson. But although Emily Dickinson has been at the center of this study, she has not, as might have been expected, been approached through the concept of biography. Instead, this study has focused on the idea that to edit a text is also always to edit an 'author' and that what is produced in this process is a specific authorship. The textual scene left behind after Emily Dickinson's death initially required that quite literally the manuscripts received by her vast number of correspondents be gathered together along with the manuscripts left in her own possession. Such a gathering together of Dickinson's work is cumulative, as new editions of these writings appear. In the process, as I have emphasized, editions and archives have produced new texts but also new interpretations of the author. While it is true that any edition will in some sense script a life, the case of Emily Dickinson is special because of the ways in which her work and her 'life' have been made simultaneously available to a general reading audience precisely through these negotiations of a widely dispersed body of works. As they emerged posthumously, both Dickinson and her work (as critical categories) had to be defined simultaneously. Dickinson did not posit herself a public author even if she sent poems in letters to various figures in the New England literary field of the mid-nineteenth century. Her public persona then entered the stage already derived and constructed.

This study could be described as an 'alternative' or 'textual' biography. While acknowledging the facts of Emily Dickinson's biographical life and the import of criticism in general for the production of the author, I have approached this author as a figure produced through specific editorial and critical renditions of her and debates about such editorial productions. Such a construction of the author seems warranted at the present time. Like all criticism, this study is conditioned by its historical moment, a period when critical interest in Dickinson's manuscripts and editorial considerations of Dickinson's work has reached a peak.

More specifically this study has attempted to negotiate what has been interrogated here as old and new idealistic versions of Emily Dickinson as an authorial presence in editorial and critical projects that trace and locate her either in the depths of her intention or in the surfaces of her 'script.' Emily Dickinson has always been a site for questions regarding editorial proprieties.

In 1949 George Whicher pointed out the need of a full canon of Dickinson's texts: he writes "every scrap of her writing deserves a respectful consideration. Even the failures of such an artist in words are of interest (436). Critics have continually been intrigued with Dickinson's scraps—with the way in which her poetry was left to the world. In the early twentieth century, Richard Blackmur described what he thought of as the "disarray" of Emily Dickinson's work, a comment reflecting the seemingly endless process of publishing 'new' and 'further' poems of Emily Dickinson (200). Indeed, this process of 'new' and 'further' poems of Emily Dickinson continues into the present day as editors produce explicitly interpretive versions of the poet's texts. This means that Dickinson studies is the perfect testing ground for ideas regarding 'unediting,' the merging of textual and literary criticism, and the kind of archival thinking that is part of such a merger. Leah Marcus has proposed the idea of 'unediting the Renaissance' in order to read early modern texts anew, cleared from the editorial biases that produced such canonical authors as Shakespeare in the eighteenth and nineteenth centuries. Thomas Johnson's edition of Dickinson's work has been critiqued in a similar fashion. However, there is clearly no 'pure' text to be discovered once such editorial impurities are removed: Emily Dickinson's 'original' holograph is, that is, conditioned precisely by the 'excavation' process through which it emerges. The original holograph cannot be read as an innocent and 'intentionally pure' document. We can only read Dickinson by meandering through the archive of her reception.

Jerome McGann's notion of 'bibliographic' codes may seem an obvious solution to the discussion of how not only a text's 'linguistic' code but also the materiality of a text informs the reader's experience and interpretation of that text. But I have also shown that the risk with this binary solution to reading textual matter itself invokes a valorization of the 'bibliographic' to the extent of rendering 'natural' such matter. Beyond descriptive markers of textual matter, these terms offer us a tool with which to describe how literary works have been understood. At the present moment, the historical contextualization of a literary work has come to privilege bibliographical codes as a means of interpreting how a text quite literally is embedded in a historical production: in literal matter. The linguistic code has come to stand for the (naïve) ideal and aesthetic while the bibliographic seemingly locates the text politically. In my exploration of the figures of 'manuscript Dickinson' and 'digital Dickinson' I have suggested that these figures depend on an extension of this dichotomization of the 'linguistic' and the 'bibliographic' as the 'bookish' and the 'handwritten.' I have emphasized the temptation of easily categorizing the handwritten as 'natural' because unfixed and print as 'fixed' when, in fact, all these editions are part of the social text we refer to as 'Emily Dickinson' and one version cannot be understood as more authentic and natural than another, not even the holograph (which is already coded, already imbued with intent/meaning). Nevertheless I have implied that one cannot easily read Dickinson in print in the current critical climate of unediting. This argument has been made in debate with a manuscript criticism that valorizes the original document. I have wanted to test the validity of such a position.

I have characterized this textual and critical situation as made up of two superficially diametrically opposed versions of how one might read Emily

Dickinson. These two opposed versions are represented paradigmatically by R. W. Franklin on the one side and Marta Werner on the other. But both Franklin's notion of the immateriality of the work of art—its 'existence' as a purely 'intellectual' event and Werner's reading of surfaces fraught with material 'meaning' lose sight of the historical mediation and production of such meanings. It is through a consideration of and moving beyond this division that criticism might be able to elaborate a less ideal 'Emily Dickinson.' Such criticism locates the meaning of 'Emily Dickinson' in the social text that is the editing and criticism of her. While manuscript criticism insists that it is the Book that has been used to make 'pure' Dickinson's messy documents, I have thus approached all editions of Dickinson's work as part of that wider 'social text' which is Emily Dickinson's work and which, as such, is part of and cannot be separated from the manuscripts. That is to say that there can be no easy distinction between a holograph and an edited page: they each condition the interpretation of the other.

Cristanne Miller writes, reviewing the effect on criticism of "the competing editions" on the market, "one cannot even quote [Emily Dickinson's poems] without identifying one's critical position as to what constitutes a Dickinson line or poem" ("The Sound of Shifting Paradigms" 205). We could add that the effect of these competing editions is also a choice of what figure of the poet one reads. But, this study has argued that this editorial situation warrants a production of Emily Dickinson as versioned—as versioned as her holographic productions sometimes are. Rather than choosing which version of a poem or indeed what version of the author one prefers the reader may consider each edition as part of a wider social text that includes all editions and versions of the poet. Such a text offers us the practice of negotiation rather than definition.

Editing remains a powerful tool with which to better present an author. Such practice of shaping texts according to an implicit model of progression runs the risk of fixing the text according to an ideal author. Indeed Leah Marcus writes that within the conventions of editing a reliance on authorship is both fundamental and potentially problematic: "[. . .] Editing is a matter of life and death. It aims at revitalising its author, but, through its strong desire for memorialisation, risks entombing the author anew" (211). That is to say that, within the disciplinary boundaries of 'editing,' a conservative mechanism is at work. Such a mechanism is, as we have seen in the analysis of the 'archive,' both productive and destructive. If the editorial ambition remains to be to render the author's intentions rather than the social text that is the historically received idea of the author and her work, then, editing risks "entombing" the author in a return to an unmediated text, whose intention, intimate collaboration, and scripting hand will reveal the import of her work. The development of electronic tools with which to compare versions of a work seems to suggest that authorial intention no longer serves as a guiding principle in editorial ventures. However, precisely by emphasizing the author's original manuscript versions to the point of the shape of single letters, Dickinson editors remain attached to a genetic conception of literary studies as based in the author's process of writing and ultimately in the author's intentions. That the author has a role to play in her own writings is commonsensical but how to navigate this role in critical inquiry is not straightforward.

This study has contributed to the consideration of how authorship may be built by appreciating that the editorial notion of 'versioning' the text is also a 'versioning' of the author. Such a choice is also a choice of what author is presented. It is for this reason that this study has scripted an alternative to biographical narrative and editorial fixity, by constructing an 'editorial' or 'textual' biography of this poet. Such a 'biography' is characterized by a negotiation of the various texts and figures of the author rather than by the choice of one Emily Dickinson. It could be argued that this position leaves out a kind of center: but, who, then, was Dickinson? What did she write? The goal of this book has been to show that these questions inevitably lead to totalizing and monological responses, responses that do not, finally, leave it to the reader to figure these things out. The challenge for a reader-oriented editorial practice, is, then, how exactly to empower readers to become competent editors.

This study has tapped into the energies of a field in rapid change. The merging of textual criticism and literary scholarship in an age of digital dissemination seems only logical as the resources of various disciplines are needed for the large-scale ventures that the new medium seems to encourage. But the exuberant and idealistic formulations of the electronic medium as the answer to longstanding editorial dilemmas and to questions of access to rare material need to be tempered by reflection. As an outsider to Digital Humanities—as the kind of scholarly user that makes use of the end-results of electronic archiving and editing—I have approached the electronic editing and formulation of Emily Dickinson. Morris Eaves has used the term "settlement" to characterize the effect an editorial project has on the formation of a work. He accentuates the temporality and specificity of settlements—their contingency (pars 6, 25). I have discussed the settlement of Dickinson's texts in the twentieth century as a meandering negotiation of who the figure of Dickinson-as-author is.

Dickinson's 'life' in electronic form has only just begun. This study also has attempted to consider in some detail the field of Digital Humanities "from the outside" as it were. Discussing the editing of poetry on-line, Harold Short and Marilyn Deegan write "this is an exciting but problematic concept, as it means that a text could change constantly, and therefore calls into question the notion of the fixed edition and the stable referent that scholars have long relied on" (225). The dichotomy set up here between "fixed edition" and a text in constant change is foundational for current textual criticism which tends to reject the idea of a stable work in favor of multiple version presentation, for the benefit of the reader to become her own editor. But as Short and Deegan suggest, in this offering of freedom to the reader is embedded a potential for anxiety: how to make sense of all this, this potential disarray. Digital humanities' is not only an emerging interdisciplinary practice but signifies a real shift in the way in which Humanities research is conducted (both in terms of the practices of researching and the practices of disseminating that research). Perhaps one of the impacts that the electronic medium will have on literary studies is precisely the making explicit of the interpretive aspects of any editorial project. That is to say that the conventional divorce of two related and indeed interdependent disciplines will be broken as readers of literary texts become aware of the text's mediated form by being forced to edit, forced to make decisions on what text to read. Yet in the very naming of electronic archives lurks desire to appropriate texts into collectable works and so it would seem that the concepts of 'archive' and 'edition' used to describe projects in electronic media produce the same kind of effect that these archives/editions would theoretically seem to reject: they gather in and create implicit borders. There is a tension in the very 'nature' of electronic archiving and editing. While digital projects in literature wish to accentuate multiplicity and interconnections, they also somewhat paradoxically make large claims: of being 'archives' and ever-more complete repositories of the matter associated with a specific topic, a specific author. Emily Dickinson figures prominently in the canon. So this name, this figure, is not easily un-edited, not easily un-archived. And so we need to think more about the disciplining drive of even a medium as flexible as the electronic medium.

Notes

NOTES TO THE INTRODUCTION

1. Fully aware of the influential image of Emily Dickinson produced by the earliest editions of Dickinson's poems edited by Mabel Loomis Todd and Thomas Higginson in the 1890s I have excluded these editions from sustained analysis. My focus is on what may be described as an increasingly academic production of Emily Dickinson through 'scholarly' editions of her work and 'critical' analysis of the same. This is a bias of my study but such a choice is valid as I am interested with how Emily Dickinson has become canonized through the academy. Although I consider the 'family' editions of the early twentieth century, I do so to offer a contrast to Thomas Johnson's *Variorum* edition, to which they were the direct precursors.

2. I refer to this tendency in Dickinson studies as 'manuscript criticism' in accordance with Domhnall Mitchell's usage of this phrase in "'A Foreign Country'" (176). This implies a criticism which emphasizes the artistic aspects of Emily Dickinson's handwritten manuscripts. Unediting is perhaps most explicitly formulated as a critical practice in Leah Marcus' *Unediting the Renaissance: Shakespeare, Marlowe, Milton*. In the context of Renaissance studies, such 'unediting' involves a poststructuralist critique of the editorial strategies that governed much editing until the 1960s. Such practice typically served to hide the editor's choices, presenting such culturally specific choices as 'transparent' and 'unmediated' presentation of the work in question. In line with the paradigmatic challenge of modern textual criticism, more recent editorial practice "is revealing, even flaunting" of the editor's choices (4). The 'unediting' of the Renaissance proposed by Marcus involves an investigation into the cultural specifics that shaped those earlier "standard editions many of us still accept unquestioningly" (4). Such 'unediting' is not meant to undo editorial practice but rather to serve as a heuristic for both editors and readers as it is proposed "as an activity that all editors should engage in as part of their own revisionary efforts, that all readers should practice mentally even as they make use of edited texts" (5). As such,

'unediting' should ideally serve as a historicist heuristic, challenging any 'objective' editing or reading.

3. Jonathan Goldberg's introduction to *Shakespeare's Hand* directed my attention to Karen Newman's study *Fashioning Femininity and English Renaissance Drama* in which in a 'melancholy coda' she writes, and I quote at length, "In my university, and in the secondary school curriculum in New England at least, any text from the Renaissance, however marginal, however decentered—ballads, jigs, penny histories, long ignored and forgotten plays—produces 'canonical effects.' That is, any text from an historical period before the French revolution is construed as 'canonical.' History itself, mere pastness, produces canonical effects. Similarly, the turn to history, however textualized, however problematized or theorized, produces a similar 'history effect' that is powerfully conservative and that explains why cultural studies is being institutionalized as the study of contemporary mass culture—not popular culture of the past, only the present, a present that continues to include the nineteenth century so as not to jettison Marx or Freud. Given the commanding force of what I have turned the history effect to construct any cultural production of the past as canonical, is political criticism possible in the Renaissance?" (146). I argue that the canonizing effect through a 'history effect' shape also the periodization and essentially canonization of authors in the nineteenth century.

4. While this study is not concerned with the self-fashioning of Emily Dickinson, it is interesting to note that her insistence on the manuscript miscellany and the letter form for the private circulation of her work retains an earlier, specifically anti-commercial and exclusive notion of the author-function. See further discussion on the author-function in Chartier.

5. In his survey of French language explorations of the 'archive,' that he describes as articulating an "archival consciousness or obsession." Sheringham considers artistic and philosophical narratives expanding on the 'archive.' Lacking from his survey is, however, the specifically electronic form of archives that appears as important tools for re-imagining the archive's form and significance. It is this specific kind of archive that I analyze in Chapter Three.

6. As outlined in note 3 the idea of 'unediting' governs this study.

7. The ideas of a 'scene of writing' and a scene of reading are frequently used in Dickinson studies, frequently used to denote Emily Dickinson's work habits and context. In particular, see Marta Werner, *Open Folios*. In "Freud and the Scene of Writing," Derrida analyzes how Freud "renders enigmatic [. . .] what we believe we know by the name of writing" (75). Freud's dependence on metaphors of writing allows Derrida to make the argument that 'writing,' rather than being the 'record' of perception, is in fact that which conditions perception. We are 'written' by previous writings: "If there is neither machine nor text without a psychic origin, there is no psyche without text"

(74). Dickinson's 'scene of writing' is thus an inscription of previous writings and our interpretations of her and her work equally 'written.'
8. For a long introduction to this 'war' see Richard Sewall's biography of Dickinson. Sewall titles a chapter in his biography of Dickinson "'War Between the Houses.'" Because Sewall's biography in fact was commissioned by one of the participants in this 'original' war, it is necessarily partial. Sewall writes "It was in 1946, or shortly thereafter, that Mrs Bingham first breathed to me the possibility of this work. Ten years later she gave me the first full view of its possible dimensions; and shortly after that her papers, indispensable to the project, came to Yale. She wanted, she said, 'the whole story' of her mother's involvement told—but told in the setting of the larger story of Emily Dickinson" (*xiv*).
9. For such indulgent readings of the text, consider for example Allen Tate's reading of Emily Dickinson as a solid representative of a lost past and Richard Blackmur's location of Dickinson as a domestic female. Such readings stabilize the text as, in Tate's case, a cultural heritage, and in Blackmur's case, paradoxically, an almost freak accident of an unthinking mind. Such a pseudo-biographical approach to Emily Dickinson's poems is of course not limited to the New Critical period. As Martha Nell Smith writes, "Literary criticism in general, but especially, it seems, criticism of Emily Dickinson, seems prey to developing into gossip, armchair psychoanalysis, or everybody's autobiography." Clearly, as will be considered in Chapter One, a very real reason for the reluctance to include Emily Dickinson in the ranks of American canonical authors is her status as a female author. That is, not only did the textual uncertainties hinder a serious consideration of the poet's art: an institutional sexism plagued early Dickinson studies. Such sexism has been fully critiqued by critics like Adrienne Rich ("Vesuvius at Home"), Timothy Morris (*Becoming Canonical*) and Robert McClure Smith ("Reading Seductions").
10. Christopher Benfey discusses New Critical analyses of Emily Dickinson in "Emily Dickinson and the South."
11. In our consideration of such 'luxurious' bibliographic codes we must also remind ourselves of Emily Dickinson's gilt edged stationery and how the poet shaped herself an exclusive author. To posit Emily Dickinson as a writer working against an elitist notion of literature and its dissemination means to negotiate the author's own employment of the effects of 'gold.' Marta Werner has dwelled the most extensively on the bibliographic codes of Harvard University Press 'packaging' of Dickinson. I discuss her analysis in Chapter Two.
12. In Chapter Three I analyze more fully the 'digital Dickinson' figure that emerges in this edition/archive. Electronic transmission of literary texts is now a commonplace. There are basically two kinds of literary texts on the web. Many editions of texts that are published on-line on the Internet rely upon

the bibliographic codes of the medium of the book. Such enormous web sites as *Project Gutenberg* and *Project Runeberg* are examples of electronic libraries of transcribed texts. The rationale for these kinds of electronic editions is that it provides simple and typically free access to texts for readers. *The Walt Whitman Archive, The Rossetti Archive* and *The Blake Archive* are examples of how the electronic medium reaches 'beyond' this kind of simple amassment of texts first produced in print as they move beyond the typographical domain of the Book by incorporating digitized images of manuscripts and by offering screen environments that allow reader-users to browse the 'stacks' of documents, typically only available at a 'real' archive, as it were. All the archive-editions mentioned so far contain texts that were once produced in a different medium, handwriting or typographic print; they are texts 'remediated' in a new medium. The other kind of text is produced directly for the electronic medium, they are 'digital born' hypertexts. These are not of particular interest to this study but it is worth noting that such texts are not easily reconciled with and transmitted through printed versions. Yet, in spite of such apparently neat categorization, according to Johan Svedjedal, hypertext is a contentious concept. Some argue that as a form hypertext is restricted to the computer; that it depends on a certain kind of technology for its manifestation. Others, however, argue that it should be interpreted as a distinct textual form with certain structures—a form that could be realized in different media ("A Note on Hypertext" 2–3). If we agree on the latter definition, works that were produced before that physical advent of hypertext could also be understood as such. For example, we could describe Emily Dickinson's variants of particular words in a poem as hypertextually linked to the reading given in the 'body' of the poem. A reader would in such a scenario choose the link she preferred and later come back and choose a new 'direction' of reading. This would be a kind of literalization of the kind of versioned reading that is demanded by Dickinson's variants. The question is whether hypertext is a useful metaphor for describing Dickinson's texts. Dickinson criticism concerned with digital editing does not usually consider Dickinson's work to be hypertextual (which is also intertextual) in this sense. But in fact to read Dickinson's word variants as hypertextual layers, interchangeable, according to the paradigm of the scroll window, is a fruitful way of understanding her variants.

13. The most explicitly biographical studies of Emily Dickinson are George Whicher's *This Was a* Poet: *A Critical Biography of Emily Dickinson,* Richard Sewall's *Emily Dickinson,* Cynthia Wolf's *Emily Dickinson,* Judith Farr's *The Passion of Emily Dickinson,* and Alfred Habegger's *My Wars are Laid Away.* Whicher's study, the first full-length study of the poet (1936) with its subtitled phrase "Critical Biography" sets Dickinson in her culture by investigating and cataloguing her place in New England, offering narratives about Amherst and its people as a kind of 'background' to Dickinson's life. While Sewall's study aims to produce a kind of totalizing covering of each aspect of Dickinson's life it must be

emphasized that all these studies offer specific interpretations of the poet's life. Wolf and Farr offers more specifically interpretive frameworks for their readings of the poet, Wolf reading the poet through theology, Farr through visual art. Habegger's study is the most recent attempt to narrate Dickinson's biography in the full-length book format. Habegger starts out by correcting what he sees as a misconception in much study of Dickinson, namely that she did not have a project that developed through and in time (xiv). Thus he connects Dickinson's work tightly to a temporal chronology and hence can merge poetry and life into a narrative of the life of the poet (xiv). Much criticism of Dickinson produces biographical accounts. Martha Nell Smith's *Rowing in Eden* is an important revision of Emily Dickinson through the lens of two specific arguments: that Dickinson must be read through the relationship between Dickinson and Susan Huntington Dickinson and that Dickinson cannot be simply understood according to the binary model of 'private' and 'public' poets, that is to say that Dickinson published her work without printing it. Such a proposition is not to be taken lightly and deserves serious consideration to combat the insidious sexism that seems to stick to the commentary on Emily Dickinson. Harold Bloom's reading of Dickinson in *Genius* is only a too telling case in point. While quickly brushing of the idea that Dickinson's letters to Susan Dickinson need to be understood as part of a particular and all-important dynamic between these two women (a poetic workshop) Bloom goes on, in line with a hundred years of mythologizing, to elevate Dickinson's letters to Judge Otis Lord (346). Hence Bloom writes "Wary as one has to be with Dickinson, I follow Sewall in crediting her love for Bowles and what almost became a marriage with Lord" (347). Smith's arguments towards producing Dickinson's 'private' poetic workshop and means of 'publication' will be interrogated in Chapter Three. While I disagree with her in many respects her aggressively challenging a norm in the reception of Dickinson that seems literally impossible to wash out is crucial for, although Blooms's narrative of the author as 'genius' must be understood as part of his intervention in favor of the irreducibly canonical artist in the wake of the 'culture wars' of the 1980s, it must be taken seriously. Jay Leyda's *The Years and Hours of Emily Dickinson* offers a .kind of biographical study in its amassment of historical data and information regarding Emily Dickinson's life. The notion of 'biography' is typically treated straightforwardly in Dickinson criticism. In a recent survey of biographical approaches to Dickinson Martha Ackmann presents such 'biographical studies' in opposition to the kind of myth making that plagued the construction of the poet for a long time. Instead biographical studies have typically served as a corrective to such mythology by situating the poet in her culture (rather than presenting her as that ephemeral woman in white, dwelling melancholically and childlike in her upstairs bedroom) (12). Such a biographical criticism moves away from the construction of an ideal poet, a saint-like figure ahistorically sealed from the ideas and practices of nineteenth-century American upper middle-class culture.

14. Clearly much criticism had considered the difficulty inherent in the editorial choice of separating poems from prose (letters). Hence Brita Lindberg-Seyersted writes "scholars do not always agree on what is and what is not verse in the Dickinson canon" (22). Lindberg-Seyersted accentuates that both forms of writing "were artistic products" (22).
15. All writers can be understood as re-writers of their own texts: the 'avant-texte' of the 'final work' can be smaller or larger. But some writers' rework a text into a 'new' text that must in some sense be understood as a 'different' work. Common examples of such revisers are Shakespeare and Marianne Moore. Emily Dickinson must be included in any history of 'revisers' or, perhaps, rather, of 're-writers.'
16. In *A Vice for Voices,* Marietta Messmer has developed this thesis.
17. Indeed, Eleanor Heginbotham argues that Emily Dickinson herself was an 'editor' and that her manuscript collections, known as fascicles,' are examples of edited material (*x*).
18. It is important to consider here how, clearly, much Dickinson criticism continues to rely on the typographical translations in printed editions of the poet's work. It would appear, that is, that 'manuscript criticism' is *one* among several approaches to Dickinson's work. It is worth considering here whether the 'instability' of the Dickinson text in fact in a serious way troubles Dickinson studies in general, in the sense of directing it away from a focus on 'the work' as still a relatively stable entity that critics can perform readings of for the promotion of stable formulations of the author's poetics and poetic project, as if the stable text references such a project.
19. I analyze *The Dickinson Electronic Archives* at length in Chapter Three, where I consider the potential of electronic editing for the display and dissemination of Emily Dickinson's manuscripts.
20. Incidentally, the connection of the visual poetic of Dickinson's work to Olson is one that Edith Wylder made in 1971 (1).
21. We could consider here if it is possible for an author centered discipline as ours is (as *Dickinson* studies is) to radically practice the versioning of texts, the privileging of the variant, multiple text. The author always lurks in the background, as the gatherer-in of the multiplicity of meanings into 'the texts of Emily Dickinson.' As such the texts are pre-canonized, pre-historicized into poems with a certain stability given by the concept of the author.

NOTES TO CHAPTER ONE

1. Much critical attention has been given the various ways in which early criticism of the poet is colored by unselfconscious heterosexist assumptions. It is clear that gender played a pivotal role in the New Critical imagination and production of Emily Dickinson. In 1936, George Whicher in the Preface to his biographical interpretation of the poet's achievement, *This*

Was a Poet, emphasized his desire to "terminate the persistent search for Emily's unknown lover" (no pagination). Insidiously, however, the preference for referring to the author by her first name recurs even in Whicher's writing, thus undermining decidedly his neutrality: "this" poet was female and hence, for this male critic, figures on a first name basis. Furthermore, Whicher reveals a rather romantic notion of the poet as the unique and separate *isolato* in his assumption that her 'love poems' are "no more" than "reverberations" of "a devotion whispered in the heart's chambers" (Preface). To Whicher, such "reverberations" does not in any possible way represent a 'real' experience (that is, it didn't 'really' happen) but only the imaginations of this isolated poet, which is really just another oblique way of arguing for a specific interpretation of Dickinson's biographical self, thereby continuing the mythology of the spinster who spun her poetic webs in her Amherst bedroom, far away from any experience of 'real' life. Thus, the critic manages to elevate Dickinson's lowly female-ness onto a pedestal above the daily business of 'life' and hence manages to justify his allocating her the role of the representative of an entire era and an entire region, what Whicher calls the "New England spirit" (Preface). Similarly, Conrad Aiken, in a preface to an English edition of Dickinson's poetry, describes the "spinsterly angularity of the mode" of her poetry (117). Similarly, the formal effects of the poet's "singular perversity, her lapses and tyrannies" are accepted, in the end, with a sigh, as "an inevitable part of the strange and original genius she was" (117). These tyrannies became "charms" in her work and 'we' supposedly "surrender" "completely" to her personality's "singular sharp beauty" (117). The woman and the poem creep, in this discourse, in and out of each other, into a final confusion of which is which and what is what (apart from the connotations of the ideology of the married woman being fulfilled). In a similar attempt to rid criticism of biographical bias (with the added crux of Dickinson's decidedly *female* gender), Allen Tate comments on the critical puzzlement with the apparent contrast between Dickinson being a "virgin" and the fact that there is so much experience in her work: It is *dangerous* to assume that her 'life,' which to the biographers means the thwarted love affair she is supposed to have had, gave to her poetry a decisive direction. It is even more dangerous to suppose that it made her a poet (157 my italics). It was not, then, Dickinson's 'virginity' nor her 'thwarted love affairs' nor her eccentric dressing in white, secluding herself in her room, that made her a great poet. Rather, Dickinson 'rejected' life so that she could explore the cultural pressures that were shaping New England culture in the mid 1800s. This attempt to reach an understanding of Dickinson's work from a wider cultural analysis, rather than pinning her work to her person, however, fails even Tate, as he himself falls into his own trap by explaining Dickinson's greatness. For, he traces her poetic greatness to "her very ignorance, her lack of formal intellectual training," continuing to say that "She cannot reason at all. She can only see" (159–160). Indeed, "She could not in the proper sense think at all" (161). This leads to the realization for Tate that 'biography' connotes rumors of love affairs, whereas apparently 'biographical' aspects of a writer's life such as the kind of education she received, is deemed to be on a different, and indeed, analytical level. The 'intellectual' aspects of a person's life may, then, legitimately, be explored. It was the popular myth-making Tate wanted to stay clear from: "[p]oets are mysterious, but a poet, when all is said, is not much more mysterious than a banker." Tate grants that, "[p]ersonality is a legitimate interest because it is an incurable interest, but legitimate as a personal interest only; it will never give up the key to anyone's verse" (157). Intellectual training, however, gives up such "keys." And thus is able, finally and in spite of the poet's supposed ignorance, to insert Dickinson into a lineage of other 'reclusive' thinkers such as Cotton Mather, Jonathan Edwards, Nathaniel Hawthorne and Henry James. F. O. Matthiessen concedes that Dickinson was a private poet but not in the sense in which, for example Gerard Manley Hopkins, was one. For whereas that latter male poet reacted consciously against current poetic styles he did not care for, consciously crafting his own poetic form, Dickinson on the other hand, was "wholly instinctive" (230). In this she embodies Emerson's ideal poet, the poet who composes in the moment of inspiration (230). In this production of a poet "overwhelmed," an image of the poet emerges through a patriarchal bow that allows both for that 'greatness' with which all critics praise her, all along with a modification of such judgments by calling forth the woman poet's presumed eccentricity and intuition. It was, then, in paradoxical terms, that Tate and the other New Critics, were strained to express Emily Dickinson's greatness: *in spite of* their depreciating biographical construction of the poet-as-spinster, she was made "great" (Tate 159).

2. Lowell thus serves as a precursor to late twentieth-century readings of Emily Dickinson. The focus on materialities of text is also governed by the profusion in the twentieth century of artistic explorations of visual/material aspects of print/typography. Modernist writers explored the possibilities of the print medium for experimentation. The focus on Emily Dickinson's manuscripts as art objects, then, can possibly be traced to critical interest in Modernist conventions. Thus Susan Howe calls Dickinson a 'protomodernist' (*My Emily Dickinson* 11) and Jerome McGann writes that, "Eventually [Dickinson] would elaborate a complex set of writing tactics from this elementary textual move [from/between a poetics of the ear to a poetics of the eye]. *In a very real sense, Modernism's subsequent experiments with its many 'visible languages' are forecast in the textual ventures of Emily Dickinson*" ("Visible Language" 248–49, my italics).

3. It is surprising how the idea of a 'new world' is here used. When its references of the 'discovery' of 'new' worlds by European 'explorers' in the fifteenth century are considered, the usefulness of the image as a metaphor of

Dickinson's manuscripts (as territories to be explored) and their readers as 'explorers' seems less appealing.

4. Morris bases his notion of the 'monologic' on Mikhail Bakhtin's theorization of the 'monologic' and 'dialogic' modes of language production. Bakhtin associates the 'dialogic' with prose and the 'monologic' with poetry. Whereas in Bakhtin's theory this distinction is relatively neutral, the concepts have developed a life of their own in subsequent critical employment so that, as Morris puts it, "the dialogic has come more and more to mean merely good and monologic merely bad" (3). Hence, "in response there has been a trend in criticism to reinterpret poetry as dialogic" (3). The 'monologic' thus appears a fiction impossible to uphold: all language is dialogic. Instead of employing the term 'monologic' to analyze literary texts, Morris appropriates the term for metacritical analysis as "the concept of monologism is perhaps a better heuristic for ordering critical practices than for reading literary texts" (4). It comes to serve as one component of Morris' construct of a 'poetics of presence' that serves to describe the kind of literary criticism that aims to ensure "the purity of the author's original, organic expression, untainted by other influences, and making that pure idiom available as a founding standard for a national literary dialect" (4).

5. I do not suggest that editorial history can be delineated as a linear progression. However, there seems to remain, in textual criticism, a desire towards 'better' productions, 'better' editions. Rather than seeing editorial history as linear we can see it as an expanding text, in accordance with the notion of the socialization of texts posited by McGann and Waller's analysis of the social context/effect on texts.

6. In *The Rules of Art* Bourdieu writes of 'position-takings' in the field (of cultural production) that they are "the product and the stake of a permanent conflict. In other words, the generative and unifying principle of this 'system' is the struggle itself" (232).

NOTES TO CHAPTER TWO

1. Wylder brings up Modernist experiments in typography as graphic or visual 'markers' of meanings and Charles Olson's theory of 'visual projection' as similar in kind to Dickinson's manuscript punctuation (*The Last Face: Emily Dickinson's Manuscripts*)

2. Wylder's distinction can be compared to more recent trends in the study of poetry. Concerned with a similar distinction between 'actual' speech and 'voice,' Yopie Prins asks, "why do we insist on reading literally what the Victorians understood to be a metaphor? What is the voice we are looking for, or think we hear, when we read a Victorian poem? How can we reverse the tendency to read these poems as the utterance of a speaker, the representation of speech, the performance of song? ("Voice Inverse" 44) Prins'

question conjures up a Derridean questioning of the privileging of speech over writing and his argument that speech retains traces of the written so that the traditional privilege cannot be upheld. It is the seeming 'naturalness' of 'speech' which is questioned, not 'speech' as an act. Hence we can study 'voice' in written poetry but, as Margaret Linley suggests, such voice returns "as an organic (though mechanically enhanced) prosthesis for the machine-made word" (46).

3. In the following *The Manuscript Books of Emily Dickinson* will be referred to as *The Manuscript Books*.

4. Jerome McGann has argued that literary critics seem less inclined to integrate editorial thinking, or attention to bibliographic detail, in their work than the opposite. ("The Case of *The Ambassadors* and the Textual Condition" 151–52). David Greetham challenges instead what he sees as some textual critics' tendency to withdraw into 'bibliography' and argues that "bibliography is not a safe positivist redoubt resistant to the onslaughts of post-structuralism, culture criticism, and so on, but that the gates are already open and the traffic two-way" (*Theories of the Text* 2). George Bornstein urges that these trends in textual criticism must work against a habit, still existing, according to him, among many literary critics, to regard their copies of a classic work as 'the real thing'—that, as Bornstein puts it, their paperback version of *Pride and Prejudice* 'is' Jane Austen's *Pride and Prejudice* (2). Bornstein argues that, in an otherwise "age of relentless demystification," many critics still assume that the text they have in their bookcase is 'the text' (*Material Modernism* 5). Leah Marcus, however, offers a more optimistic account, claiming that this traditional divide between 'editors' and 'critics' has more or less dissolved ("Afterword: Confessions of a reformed uneditor" 211). What this all testifies to is an increased awareness, among textual critics, of the 'two-way' traffic of ideas between their own editorial territory and related humanities disciplines.

5. Leah Marcus argues that the challenge of 'old' editions should not lead to a "purist position that all previous editions must be avoided" because it "would bring scholarly writing and research to a halt" (4). Certainly the editorial debates in Dickinson studies have not substantially affected 'criticism'—for critics continue to cite Emily Dickinson's poems in their Johnson and Franklin instantiations. But the point of this study is precisely to take the argument of manuscript criticism to its logical end, which is precisely that readers should exactly not rely on printed typographical editions of Emily Dickinson's writings.

6. A most important study of Emily Dickinson and the visual arts is Judith Farr's chapter on "A Vision of Form" in *The Passion of Emily Dickinson* in which she locates the poet in a Romantic tradition. Farr considers Dickinson's thematic use of 'light' and connects her work intertextually with the theory and paintings of the American painters associated with the Luminist painters but also

with the English Romantic poets. For some important studies of the fascicles see Sharon Cameron, *Choosing Not Choosing* (1992), Dorothy Huff Oberhaus, *Emily Dickinson's Fascicles: Method and Meaning* (1995), and Domhnall Mitchell, *Monarch of Perception* (2000).

7. Certainly we need to take into consideration that we may see Dickinson as 'producing' a radically new form of art but I insist that this 'radical' reading of Dickinson can be located in McGann's (and others') investments in Modernist poetries. Is it viable to transpose Modernist poetic strategies onto Dickinson's work? If we accept that "time, space, and physicality" are the "bounding conditions" of the study of literature, then we realize that all engagements with literary texts will 'change' those texts (*The Textual Condition* 9). The growing 'archive' of the 'textual condition' of 'a poem' then must incorporate 'positively' all editorial versions of that poem, taking into consideration also the 'effects' of the specific editions on for example the critical reception of the poem (in that specific form). The reading of Dickinson through a modernist template thus must be viable, but we must acknowledge this as a mediated *effect* rather than something 'intrinsic' to the text 'itself.' Cristanne Miller, considering the effect that the privileging of the visual has on the reading of Emily Dickinson, has similarly suggested that that the return to the site of Emily Dickinson's original production as a visually oriented production is conditioned by the increasing privileging of the *visual word* in twentieth-century poetic theory and practice ("The Sound of Shifting Paradigms" 202–203). It appears fortuitous that the development of theories of the visuals of Dickinson appeared more or less at the same time as developments in digital media have made it easier to 'reproduce' a handwritten manuscript for general perusal. There is a potent mixture at stake here, I argue. That is to say that digital media appear to condition our return to the manuscript, or, at the very least, reinforce our production of a visual-as-digital Dickinson text. I return to this Digital Dickinson in the third chapter.

8. By 'experimental' I refer explicitly to the word's connotations of 'radical' or 'avant-garde.' I do not use the term 'experimental' here in the general sense of thinking about a text as a conscious artistic craft. Cristanne Miller so uses the term in her discussion of "Emily Dickinson's Experiments in Language." In this essay Miller uses the term to repudiate the long-standing formulation of Emily Dickinson as essentially an art-less artist, whose mind was genius but whose poetic craft was flawed (246).

9. This does not mean, however, that 'meaning' is somehow necessarily meant to be literally read: indeed Emily Dickinson's handwriting is so difficult to 'read' in the 'normal' sense that readers need 'transcriptions.' While some manuscript critics prefer to decisively make 'meaning' out of Dickinson's handwriting, by taking recourse to 'calligraphy' (and thereby insert Dickinson's texts into a referential context), Marta Werner considers this *illegibility*

in a serious way and suggests that "For Dickinson the aim of transcription is neither greater legibility—the production of a 'fine' hand—nor the government of a multiplicity of hands in conformity with a prescribed model" (27). This is an attractive kind of metaphorical reading of Dickinson's writing, a literal blurring or dispersal of the linguistic-semantic meaning of the script. I read Dickinson's difficult script as a literal/visual metaphor or thematization of her continual return to the problem of 'knowing' (as her poems continually 'break down' in the search for 'knowledge).

10. Domhnall Mitchell refers to how "Marjorie Perloff's understanding of Dickinson's poetry was subjected to criticism on the grounds that she had not looked at manuscript versions of the poems she discussed" ("The Grammar of Ornament" 494n39). I bring this comment up in my discussion of what I see as Martha Nell Smith's 'scriptural' formulation of Emily Dickinson's work. See p. 103. Connected to this notion that the 'original' is necessarily the best source for knowledge about Dickinson's texts is the insistence in Martha Nell Smith's work in particular on various "facts" about Emily Dickinson's life that should be taken into account if we wish to understand Dickinson's work more properly. See for example "Corporealizations" and "Susan and Emily Dickinson: their lives, in letters." There is, I argue, a tendency towards assigning a positivist idealist truth-factor in such 'facts' and such 'originals' as if the critical assumptions through which such 'facts' and 'origins' are construed were not socially contingent and necessarily interpretive.

11. We could say that Emily Dickinson's manuscripts visualize a thematic concern with 'not knowing' in the sense that Dickinson's script is so difficult to 'decode' that it becomes a play on the poet's continual return to the question of the 'beyond' what is legible, what is possible to frame through human 'knowledge' of 'this world' and that theological or metaphysical 'beyond.' In a similar (but different) interpretation of the interconnectedness between linguistic and bibliographical codes, Jerome McGann reads the poem beginning with the line "Many a phrase has the English language" (Fr 333). Dickinson breaks the 'line' "Breaking in bright Orthogra/phy,' a break that materializes the 'idea' of the poem's linguistic codes. Most editions, including those of Johnson and Franklin 'conventionalize' this poem to be a single line.

12. This study is not concerned with the *sound* of Emily Dickinson's work. This does not mean that sound is unimportant to the study of Emily Dickinson's poetics. As noted above, Miller points out, in "The Sound of Shifting Paradigms," that there is a tendency in the current critical climate to privilege the visual at the expense of the aural. Brita Lindberg-Seyersted has offered one of the most sustained analyses of the sound effects of Dickinson's work. From a formalist methodology derived from Roman Jakobson and other critics associated with Russian and Czech formalism she considers Emily Dickinson's "versification" in terms of meter and rhythm (118–127). My intention is not to devalue such an analysis of Emily Dickinson's work but

at the present moment it is important to consider the arguments of visually oriented criticism.

13. Not the least their centrality stems from their prominent positions as the editors (along with Ellen Louis Hart) of the two editions of Emily Dickinson poems that attempt to render the poems as closely as possible to the manuscript original. Marta Werner's *Emily Dickinson's Open Folios* is an edition of late poetic fragments and scraps, and it provides both facsimiles and print transcriptions of the poem. Werner also puts the history of Dickinson criticism and editing in a critical perspective. Ellen Louise Hart and Martha Nell Smith's edition of the correspondence between Emily Dickinson and her sister-in-law Susan Huntingdon Dickinson, *Open Me Carefully: Emily Dickinson's Correspondence with Susan Huntington Dickinson* was published in 1999.

14. Judith Farr discusses the interest in the materiality of Emily Dickinson's language on the page, the visible word, and argues that Dickinson indeed must have experimented with her script but that such experimentation as is attributed to Dickinson today might have more to do with a Modernist aesthetics than with Dickinson's 'intentions' as an artist. On the question of lineation, she points out that Emily Dickinson sent Susan, supposedly the poet's collaborator and muse, a standardized version of one stanza of "This Consciousness that is aware," and asks, "Since she shared other poetic experiments with Sue, why not such crucial ones?" (373–74n13). As Farr points out, the 'problem' is, as always, one of ascribing 'intention' onto the figure of the artist. Not rejecting the idea of Dickinson's artistic material engagement with language, Farr notes that "The young Emily Dickinson called her letters to friends 'symbols traced upon paper' [L146]. She was, then, "highly conscious of the physical process of recording, of her lines as designs, verbal arrangements" (252).

15. This 'genetic criticism' is concerned with "the production of writings, especially of literary texts" (Louis Hay 18). Developed as a theory and methodology in the 1960s and 1970s, genetic criticism builds on a tradition of literary manifestos and theories that engage the 'birth' of the literary work. Louis Hay, one of the major practitioners of this method, traces its origins to the aesthetics of Novalis, Goethe, and Schlegel. He cites Goethe's remark that "One cannot embrace the works of nature and art when they are finished: they must be taken on the wing, in the nascent state, if one wishes to comprehend them" (quoted in Hay 18). The practice of such a study of the 'nascent state' involves, for Hay, first the entrance into the writer's workshop and, second, a methodological means of analyzing what one finds there, in the manuscripts, what he calls the 'internal mechanisms' of the production of the literary work (19). Importantly, Hay traces the access to manuscripts that is required for such a study as an effect of a historical "construction of literary-manuscript collections" (19). Hay traces this development to the

Germany of the Romantic era. The idea of the vernacular literary tradition as part of the building of the nation state was an incentive for the collection of German literary texts, in the same way as Greek and Roman texts had previously been collected (20). (We can see a similar 'nationalist' movement in current-day employment of digital media, in the name of 'democratization' of culture: I return to this aspect of the 'cultural archive' in the third chapter's engagement with digital archives of text).

16. Such a 'blank' could be seen to allow the reader to inscribe any meaning onto/from the Dickinson text, but Werner's construction of such a blank is decisively based in a pre-articulated 'meaning' of the manuscript page as indicative of Emily Dickinson's artistic practice.

17. Compare Pierre-Marc De Biasi's description of the function of the 'rough draft' for genetic critics. "From the point of view of a work's genesis, the rough draft can be considered as a sort of text laboratory in which it becomes possible to piece back together an essential phase of the writer's work by tracing each one of the writing movements, observing, as if at the time they took place, choices, hesitations among the array of invented possibilities, bursts of speed and moments of discouragement or block in the composition, sudden intuition or happy accidents that sweep aside the difficulties and set the writing off again in a new direction. The rough draft tells a kind of day-by-day story at once logical, symptomatic of affect, and phenomenological—non other than that of the life of the writer at work: a secret tale, almost always absent from literary biographies, and which nevertheless constitutes the crux of what we would like to know about the author" ("What is a Literary Draft? Toward a Functional Typology of Genetic Documentation" 29).

18. The usage of words related to 'scriptural' range from the writing-oriented "inscriptions" and "scripturally" to the more metaphorically invested "scriptures" as a description of Dickinson's work ("Corporealizations" 199, 197; "Because the Plunge" 3).

19. Compare Leah Marcus' discussion of the 'purist' position in *Unediting the Renaissance,* 3–4.

20. Peter Shillingsburg defines five different 'orientations' in editorial practice. These are the sociological, bibliographic, aesthetic, documentary and authorial orientations (*Scholarly Editing* 16–23). It is useful to consider Shillingsburg's suggestion that "it is important for scholars, as well as critics, to accept the legitimate existence of this variety of approaches [. . .]" (*Scholarly Editing* 73).

NOTES TO CHAPTER THREE

1. Katherine Sutherland writes in *Jane Austen's Textual Lives* "literary works exist not as things or work-of-art particulars, so the standard explanation

goes (. . .); as a consequence we do not hold a notion of their uniqueness as in some sense we do of a painting" (315).

2. Quotations are from the digital article "The Flights of A821: Dearchiving the Proceedings of a Bird Song" in *Electronic Book Review* 6 (1998) (accessed March 16, 2005). This article is also available in printed form in *Voice, Text, Hypertext: Emerging Practices in Textual Studies*. Eds. Raimonda Modiano, Leroy F. Searle, and Peter Shillingsburg. Seattle: Walter Chapin Simpson Center for the Humanites in Association with the University of Washington Press, 2004. 298–329.

3. Members include Susan Howe, Marta Werner, Ellen Louise Hart, Jerome McGann and Martha Nell Smith (Smith, "Plunge" 2). Smith reveals an identification between the collective and 'Susan and Emily': "This ongoing collective thinking about the identities and meanings of documents is, informed as it is by different sensibilities, different talents, different opinions, akin to the long-term collaboration of Susan and Emily: at its heart is a generative, capacious poetics accommodating different sensibilities, different talents, different readers" ("Plunge" 2).

4. In the following, *Dickinson Electronic Archives* is abbreviated *DEA*.

5. See Susan Howe, *The Birth-mark*; Marta Werner, *Open Folios,* Jerome McGann, *Black Riders* and Martha Nell Smith, *Rowing in Eden*.

6. See the "Proposal for *Dickinson Electronic Archives*" <http://www.emilydickinson.org/archive_description.html>.

7. Katherine Hayles writes that electronic text is more accurately described as a 'process' rather than an 'object' (274). Since the building of the *DEA* is a work-in-progress, this description of electronic text as 'process' seems doubly apt in this case.

8. Marta Werner has published an electronic archive of Dickinson's "late writings," *Radical Scatters*. This edition is available only through the subscription of a university library. .

9. In fact, the practice of archiving, with its widening of the scope of the traditional 'edition,' seriously asks the question of what is an object of 'study' in the study of Emily Dickinson. For example, if letters are seen to comprise the archive not merely as 'background' material, then we may wish to ask if this 'poet' should not be called a 'writer,' that is, the 'writer' of the materials in the archive. That is, how useful is the conventional characterizations of 'Emily Dickinson' as 'poet'?

10. Julia Kristeva, building on Mikhail Bakhtin's work on the dialogic produces the concept of 'intertextuality' as "any text is constructed as a mosaic of quotations; any text is the absorption and transformation of another. The notion of *intertextuality* replaces that of intersubjectivity, and poetic language is read as at least *double* ("Word, Dialogue, Novel" 66). In *Revolution in Poetic Language* Kristeva usesthe term 'transposition' to describe her development of a notion of 'inter-textuality' that does not merely signify the

"study of sources" (59–60). However, 'intertextuality' is the term Kristeva has gone on to use. To Roland Barthes the notion of 'text' serves to subvert the notion of 'work' as the object of a reading. Rather than reading a work, the ideal 'reader' is a writer who scripts texts. See *S/Z* 3–6.

11. Johan Svedjedal refers to Manuel Castells, and I quote at length: "As Manuel Castells has pointed out, this process should be understood as a restructuring of capitalism into informational capitalism, a network society permeated with modern information technology working globally and in real time—that in fact, "globalization" is mainly the consequences of advances in information and communications technology. [. . .] Predictably, the Western World is leading this industrial change. The result is reinforcement of traditional global structures and further Americanization of economies and minds. In sociological variables, the winning sides are the expected ones—men still dominate over women, the educated over the uneducated, white over non-white, the Western World over the Third World. Such is the larger sociocultural framework of the present digitization of literature" (*The Literary Web* 10–11). For a discussion on democracy of access in the specific context of national and university libraries see Christine L. Borgman *From Gutenberg to the Global Information Infrastructure,* in particular the chapter "Toward a Global Digital Library."

12. As Domhnall Mitchell points out, "a cousin of marble (for which it is sometimes mistaken), though it does not have quite the same pedigree: marble is monumental, while alabaster (especially in the nineteenth century) was more often employed as an imitation" (*Monarch* 267)

13. Here it is fruitful to consider Walter Ong's theorization of print as an intertext: Ong writes "Print situates words in space more relentlessly than writing ever did. Writing moves words from the sound world to a world of visual space, but print locks words into position in this space. Control of position is everything in print" (119)

14. The question of 'how to read' the Dickinson page consciously echoes George Bornstein's study of *Material Modernism* in which he asks how to read various cultural-material instantiations of 'the same' Modernist texts. George Bornstein argues that in order to better understand a literary work we need to pay detailed attention to the material form which, really, *constitutes* that work: we cannot, that is, separate a linguistic text from its materiality. A book is not simply a vessel of a textual ideality but in fact conditions the very act of reading, what the text in question will 'mean' to a reader. Bornstein's work is part of a wider critical investigation of the materiality of the book. I outlined the theorization of this very 'physical' notion of 'materiality' in detail in Chapter Two. *See also* the Introduction.

15. Martha Nell Smith's and Domhnall Mitchell's readings are the most important contemporary studies of this poem. See *Rowing in Eden* and *Monarch of Perception.*

16. Richard Sewall writes "The extent of Sue's help with Emily's poetry is impossible to document, except for the one instance of the poem 'Safe in their Alabaster Chambers'" (201). Smith expands from this one example to produce her argument of the necessity of reading Dickinson in her correspondences and as a decisively not isolated figure. We may question the weight of an argument based in one single example but Smith's usage of the 'Safe' texts as a key to Dickinson's poetics is nevertheless powerful: the Safe texts have become, in a sense, the symbol of the relationship between 'Emily' and 'Sue.'
17. <http://www.iath.virginia.edu/dickinson/safe/preintro.html> accessed on March 10 2003)
18. <http://mith2.umd.edu/products/ver-mach/description.html>.
19. Smith and Vetter <http://www.emilydickinson.org/safe/exercises>.

Bibliography

Ackmann, Martha. "Biographical Studies of Dickinson." Grabher, Hagenbüchle, and Miller 11–23.
Alfrey, Shawn. "The Function of Dickinson at the Present Time." *Emily Dickinson Journal* 11:1 (2002): 9–20.
Allen, Graham. *Intertextuality.* London and New York: Routledge, 2000.
Anderson, Charles R. *Emily Dickinson's Poetry: Stairway of Surprise.* New York: Holt, Rinehart and Winston, 1963.
———. "From a window in Amherst: Emily Dickinson looks at the American scene." *New England Quarterly* 31 (1958): 147–171.
"Archive." *Oxford English Dictionary.* 2nd ed. 1989.
Arvin, Newton. "The Poems of Emily Dickinson." *American Literature* 28 (1956): 232–236.
Barthes, Roland. "The Death of the Author." *Image-Music-Text.* Trans. Stephen Heath. New York: Hill and Wang, 1977. 142–148.
———. "From Work to Text." *Image-Music-Text.* Trans. Stephen Heath. New York: Hill and Wang, 1977. 155–164.
———. *S/Z: An Essay.* Trans. Richard Miller. New York: Hill and Wang, 1974.
Bellemin-Noël, Jean. "Psychoanalytic Reading and the Avant-texte." Deppman, Ferrer, and Groden 28–35.
Benfey, Christopher. "Emily Dickinson and the American South." Martin 30–50.
Benjamin, Walter. "The Work of Art in the Age of Mechanical Reproduction." *Illuminations.* Ed. and trans. Hannah Arendt. New York: Schocken Books, 1968. 217–251.
Bennett, Paula Bernat. "Emily Dickinson and her American Women Poet Peers." Martin 215–235.
Bingham, Millicent Todd. *Ancestors' Brocades: The Literary Debut of Emily Dickinson.* New York: Harper & Brothers, 1945.
———. *Emily Dickinson: A Revelation.* New York: Harper & Brothers, 1954.
Blackmur, Richard P. "Emily Dickinson: Notes on Prejudice and Fact." *Southern Review* 3 (1937): 323–47. Rpt. In Blake and Wells, eds. 201–223.

Blake, Ceasar R. and Carlton F. Wells, eds. *The Recognition of Emily Dickinson. Selected Criticism Since 1890.* Ann Arbor: U of Michigan P, 1964.
The William Blake Archive. Morris Eaves, Robert N. Essick, and Joseph Viscomi, eds. May 10, 2007. <www.williamblake.org>.
Bloom, Harold. *Genius: A Mosaic of One Hundred Exemplary Creative Minds.* London: Fourth Estate, 2002.
Boisseau, Michelle. "The Industry of Emily Dickinson" *Kenyon Review* 23(2001): 178–188.
Bolter, Jay and Richard Grusin. *Remediation: Understanding New Media.* Cambridge: MIT P, 1999.
Borgman, Christine L. *From Gutenberg to the Global Information Infrastructure: Access to Information in the Networked World.* Cambridge and London: MIT P, 2000.
Bornstein, George. *Material Modernism: The Politics of the Page.* Cambridge: Cambridge UP, 2001.
Bornstein, George, and Tinkle, eds. Introduction. *The Iconic Page in Manuscript, Print, and Digital Culture.* Ann Arbor: U of Michigan P, 1998.
Bourdieu, Pierre. *The Field of Cultural Production. Essays on Art and Literature.* Edited and Introduced by Randal Johnson. New York City: Columbia UP, 1993.
———. *The Rules of Art. Genesis and Structure of the Literary Field.* Trans. Susan Emanuel. Stanford: Stanford UP, 1995.
Brooks, Cleanth and Robert Penn Warren. *Understanding Poetry.* 3d ed. New York: Holt, Rinehart & Winston, 1960.
Buell, Lawrence. *New England Literary Culture.* Cambridge: Cambridge UP, 1986.
Cameron, Sharon. *Choosing Not Choosing. Dickinson's Fascicles.* Chicago and London: Uof Chicago P, 1992.
Chartier, Roger. *The Order of Books. Readers, Authors, and Libraries in Europe between the Fourteenth and Eighteenth Centuries.* Trans. Lydia G. Cochrane .Cambridge: Polity Press.
Clarke, Graham, ed. *Emily Dickinson: Critical Assessments.* 4 vols. The Banks, Mountfield: Helm Information Ltd, 2002
Cook, Terry and Joan M. Schwartz. "Archives, Records, and Power: From (Postmodern) Theory to (Archival) Performance." *Archival Science* 2:3–4 (2002) 171–185.
Crumbley, Paul. "The Dickinson Variorum and the Question of Home." *Emily Dickinson Journal* 8:2 (1999): 10–23.
De Biasi, Pierre-Marc. "What is a Literary Draft? Toward a Functional Typology of Genetic Documentation." *Yale French Studies* 89 (1996): 26–58.
Deppman, Jed, Daniel Ferrer, and Michael Groden, eds. *Genetic Criticism: Texts and Avant-textes.* Philadelphia: U of Pennsylvania P, 2004.
———. Introduction. Deppman, Ferrer, and Groden 1–16.
Derrida, Jacques. *Archive Fever: A Freudian Impression.* Trans. Eric Prenovitz. London: U of Chicago P, 1998 (1996).
———. "Freud and the Scene of Writing." *Yale French Studies* 48 (1972): 74–117.

———. *Of Grammatology.* Trans. Gayatri Chakravorty Spivak. Corrected ed. Baltimore and London: The Johns Hopkins UP, 1997.
Dickinson, Emily. *Bolts of Melody. New Poems of Emily Dickinson.* Eds. Mabel Loomis Todd and Millicent Todd Bingham. New York and London: Harper and Brothers Publishers, 1945.
———. *Emily Dickinson: The Complete Poems.* Ed. Thomas H. Johnson. London: Faber and Faber, 1970.
———. *The Letters of Emily Dickinson. Including variant readings critically compared with all known manuscripts.* Ed. Thomas H. Johnson. 3 vols. Cambridge: Harvard UP 1958.
———. *The Manuscript Books of Emily Dickinson.* Ed. R. W. Franklin. 2. vols. Cambridge, Mass.: Harvard UP, 1981
———. *Poems by Emily Dickinson.* Third Series. Ed. Mabel Loomis Todd. Boston: Roberts Brothers, 1896.
———. *The Poems of Emily Dickinson: Including Variant Readings Critically Compared with all Known Manuscripts.* Ed. Thomas H. Johnson. 3 vols. Cambridge: Harvard UP, 1955.
———. *The Poems of Emily Dickinson: Variorum Edition.* Ed. R. W. Franklin. 3 vols. Cambridge, Mass.: Harvard UP, 1998
———. *The Single Hound: Poems of a Lifetime by Emily Dickinson.* Ed. Martha Dickinson Bianchi. Boston: Little, Brown, and Company, 1914.
The Emily Dickinson Archives. Eds. Martha Nell Smith, Marta Werner and Lara Vetter. Institute for Advanced Technology in the Humanites, University of Virginia. May 10, 2007 <www.emilydickinson.org>.
Eaves, Morris. "Crafting editorial settlements." *Romanticism on the Net.* 41–42 (2006): 33 pars. 10 May 2007 <http://www.erudit.org/revue/ron/2006/v/n41–42/013150ar.html>.
Eberwein, Jane Donahue, ed. *An Emily Dickinson Encyclopedia.* Westport: Greenwood Press, 1998.
———. Preface. Eberwein xi-xiv.
———. "'Safe in their Alabster Chambers–'" Eberwein 256–57.
Eliot. T. S. "Tradition and the Individual Talent." *The New Criticism: An Anthology of Modern Aesthetics and Literary Criticism.* Ed. Edwin Berry Burgum. New York: Prentice Hall, 1930. 291–302.
Erkkila, Betsy. "The Emily Dickinson Wars." Martin 11–29.
———. "Dickinson and the Arts of Politics." Pollak 133–174.
Farr, Judith. *The Passion of Emily Dickinson.* Cambridge: Harvard University Press, 1992.
Foucault, Michel. "What is an Author? *Language, Counter-Memory, Practice: Selected Essays and Interviews.* Trans. Sherry Simon. Ed. Donald. F. Bouchard. Ithaca: Cornell UP, 1977. 197–210.
———. *Archaelogy of Knowledge and the Discourse on Language.* 1971. Trans. A. M. Sheridan Smith. New York: Pantheon Books, 1982.

Franklin, R.W. *The Editing of Emily Dickinson: A Reconsideration*. Madison: University of Wisconsin Press, 1967.
Genette, Gérard. *Paratexts: Thresholds of Interpretation*. Trans. Jane E. Lewin. Cambridge: Cambridge UP, 1997.
Goldberg, Jonathan. *Shakespeare's Hand*. Minneapolis: University of Minnesota Press, 2003.
Grabher, Gudrun, Roland Hagenbüchle, and Cristanne Miller, eds. *The Emily Dickinson Handbook*. Amherst, U of Massachusetts P, 1998.
Greetham, David. *Textual Scholarship: An Introduction*. New York: Garland Publishing, 1992.
———. *Theories of the Text*. Oxford: Oxford UP, 1999.
———. "'Who's In, Who's Out': The Cultural Poetics of Archival Exclusion." *Studies in the Literary Imagination*. 32:1 (1999): 1–29.
Habegger, Alfred. *My Wars Are Laid Away in Books: The Life of Emily Dickinson*. New York: Random House, 2001.
Hagenbüchle, Roland. "Dickinson and Literary Theory." Grabher, Hagenbüchle, and Miller 356–384.
Hamilton, Paul. *Historicism*. 2nd ed. London and New York: Routledge, 2003.
Hart, Ellen Louise. "Editorial Scholarship." Eberwein 93–95.
Haslett, Moyra. *Marxist Literary and Cultural Theories*. New York: St. Martin's Press, 2000.
Hayles, N. Katherine. "Saving the Subject: Remediation in House of Leaves." *American Literature* 74 (2002): 779–806.
———. "Translating Media: Why We Should Rethink Textuality." *Yale Journal of Criticism* 16:2 (2003): 263–290.
Heginbotham, Eleanor Elson. *Reading the Fascicles of Emily Dickinson. Dwelling in Possibilities*. Columbus: Ohio State UP, 2003.
Higginson, Thomas Wentworth. "Emily Dickinson's Letters." *Atlantic Monthly* Oct. 1891: 444–456.
———. "Letter to a Young Contributor." *Atlantic Monthly* Apr. 1862. 402–411.
Horne, Philip. "The Poetry of Possibilities: Dickinson's Texts." *Women's Studies* 31 (2002): 725–74.
Howe, Susan. *The Birth-mark: unsettling the wilderness in American literary history*. Hanover and London: Wesleyan UP, 1993.
———. *My Emily Dickinson*. Berkeley: North Atlantic Books, 1985.
Ickstadt, Heinz. "Emily Dickinson's Place in Literary History; or, The Public Function of a Private Poet." *Emily Dickinson Journal*. 10:1 (2001): 55–69.
Jackson, Virginia. *Dickinson's Misery. A Theory of Lyric Reading*. Princeton: Princeton UP, 2005.
Jenny, Laurent. "Genetic Criticism and its Myths." *Yale French Studies*. 89 (1996): 9–25.
Juhasz, Suzanne. "Materiality and the Poet." Grabher, Hagenbüchle, and Miller 427–439.

Keller, Karl. *The Only Kangaroo among the Beauty: Emily Dickinson and America.* Baltimore: Johns Hopkins UP, 1979.

Kristeva, Julia. *Revolution in Poetic Language.* Trans. Margaret Waller. New York: Columbia UP, 1984.

———. *Desire in Language. A Semiotic Approach to Art and Literature.* Ed. Leon S. Roudiez. Trans. Thomas Gura, Alice Jardine, and Leon S. Roudiez. New York: Columbia UP, 1980.

Ladin, Jay. "'So Anthracite—to live': Emily Dickinson and American Literary History." *Emily Dickinson Journal.* 13:1 (2004):19–50.

———. "Soldering the Abyss: Emily Dickinson and modern American Poetry." Diss. Princeton University, 2000.

Landow, George P. *Hypertext.* Baltimore and London: Johns Hopkins UP, 1992.

Leavell, Linda. "Marianne Moore's Emily Dickinson." *Emily Dickinson Journal* 12:2 (2003): 1–20.

Leyda, Jay. "The Poems of Emily Dickinson." *New England Quarterly* 29:2 (1956): 239–245.

Lindberg-Seyersted, Brita. *The Voice of the Poet: Aspects of Style in the Poetry of Emily Dickinson.* Cambridge: Harvard UP, 1968.

Loeffelholz, Mary. "Corollas of Autumn: Reading Franklin's Dickinson." *Emily Dickinson Journal* 8:2 (1999): 55–71.

———. "The Incidental Dickinson." *New England Quarterly* 72 (1999): 456–472.

Lowell, Amy. "Emily Dickinson." *Poetry and Poets.* Boston: Houghton Mifflin Co., 1930. 88–108. Rpt. in Clarke vol 2. 339–349.

Lubbers, Klaus. *Emily Dickinson. The Critical Revolution.* Ann Arbor: U of Michigan P, 1968.

Manoff, Marlene. "Theories of the Archive from Across the Disciplines." *Libraries and the Academy* 4 (2004): 9–25.

Marcus, Leah S. *Unediting the Renaissance: Shakespeare, Marlowe, Milton.* London and New York: Routledge, 1996.

———. "Afterword: Confessions of a reformed uneditor." *The Renaissance Text.* Ed. Andrew Murphy. Manchester: Manchester UP, 2000. 211–216.

Martin, Wendy, ed. *The Cambridge Companion to Emily Dickinson.* Camridge: Cambridge UP, 2002.

Matthiessen, F. O. "Emily Dickinson. A Private Poet." *Kenyon Review* 2 (1945): 584–97. Rpt. in Blake and Wells, eds. 224–234.

McGann, Jerome. *Black Riders: The Visible Language of Modernism.* Princeton: Princeton UP, 1993.

———. "Emily Dickinson's Visible Language." *Emily Dickinson: A Collection of Critical Essays.* Ed. Judith Farr. Upper Saddle River: Prentice, 1996.

———. "The Monks and the Giants: Textual and Bibliographical Studies and the Interpretation of Literary Works." 180–199. *Textual Criticism and Literary Interpretation.* Ed. Jerome McGann. Chicago: U of Chicago P, 1985.

———. *The Textual Condition.* Princeton: Princeton UP, 1991.

Messmer, Marianna. *A Vice for Voices: Reading Emily Dickinson's Correspondences.* Amherst: U of Massachusetts P, 2001.
Miller, Cristanne. "'Because I could not stop for Death–' (P712)." Eberwein 13–14
———. "Dickinson's Experiments in Language." Grabher, Hagenbüchle, and Miller 240–257.
———. "The Sound of Shifting Paradigms." Pollak 210–234.
———. ."Whose Emily Dickinson?" *American Literary History* 12:1 (2000): 230–253.
Miller, J. Hillis. "The Critic as Host." *Deconstruction and Criticism.* Harold Bloom et al. New York: Continuum. 1979. 217–253.
Miller, Perry. "Emily Dickinson: An Interpretive Biography." *New England Quarterly* 29 (1956):101–103.
Mitchell, Domhnall. "'A Foreign Country' Emily Dickinson's Manuscripts and their Meanings." *Legacy* 17 (2000): 174–186.
———. *Emily Dickinson: Monarch of Perception.* Amherst: U of Massachusetts P, 2000.
———. "The Grammar of Ornament: Emily Dickinson's Manuscripts and their Meanings." *Nineteenth-Century Literature* 55:4 (2001): 479–514.
Morris, Timothy. *Becoming Canonical in American Poetry.* Urbana: U of Illinois P, 1995.
———. "The Franklin Edition of Dickinson: Is That All There Is?" *Emily Dickinson Journal* 8:2 (1999): 1–9.
Morse, Jonathan. "Bibliographical Essay." Pollak 255–283.
Newman, Karen. *Fashioning Femininity and Renaissance Drama.* Chicago: U of Chicago P, 1991.
Oberhaus, Dorothy Huff. *Emily Dickinson's Fascicles: Method and Meaning.* University Park, PA: Pennsylvania State UP, 1995.
Ong, Walter J. *Orality and Literacy. The Technologization of the Word.* 1982. London: Routledge, 2002.
Orgel, Stephen. "Margins of Truth." *The Renaissance Text.* Ed. Andrew Murphy. Manchester: Manchester UP, 2000. 91–107.
Oxford English Dictionary. 2nd ed. Oxford: Clarendon Press, 1982.
Pask, Kevin. *The Emergence of the English Author: Scripting the life of the poet in early modern England.* Cambridge: Cambridge UP, 1996.
Perloff, Marjorie. "Emily Dickinson and the Theory Canon." May 10 2007 <http://epc.buffalo.edu/authors/perloff/articles/dickinson.html>.
Petrino, Elizabeth. *Emily Dickinson and Her Contemporaries: Women's Verse in American, 1820–1885.* Hanover and London: UP New England, 1998.
Pollak, Vivian R. *A Historical Guide to Emily Dickinson.* Ed. Vivian R Pollak. Oxford: Oxford UP, 2004
———. Introduction. Pollak 3–11.
Porter, David. *Emily Dickinson: The Modern Idiom.* Cambridge: Harvard UP, 1981.
———. "Searching for Emily Dickinson's Themes." Grabher, Hagenbüchle, and Miller 183–196.

Prins, Yopie. "Voice Inverse." *Victorian Poetry.* 42:1 (2004): 43–59.
Rich, Adrienne. "Vesuvius at home: The Power of Emily Dickinson." *Parnassus: Poetry in Review* 5 (1976): 49–74. Rpt. in Clark vol. 2. 319–338.
The Complete Writings and Pictures of Dante Gabriel Rossetti: A Hypermedia Archive. Ed. Jerome McGann. May 10, 2007 <www.rossettiarchive.org>.
Schreibman, Susan, Ray Siemens and John Unsworth, eds. *A Companion to Digital Humanities.* Oxford: Blackwell, 2004. May 10, 2007 http://digitialhumanities.org/companion. "Scriptural." *Oxford English Dictionary.* 2nd ed. 1989.
Sewall, Richard B. *The Life of Emily Dickinson.* Cambridge: Harvard UP, 1974.
Sheringham, Michael. "Memory and the Archive in Contemporary Life-Writing." *French Studies* 59:1 (2005): 47–52.
Shillingsburg, Peter L. "Principles for Electronic Archives, Scholarly Editions, and Tutorials." *The Literary Text in the Digital Age.* Ed. Richard J. Finneran. Ann Arbor: U of Michigan P, 1996. 23–35.
———. *Scholarly Editing in the Computer Age. Theory and Practice.* 3d. ed. Ann Arbor: U of Michigan P, 1996.
Short, Harold and Marilyn Deegan. "ICT as a Research Method." *Research Methods for English Studies.* Ed. Gabriele Griffin. Edinburgh: Edinburgh UP, 2005. 214–235.
Smith, Martha Nell. "'Because the Plunge from the Front Overturned Us': The *Dickinson Electronic Archives* Project." *Dickinson Electronic Archives.* Martha Nell Smith, Marta Werner and Lara Vetter, eds. Institute for Advanced Technology in the Humanities. University of Virginia. May 10, 2007. http://www.emilydickinson.org/plunge1.html
———. "Computing: What's American Literary Study Got to do with IT?" *American Literature* 74:4 (2002): 833–857
———. "Corporealizations of Dickinson and Interpretive Machines." *The Iconic Page in Manuscript, Print, and Digital Culture.* Eds. George Bornstein and Theresa Tinkle. Ann Arbor: U of Michigan P, 1998.
———. *Rowing in Eden: Rereading Emily Dickinson.* Austin: U of Texas P, 1992.
Smith, Martha Nell, and Ellen Louise Hart. "On Franklin's Gifts and Ghosts." *Emily Dickinson Journal* 8:2 (1999) 24–38.
Smith, Martha Nell, and Lara Vetter. "Emily Dickinson Writing a Poem." *Dickinson Electronic Archives.* Ed. Martha Nell Smith. 10 May 2007 <http://emilydickinson.org/safe/safedex.html>.
Smith, Robert McClure. "Dickinson and the Masochistic Aesthetic." *Emily Dickinson Journal* 7:2 (1998): 1–21.
———. "New Critical Approaches." Eberwein 206–207.
———. "Reading Seductions: Dickinson, Rhetoric, and the Male Reader." *Dickinson and Audience.* Ed. Martin Orzeck and Robert Wesibuch. Ann Arbor: U of Michigan P, 1996. 105–131.
Stoneley, Peter. "'I Pay—in Satin Cash–': Commerce, Gender, and Display in Emily Dickinson's Poetry." *American Literature* 72:3 (2000): 575–594.

Sutherland, Kathryn. Introduction. *Electronic Text.* Ed. Kathryn Sutherland. Oxford, Oxford UP, 1997.

———. *Jane Austen's Textual Lives: from Aeschulus to Bollywood.* Oxford: Oxford UP, 2005.

Svedjedal, Johan. "A Note on the Concept of 'Hypertext'" *Human IT: Tidskrift för studier av IT ur ett humanvetenskapligt perspektiv.* May 10 2007 <http://www.hb.se/bhs/ith/3-99/htm>.

———. *The Literary Web. Literature and Publishing in the Age of Digital Production. A Study in the Sociology of Literature.* Stockholm: Kungliga Biblioteket, 2000.

Tate, Allen. "New England Culture and Emily Dickinson." *Symposium* 3 (1932): 206–226. Rpt. in Blake and Wells, eds. 153–167.

Todd, Mabel Loomis. Preface. *Poems of Emily Dickinson.* Second Series. Eds. Thomas Higginson and Mabel Loomis Todd. 1891. Boston: Little Brown, and Company, 1910. *The American Verse Project.* 10 May 2007 <http://name.unmdl.umich.edu/BAE0074>.

Waller, Gary. *English Poetry of the Sixteenth Century.* London and New York: Longman, 1993.

Weil-Garris Brandt, Kathleen. "The Grime of the Centuries is a Pigment of the Imagination: Michelangelo's Sistine Ceiling." *Palimpsest: editorial theory in the humanities.* Eds. George Bornstein and Ralph G. Williams. Ann Arbor: U of Michigan P, 1992.

Wells, Anna Mary. "Early Criticism of Emily Dickinson." *American Literature* 1:3 (1929): 243–259.

Werner, Marta. *Emily Dickinson's Open Folios: Scenes of Reading, Surfaces of Writing.* Ann Arbor: U of Michigan P, 1995

———. "The Flights of A821: dearchiving the proceedings of a birdsong." *Electronic Book Review* 6 (1998). 10 May 2007 <http://www.altx.com/ebr/ebr6/6werner/6werner.htm>.

Whicher, George Frisbie. *This Was a Poet: A Critical Biography of Emily Dickinson.* Ann Arbor: U of Michigan P, 1938.

———. "Some Uncollected Poems of Emily Dickinson." *American Literature* 20 (1949): 436–440.

The Walt Whitman Archive. Ed Folsom and Kenneth M. Price, eds. 10 May 2007 <www.whitmanarchive.org>.

Williams, Raymond. *Marxism and Literature.* Oxford: Oxford UP, 1977.

Wilson, Gay Allen. "Emily Dickinson's Versification." *American Prosody.* New York: American Book Co., 1935. Rpt. in Blake and Wells 176–186.

Wolosky, Shira. "Emily Dickinson: Being in the Body." Martin 129–141.

———. "Emily Dickinson's Manuscript Body: History/Textuality/Gender." *Emily Dickinson Journal* 8:2 (1999): 87–99.

Wylder, Edith. *The Last Face: Emily Dickinson's Manuscripts.* Albuquerque: U of New Mexico P, 1971.

Index

A
Alfrey, Shawn 23, 26
Allen, Gay Wilson 50
Allen, Graham 137, 148
American literature 33, 35
American literary canon 31, 51
Anderson, Charles 56, 60–61
Archive 11, 122–123, 153
Archiving 10–11, 29, 117, 119, 120, 121; *see also* Electronic archiving
Archive Fever 122–123, 138–139
Arvin, Newton 59
aura 74–76, 88, 115
autograph 1, 97
authorship 2–3, 6, 7, 9, 110, 152
avant-texte 119, 124

B
Barthes, Roland 13, 132–133; *S/Z* 133, 154
Bellemin-Noël, Jean 124–125
Benfey, Christopher 46–47
Benjamin, Walter 74, 115, 150
bibliographical codes 10, 62, 73–74, 90, 159
Biography 1,2, 4, 6, 8, 20, 23, 59
Bloom, Harold 167
Blackmur Richard 36, 38, 48–49
Bolter, Jay and Richard Grusin 128, 135
Bolts of Melody 8–9, 79
book, the idea of the 133, 140, 160
Borgman 178n11

Bornstein, George 4, 74, 172n4, 178n14
Bourdieu, Pierre 65
Brandt, Kathleen Weil-Garris 115

C
Cameron, Sharon 24, 77
canonization 3, 6, 8, 20, 29, 36
Chartier, Roger 8, 165n8
chest-of-drawers, symbolic value of, 17
Choosing not Choosing 24, 77
computer screen 137–138
computing 113
consumerism 137
correspondence, Dickinson's as publication form 60
critic, role of 69

D
"Death of the author" 8
democratic reading 101–102; editing 135
Derrida, Jacques 63, 100, 122
de Biasi, Pierre-Marc 92, 176n15
Dickinson Editing Collective 103,104, 137, 177n3
Dickinson Electronic Archives 21, 99, 139, 146, 147, 152; Dickinson, Emily 2, 15–16, described by Thomas Higginson 19, 52; described by Thomas H. Johnson 59; as academic subject 65–66; as intertext 2; as

189

manuscript poet 61, 69, 87, 104, 105, 118, 120, 142; as name 1–2, 7; as 'spinster' 23, 65; *see also* Biography; *see also* Genius; *see also* Handwriting
Poems: "Because I could not stop for death" 39–46; "In Ebon box, when years have flown" 80–82; "It sifts from leaden sieves" 83; "Safe in their alabaster chambers" 141–145, 150; "The Sea said 'come' to the brook" 84–85; "Success is counted sweetest" 62
Dickinson, Lavinia 16
Dickinson studies 16
Dickinson, Susan 21, 26, 142, 143, 144–145
Digital Humanities 161
digital scholarship 119
digitization 119

E
Eaves, Morris 161
Eberwein, Donahue, Jane 120
editing 3, 82, 93, 97, 98, 101, 163, 176n20; effect on the biography of Emily Dickinson, 19; in relation to biography 20; function of 33; as critical topos, 33; digital 119, 133 153; tropes of 68; reader-oriented 161
editor as poet/writer 8
electronic archiving 3, 21, 118, 124, 138, 146, 149, 152, 155, 161, 162
Eliot, T. S. 65
epitext 45
Erkkila, Betsy 26, 35, 48, 141
Evergreens, the 154

F
Farr, Judith 22, 90–91, 172n6, 175n14
fascicles 76
Foucault, Michel 7, 8, 124, 157
Franklin, R. W. 14, 21 26, 85, 160; *Reconsideration* 61–63; *Poems* 41, 45, 105–107, 112; *The Manuscript Books* 23–24, 60, 68, 76, 88–89, 90, 95, 138

G
genetic criticism 12–13, 91–93, 119, 124, 126, 127, 152, 175n15
Genette, Gérard 10, 45
genius 48, 167, 169, 173
Greetham, David 9, 91, 172n4

H
Habegger, Alfred 121
Hagenbüchle, Roland 64
Hamilton, Paul 15
Hampson, Alfred Leete 51
handwriting 78, 86, 87, 91, 105, 11, 116
Hart, Ellen Louise 14, 69, 107
Haslett, Moyra 76
Hayles, Katherine 13, 145, 177n7
Heginbotham, Eleanor 168n17
Higginson, Thomas 1, 53, 86, 87; "Letter to a young contributor" 52
Holland, Elizabeth 141
holograph 121, 159
Homestead, the 154
Horne, Philip 140
Howe, Susan 2, 25, 77, 170n2
Hubbard, Melanie 27
humanities 162
hypertext 130, 132

I
Ickstadt, Heintz 27, 28
intertextuality 18, 151, 177n10
Internet 31, 90, 131, 135, 150, 151–153, 165n12

J
Jackson, Virginia 118
Jenny, Laurent 125, 127
Johnson, Thomas H. 14, 18, 20, 33, 42, 44, 55; *Poems of Emily Dickinson* 4, 20, 24, 34, 44, 51–55, 56–57, 61
Juhasz, Suzanne 68, 75

K
Keller, Karl 22

Index

L
Landow, George 130, 134, 137, 148, 151–152
Leavell, Linda 37–38
Lightbox 146
Lindberg-Seyersted, Brita 168n14
linguistic codes 10, 73–74
Leyda, Jay 60
Loeffelholz, Mary 107
Lowell, Amy 36, 37, 38
Lubbers, Klaus 65–66

M
Manoff, Marlene 121
manuscript criticism 13, 27–31, 50, 68, 76, 77, 86, 92, 102, 104, 109–111, 124, 128, 146, 159, 163n2; and print 68
Marcus, Leah 12, 14–15, 147, 149, 159, 160, 163n2, 172n4
materiality 70, 71, 72
Matthiessen, F. O 49–50
McGann, Jerome 10, 44, 63, 71, 72–74, 76, 77, 159, 172n4
Messmer, Marietta 168n16
metacriticism 15–16; 28
Miller, Cristanne 14, 70, 136, 160, 173n7, 173n8
Miller, J. H. 1–2
Miller, Perry 56
Mitchell, Domhnall 25, 83, 86, 102–104, 120–121, 148, 174n10, 178n12
modern textual criticism 9
Morris, Timothy 46, 47, 108

N
Nelson, Theodor H. 130
nostalgia 136
New Criticism 6, 34, 35, 36

O
Ong, Walter 178n13
Open Me Carefully 21, 144

P
Paratext 10, 45

Paratexts 10
Pask, Kevin 8
Perloff, Marjorie 35, 102, 174
Petrino, Elizabeth 52
Pollak, Vivian 22
Porter, David 25, 51
possibility idea of 112

R
Radical Scatters 177n8
real, concept of 126
reader's edition 58, 59
Recognition of Emily Dickinson, The 56
remediation 128–129, 138, 145
Renaissance, the 159, 163n2, 164n4
Rich, Adrienne 35

S
scriptural 26, 99, 101, 176n18
Sewall, Richard 19, 165n8, 179n16
Sheringham, Michael 10–11
Shillingsburg, Peter 56, 121, 176n20
Short, Harold and Marilyn Deegan 162
Smith, Martha Nell, 17, 18, 90, 142, 165n9; "Because the Plunge" 117, 136; "Computing" 113, 120, 135–136; "Corporealizations" 25–26, 100, 103, 137, 139, 147; "Emily Dickinson writing a Poem"144, 149, 150; "Gifts and Ghosts" 107, *Rowing in Eden* 1, 71, 86–87, 98, 100–101, 112, 131,
Smith, Robert McClure 26, 64, 45, 64
social theory of text 72
Springfield Republican, The 143
Stoneley, Peter 43
Sutherland, Katherine 134–135, 176n1
Svedjedal, Johan 132, 166n12

T
Tate, Allan 36, 38–39, 42, 44, 65
text 13, 14
textual criticism 12–13, 69

U
Understanding Poetry 35, 44
unediting 93–94, 111, 140, 159

V

Versioning Machine 129, 146, 149

W

Waller, Gary 45
war of the houses, the 17, 18, 26
Wells, Anna Maria 37
Werner, Marta 12, 14, 27, 69, 71, 91, 100–101, 124, 174n9, 177n8; "Flights" 116–117, 155, 160 175n3; *Open Folios* 25, 70, 92–97, 104, 111, 121
"What is an author?" 8
Williams, Raymond 7
Williams, William Carlos 46
Wolosky, Shira 27, 107
writerly text 133, 134
Wylder, Edith 67

For Product Safety Concerns and Information please contact our EU
representative GPSR@taylorandfrancis.com
Taylor & Francis Verlag GmbH, Kaufingerstraße 24, 80331 München, Germany

www.ingramcontent.com/pod-product-compliance
Lightning Source LLC
Chambersburg PA
CBHW070610300426
44113CB00010B/1486